American Indian Environmental Ethics: An Ojibwa Case Study

D0075121

"Think for yourself."

prentice hall

Prentice Hall's *Basic Ethics in Action* series in normative and applied ethics is a major new undertaking edited by Michael Boylan, Professor of Philosophy at Marymount University. The series includes both wide-ranging anthologies as well as brief texts that focus on a particular theme or topic within one of four areas of applied ethics. These areas include: Business Ethics, Environmental Ethics, Medical Ethics, and Social and Political Philosophy.

Anchor volume
Michael Boylan, *Basic Ethics*, 2000

Business Ethics

Michael Boylan, ed., *Business Ethics*, 2001

James Donahue, *Ethics for the Professionals*, forthcoming

Dale Jacquette, *Journalistic Ethics*, forthcoming

Murphy, Laczniak, Bowie, and Klein, *Marketing Ethics*, forthcoming

Edward Spence, *Advertising Ethics*, forthcoming

Environmental Ethics

Michael Boylan, ed., *Environmental Ethics*, 2001

J. Baird Callicott and Michael P. Nelson, *American Indian Environmental Ethics: An Ojibwa Case Study*, 2004

Lisa H. Newton, *Ethics and Sustainability*, 2003

Mary Anne Warren, *Obligations to Animals*, forthcoming

Medical Ethics

Michael Boylan, ed., *Medical Ethics*, 2000

Michael Boylan and Kevin Brown, *Genetic Engineering*, 2002

Rosemarie Tong, *New Perspectives in Healthcare Ethics*, 2003

Rosemarie Tong and Reggie Raymer, eds, *New Perspectives in Healthcare Ethics*, 2003

Social and Political Philosophy

R. Paul Churchill, *Global Diversity and Human Rights*, forthcoming

Seumas Miller, Peter Roberts, and Edward Spence, *Corruption and Anti-Corruption: An Applied Philosophical Study*, forthcoming

Deryck Beyleveld, *Informed Consent*, forthcoming

Please contact Michael Boylan (mboylan@phoenix.marymount.edu) or Prentice Hall's Philosophy & Religion Editor to propose authoring a title for this series!

American Indian Environmental Ethics: An Ojibwa Case Study

J. BAIRD CALLICOTT
Department of Philosophy and Religion Studies
University of North Texas

MICHAEL P. NELSON
Department of Philosophy
University of Wisconsin–Stevens Point

Upper Saddle River, New Jersey 07458

Library of Congress Cataloging-in-Publication Data
Callicott, J. Baird.
 American Indian environmental ethics: an Ojibwa case study / by J. Baird Callicott and
 Michael P. Nelson.
  p. cm.
  Includes bibliographical references.
  ISBN 0-13-043121-4
   1. Ojibwa Indians—Folklore. 2. Ojibwa philosophy. 3. Environmental ethics—Case
 studies. I. Nelson, Michael P., 1966– II. Title.

E99.C6C16 2004
179'.1'089973—dc21   2003048272

Editorial Director: Charlyce Jones-Owen
Senior Acquisitions Editor: Ross Miller
Assistant Editor: Wendy Yurash
Editorial Assistant: Carla Worner
Managing Editor: Jan Stephan
Full Service Liaison: Fran Russello
Production Editor: Terry Routley, Carlisle Communications, Inc.
Prepress and Manufacturing Buyer: Brian Mackey
Director of Marketing: Beth Mejia
Marketing Assistant: Kimberly Daum
Art Director: Jayne Conte
Cover Designer: Geoffery Cassar

This book was set in Palatino by Carlisle Communications, Ltd. It was printed and
bound by Courier Companies, Inc. The cover was printed by Coral Graphics.

Pearson Education Ltd. London   Pearson Education Australia Pty. Limited
Pearson Education Singapore Pte. Ltd.   Pearson Education North Asia Ltd.
Pearson Education Canada, Ltd.   Pearson Educación de Mexico, S. A. de C.V.
Pearson Education—Japan   Pearson Education Malaysia Pte. Ltd.

10 9 8 7 6 5 4 3 2 1

ISBN: 0-13-043121-4

Contents

chapter one

Introductory Essay: *Cultural Worldview*
and Environmental Ethics 1

  I. WHAT IS ENVIRONMENTAL ETHICS? 2
    A. Anthropocentric Environmental Ethics 3
    B. Individualistic Nonanthropocentric Environmental Ethics 4
    C. Holistic Nonanthropocentric Environmental Ethics 4
    D. Comparative Environmental Ethics 5
  II. WHAT IS A CULTURAL WORLDVIEW? 6
    A. Worldview and Philosophy 7
    B. Traditional American-Indian Philosophy 9
    C. Cultural Worldview and Personal Worldview 10
    D. Worldview and Ethos 12
  III. WHAT IS CULTURE? 13
    A. The Ontological Problem 13
    B. The Methodological Problem 14
    C. Lamarckian Cultural Evolution 14
    D. Biological Unity, Cultural Diversity 16
    E. Drawing Cultural Boundaries 17
    F. The Methodological Problem Solved: The Analysis of
       Narratives 18
  IV. LANGUAGE, WORLDVIEW, AND CULTURAL RELATIVISM 20
    A. Linguistic-Cultural Relativism 20

B. Cultural Absolutism   21
C. Descartes' Subject-Object Dualism   23
D. Kant's Copernican Revolution in Philosophy   24
E. The Einsteinian Revolution in Philosophy   25
F. The Connection Between Relativity in Physics and in
   Anthropology   26
G. The Basic Principle of Relativity in Physics   27
H. Analogous Relativity in Anthropology   28
I. Relativism in Postmodern Philosophy: Truth or
   Tenability?   29
J. The Uncertainty Principle in Worldview Analysis   30
V. THE OJIBWA NARRATIVES   32
A. Four Segments of the Ojibwa People   32
B. The Role of Narratives in Oral Education   33
C. The Provenance of These Narratives   34
D. The Authenticity of These Narratives   35

chapter two

Narratives   38

1. THE ORPHANS AND MASHŌS 38
   A. The Brothers' Escape   38
   B. The Contest With Mashōs   46
2. CLOTHED-IN-FUR 58
3. THE WOMAN WHO MARRIED A BEAVER 68
4. THE BOY THAT WAS CARRIED AWAY BY A BEAR 70
5. A MOOSE AND HIS OFFSPRING 72
6. LITTLE-IMAGE 75
7. THE PERSON THAT MADE MEDICINE 78
8. THE BIRTH OF NÄNABUSHU 79
9. NÄNABUSHU SWALLOWED BY THE STURGEON 80
10. NÄNABUSHU SLAYS HEWER-OF-HIS-SHIN 85
11. NÄNABUSHU LEAVES HIS BROTHER, AND ALSO HIS GRANDMOTHER 88
12. NÄNABUSHU, THE SWEET-BRIER BERRIES, AND THE STURGEONS 90
13. NOTES ON THE MYSTIC RITE 96
    A. Explanation of Diagram   98

chapter three

Interpretive essay: *An Ojibwa Worldview and Environmental Ethic* 100

I. KEY COGNITIVE ELEMENTS OF AN OJIBWA WORLDVIEW   100
   A. The Enculturation Function of Narratives Among
      the Ojibwa   101

B. Personification   102
C. The Community Concept   104
D. Power   105
E. Metamorphosis   108
F. The Situation of Blessing   110
G. Disobedience and Its Consequences   112
H. Reciprocity, Life, and Death   113
I. Immortal Bones and Spirit   116
II. OJIBWA ENVIRONMENTAL ETHICS   117
   A. Animal Rights   118
   B. Human-Animal Marriages as a Means of Community
      Building   119
   C. The Human-Animal Gift Economy   121
   D. The Land Ethic   121
   E. Animal Communities in the Leopold and Ojibwa Land
      Ethics   123
   F. Personification in the Leopold and Ojibwa Land Ethics   124
   G. Biotic Communities in the Leopold and Ojibwa Land
      Ethics   127
   H. The Fur, Flesh, and Bones of the Land Ethics   128
   I. Pimadaziwin   130
III. THE CONTROVERSY ABOUT AMERICAN-INDIAN ENVIRONMENTAL
   ETHICS   132
   A. Proponents and Skeptics   132
   B. A Debate About Apples and Oranges   133
   C. Ethics and Behavior; Ideals and Actions   134

Literature Cited   *137*

For Thomas W. Overholt
colleague, mentor, friend

Acknowledgments

First of all, without the talent, skill, and dedication of William Jones, who transcribed and translated the narratives that are its heart and soul, this book would not have been possible to make. We also gratefully acknowledge the Ojibwa people whose stories these are and the raconteures who told them to Dr. Jones: Mrs. Marie Syrette or Kugigepinasi'kwa (Forever-Bird-Woman), John Pinesi or Kagige Pinasi (Forever-Bird), Wasagunackang (He-that-leaves-the-Imprint-of-his-Foot-shining-in-the-Snow), Midasuganj (Ten-Claw), and Madcigabo (Begins-to-Rise-to-His-Feet). We thank Dennis McPherson and Douglas Rabb of Lakehead University in Thunder Bay, Ontario, authors of *Indian from the Inside: A Study in Ethnometaphysics,* who field-tested and ground-truthed these stories and our interpretation of the worldview they convey among their Ojibwa students. Thomas W. Overholt, now retired from the University of Wisconsin–Stevens Point, did much of the original research informing the introductory and interpretive essays of this book. For that (and for sometimes appropriating his prose) we thank him; and to him we dedicate this book. We thank Pricilla Ybarra and Heather Varco for reading and commenting on drafts of the manuscript (and for their patience). We thank Carolee Cote and Becky Hughes for their secretarial assistance.

chapter one

Introductory Essay

Cultural Worldview and
Environmental Ethics

The heart of this book consists of selections from Ojibwa stories collected around the western end of Lake Superior in the very early twentieth century by William Jones, a linguist and anthropologist, who was himself an American Indian. Surrounding this core are two essays written by the present authors, who are contemporary philosophers specializing in environmental ethics and of mostly European-American descent. The interpretive essay provides an analysis of the Ojibwa narratives, with an eye to environmental ethics. This introductory essay contextualizes them in several ways.

First, in the context of environmental ethics, some environmentalists believe that, in comparison with the now dominant European-American cultural worldview, a higher regard for nonhuman natural entities and nature as a whole was a hallmark of traditional American-Indian cultural worldviews. These narratives not only provide some actual evidence to support this belief, they provide an insight, more particularly, into what norms or ideals of the relationship between people and nature were actually envisioned in one American-Indian cultural worldview. The interpretive essay attempts to bring this Ojibwa environmental ethic to light. In this introductory essay, we begin with an overview of the origin and development of environmental ethics over the latter half of the twentieth century as a point of departure for reading and interpreting the Ojibwa stories.

Contemporary environmental ethics, however, like most subfields of philosophy, consists of a body of theory developed by individual thinkers, such as Holmes Rolston, III and Paul W. Taylor. And each of these theories is embedded in a wider cognitive complex—personal assumptions about the

1

way the world is organized and the human place in such a world. The Ojibwa tales reprinted here are not associated with any particular author; rather they are told by many Ojibwa raconteurs, each of whom vary the telling depending on audience and circumstance, but all of whom draw on the same repertoire. (Several versions of the same story sometimes appear in the collection made by William Jones.) The Ojibwa environmental ethic is also embedded in a wider cognitive complex—but, again, one that is less personal and more characteristic of a shared Ojibwa worldview. This raises a nexus of questions: What is a "cultural worldview"? How is a cultural worldview similar to and different from the philosophies with which familiar Western theories of environmental ethics are associated? And how does one reliably bring to light something so ambient and diffuse as a cultural worldview? These questions are confronted and thoroughly addressed in this introductory essay.

Finally, realizing that there are many, many cultural worldviews—most of which are mutually inconsistent—we confront the inevitable question: Which is true? We argue that none is true and none is false. Rather, different cultural worldviews are simply different ways of making sense out of human experience. On the other hand, we argue that to be "tenable," a worldview must meet criteria of consistency, comprehensiveness, practicality, sustainability, goodness, and beauty.

We frankly acknowledge that the challenge of entering another cultural worldview is fraught with uncertainty, but argue that it is nevertheless richly rewarding to undertake. If even moderately successful, one can catch a glimpse into another reality—in the present case, one that evolved for at least ten thousand years in isolation from European and Asian traditions of thought. A comparative worldview study such as this can at least help one realize that one's own way of cognitively organizing human experience is not the only way. We hope, in any case, that this introductory essay will prepare readers to open their minds and hearts to an alternative habitus.

Because this book is organized with the narratives themselves in the center, the Ojibwa cognitive culture is represented here on its own terms. We believe that we have adequately and insightfully interpreted it in the concluding essay, but in the last analysis, the narratives must speak for themselves and constitute the final authority for an Ojibwa cultural worldview and the environmental ethic embedded in it. We now turn to a more thorough discussion of these themes.

I. WHAT IS ENVIRONMENTAL ETHICS?

Environmental ethics has become a robust subdiscipline of moral philosophy. It emerged during the 1970s in response to the realization in the 1960s that there existed an "environmental crisis." The air over big cities had become choked with noxious gases; rivers were polluted with synthetic chemicals and municipal sewage, and muddied with eroded topsoil; natural resources appeared to be growing scarce; ecosystem services appeared to be threatened; and the human population continued to grow alarmingly, doubling during the first half of the twentieth century (and would double again during the second). Specifying the environmental crisis was largely a task for scientists: for toxicologists to identify harmful molecules; for ecologists to monitor the impact of deforestation and industrial development on plant and animal populations; for atmospheric scientists to model climate change. Addressing the environmental crisis was partly a technological challenge for engineers: for automotive engineers to build more fuel-efficient and cleaner-burning motors; for agrochemical engineers to develop less persistent pesticides; for architectural engineers to design better-insulated buildings. But some suggested that to really address the environmental crisis, green technological innovation had to be accompanied by a profound and fundamental shift in cultural attitudes and values (Leopold 1949, White 1967). At bottom, the environmental crisis, they insisted, stemmed from a widespread belief within Western culture that the nonhuman natural world was but a pool of resources existing only to satisfy human needs and wants. The analysis of the cultural attitudes and values ultimately responsible for the environmental crisis, and the formulation of cogent alternative attitudes and values that would ground a more harmonious relationship between human beings and their natural environments was a task for philosophers. And so, environmental ethics was born.

A. Anthropocentric Environmental Ethics

Western ethical traditions have been resolutely—some even militantly—anthropocentric (i.e., human-centered). In the Judeo-Christian ethical tradition, only human beings are morally enfranchised because only human beings are alleged to be created in the image of God and to possess an immortal soul. In the more secular Greco-Roman tradition, only human beings are morally enfranchised because only human beings are alleged to be rational.

Some philosophers argue that the anthropocentric Western ethical traditions are sufficient bases for environmental ethics because human behavior that is significantly harmful to the environment is also significantly harmful to other human beings (Passmore 1974, Shrader-Frechette 1981). And, according to the major Western ethical traditions, for human beings to harm other human beings while pursuing their own self interest is wrong. Thus, if a plastics manufacturer pollutes a lake or stream with dioxins, fish and other aquatic organisms will be harmed, but so will the people who eat the fish or swim in the water. However, some kinds of human behavior that significantly harm the environment do not significantly harm other human beings. For example, a shopping-mall development that destroys the last habitat of an endangered endemic species of frog does not significantly harm human beings, but it does cause the extinction of a vertebrate species. On the face of it, this seems morally wrong, yet it would not be according to traditional Western anthropocentric ethics. Therefore, other environmental philosophers embarked on the project of constructing nonanthropocentric environmental ethics (Routley 1973, Naess 1973, Rolston 1975).

B. Individualistic Nonanthropocentric Environmental Ethics

One main approach to nonanthropocentric environmental ethics is to start with traditional Western ethical theory and modify or extend it. For example, in utilitarian ethical theory the greatest good is happiness. Happiness was at first defined in terms of pleasure and pain and later in terms of preference satisfaction. Many nonhuman animals experience pleasure and pain and have preferences that can be satisfied or frustrated. Traditional utilitarians were concerned only with human pleasure and pain or preference satisfaction, but to be entirely consistent, they should give unbiased consideration to nonhuman pleasure and pain or preference satisfaction as well (Singer 1975, 1990). Because utilitarians add up the pleasure or preference satisfaction of many individuals and permit this "aggregate utility" to outweigh the pain or frustration of a few individuals, other philosophers argued that those animals having some sense of self should be accorded the same rights to life, liberty, and the pursuit of happiness accorded human beings because such rights "trump" considerations of aggregate utility (Regan 1983).

Self-aware or even acutely sentient animals, however, make up only a part of the environment. To include plants and other insentient organisms within the purview of ethics, environmental philosophers argued that at least they all have ends or goals—to grow, to thrive, to reproduce—that can be realized or interdicted (Goodpaster 1978). Thus interests (in realizing their goals) and goods of their own (these very goals themselves) can be intelligibly attributed to all multicelled organisms—even if they are not consciously interested in their interests or care about what is good for them. Drawing on and modifying Kantian ethical theory, these capacities, not reason alone, could be grounds for attributing intrinsic value to all multicelled organisms and recognizing duties to them (Taylor 1986).

C. Holistic Nonanthropocentric Environmental Ethics

Still, this modification of traditional Western ethical theory extends only to the living beings that make up but part of the environment and the part, moreover, of least concern to the emerging breed of environmentalists. Environmentalists are more concerned about the well-being of whole species than of individual specimens and, beyond the species level of biological organization, about the integrity of biotic communities and the health of ecosystems. Some philosophers argue that ends, goals, and interests can be intelligibly attributed to whole species, biotic communities, and ecosystems (Johnson 1991). Contemporary evolutionary biology and ecology, however, do not support such an attribution. While species evolve, they are not actual individuals protracted in space and time, as some philosophers of biology have alleged (Ghiselin 1974). Certainly they do not evolve toward any end or goal; they are not, as it were, trying to become better (fitter) or even something different (Wilson 1992). Biotic communities and ecosystems are less unified than ecologists once believed; they are certainly not sufficiently unified to be regarded as "superorganisms" as ecologists once supposed (McIntosh 1998). Here we must be cautious. Species do exist per se and they may be rendered extinct. Biotic communities do exist per se and their integrity may be compromised. Ecosystems do exist per se and their functions may be impaired. But species, biotic communities, and ecosystems are not sufficiently like individual organisms that ends, goals, or interests may be intelligibly attributed to them.

A modification of Hume's ethical theory, as developed by Darwin, might reorient environmental ethics toward such loosely integrated wholes as species, biotic communities, and ecosystems (Leopold 1949, Callicott 1989)— without committing the "category mistake" of attributing to them interests or goods of their own. Hume suggested that ethics are based on moral sentiments—beneficent feelings that are directed both toward individuals and the societies or communities they compose. Darwin argued that in fact such sentiments evolved by natural selection to facilitate the integration of individuals into societies or communities—wherein they could pursue life's struggle collectively and cooperatively and thus more successfully. Aldo Leopold (1949) pointed out that we human beings are members not only of various human communities, but also of various biotic communities. If anthropocentric ethics were the evolutionary strategy for preserving the integrity of human societies or communities, then a "land ethic" might, by parity of reasoning, be the future evolutionary strategy for preserving the integrity of biotic communities, upon which we human beings also depend for our survival and well-being. (The Leopold land ethic is discussed more fully in the Interpretive Essay.)

D. Comparative Environmental Ethics

Another approach to developing nonanthropocentric environmental ethics is to look for precedents in non-Western traditions of thought. Some philosophers suggested that if the resolute and often militant anthropocentrism of Western traditions of ethics was partly to blame for the environmental crisis, then replacing the western world view altogether would be better than modifying or extending it (Jung 1972). Two non-Western conceptual resources for environmental ethics were believed to be especially promising—Asian and American Indian ethical traditions (Callicott and Ames 1989, Hughes 1983, 1996). However, the idea that a culture can simply cut itself off from its own cognitive stem and graft onto another seems most implausible. Westerners cannot hope to achieve a profound and fundamental shift in their cultural attitudes and values toward nature by adopting wholesale the attitudes and values indigenous to India, China, or Japan or those of the peoples indigenous to the Americas. Any such shift will come, if it comes at all, by an internal process of cultural evolution.

But an effective non-Western approach to environmental ethics need not be so simple and naive. Cultural cross-fertilization has occurred immemorially. The cross-cultural comparative study of environmental ethics can be fruitful in a variety of ways. First, by entering the worldview of another culture, the deeper, often hidden, assumptions and biases of one's own worldview may come more clearly to light. Second, possibilities (in the present context, possible ways of humanly relating to the natural environment), to which one may be blinkered by one's own cognitive culture, may be revealed. Third, one may find common structures that manifest themselves in very different ways in the deep grammar of very different cultures. When this happens, such common structures are mutually reinforcing and mutually validating.

II. WHAT IS A CULTURAL WORLDVIEW?

The great ethnographer of the Ojibwa, Irving Hallowell (1963, p. 258), offers the following general account of a cultural worldview:

> All cultures provide a cognitive orientation toward a world in which man is compelled to act. A culturally constituted worldview is created, which, by means of beliefs, available knowledge and language, mediates personal adjustment to the world through such psychological processes as perceiving, recognizing, conceiving, judging, and reasoning ... which, intimately associated with a normative orientation, becomes the basis for reflection, decision, and action ... and a foundation provided for a consensus with respect to goals and values.

Finally, Hallowell (1966/1976, p. 454) provides a concise definition of a cultural worldview as that which "establishes the ultimate premises for all that is involved in any comprehensive explanation of the nature of events in the universe and man's relation to them." A cultural worldview is, in short, the shared conceptual framework by means of which human experience is organized to create a common "reality" or "habitus" for the members of a given culture.

A. Worldview and Philosophy

In the tradition that begins with Pythagoras, who is reputed to have coined the term, philosophy—including ethics—has always been a distinctly idiosyncratic pursuit. While everyone shares some (at least one) cultural worldview, not everyone is a philosopher, and those few who are have generated philosophies that bear the unmistakable stamp of the highly individual temperaments and habits of mind of their authors. Consider how extraordinary or even bizarre are the following: the Socratic idea found in Plato's *Apology* that taking a person's property, or even life, does the person no real harm, but that doing evil is only harmful to the evildoer; Kant's idea that an act of charity motivated by sympathy is, though laudable, of no real moral worth, but that an act of charity coldly motivated solely by duty is; Bentham's idea that human rights are "nonsense on stilts," and that we should only consider aggregate utility in deciding the best course of action; and Singer's idea that performing a painful medical experiment on a human infant is no worse than performing the same experiment on a lab rat. Although they must be logically defended (and all philosophers are at pains to persuade their readers that theirs is the right way of thinking), philosophical systems of ethics are personal, though not arbitrary, statements of reasoned opinion. To propose a presentation and discussion of Ojibwa environmental ethics would therefore suggest, just as a discussion of Western environmental ethics would, a series of individual thinkers historically related—perhaps in a critical and dialectical sequence.

Ethical philosophy, in this sense of the original reflection of creative individual thinkers, depends on and, indeed, arises out of a more common substrate of generic ideas, a cultural worldview. A cultural worldview may be understood as a set of conceptual presuppositions, both conscious and unconscious, articulate and inarticulate, shared by members of a particular culture—about what exists and what does not (ghosts, electrons), cause and effect (magical words turning pumpkins into carriages, germs causing disease), who can think and who cannot (only humans, animals, anything at all depending on circumstances). The relationship between philosophy in the sense of manifest individual creative thought and the more deeply embedded cultural worldview may be illustrated in the familiar context of Western ethical theory. Plato and Aristotle, for example, are Greek philosophers of widely divergent temperament and opinion. Yet they share a distinctly Greek outlook, a common Greek worldview. To take but a single case in point, they think—as any ancient Greek of the classical period would—of right conduct (i.e., ethical or moral behavior) as involving centrally the idea of virtue or excellence (*arêtē*). To the modern student of ethics, this is a quite conspicuous and curious peculiarity because, under the influence of the Judeo-Christian tradition, we are more disposed to think of right conduct in terms of obedience to certain rules, commandments, or laws. Aristotle's ethical theory is very different from Plato's, but the degree of difference between them is sharply limited by the conventional conceptual link between goodness and virtue. In comparison with a rule-oriented theory of ethics such as Kant's, Aristotle's and Plato's appear to be only theoretical variations on an underlying common theme. As Michael Boylan (2000, p. 26) succinctly puts it, "the philosopher always brings his or her worldview along with him or her."

A philosopher, it must be admitted, can sometimes transcend the repertoire of generic concepts afforded by his or her cultural milieu and, more rarely still, can significantly modify or even transform the worldview of her or his culture, so that after his or her philosophy the world is differently arranged conceptually and differently perceived by almost everyone within that cultural tradition. Among the ancient Greeks, once more, Pythagoras or some of his intellectual heirs conceived of the Earth as a planet, contrary to the then-prevailing Greek worldview. His philosophy of nature therefore transcended the worldview of his culture, but it did not, in this particular, significantly modify or transform it. Almost all of the rest of the Greeks of classical antiquity remained—philosophers and laypersons alike—within a geocentric worldview. Copernicus, on the other hand, not only departed in his speculative natural philosophy from the still geocentric worldview of his culture, he managed to change that worldview to conform to his own—at the time bizarre as well as heretical—opinion. The solarcentric revolution in the European worldview was not accomplished in a decade or even in a century; but by now, in any case, after astronauts have walked on the moon and space probes have visited other planets, every thoughtful person participating in Western culture, virtually without exception, is a Copernican. What was once Copernicus's private opinion passed into the public domain, first as a consciously held doctrine or belief, and ultimately as a cognitive orientation entangled with the very way the world is presently perceived and experienced.

In contrast with and complementary to the individual or personal character of philosophy, a cultural worldview is the collective conceptual outlook of a people. A cultural worldview exists, so to speak, at the level of society; it is the common property of the culture's members. In Western society, in which literacy became augmented by print technology, a sort of dialogue between philosophy—in the most general sense of the term, including creative thought about nature—and cultural worldview emerged as a distinct cultural phenomenon. Copernicus was by no means the only thinker to reshape the Western worldview. Newton's mechanistic natural philosophy, Descartes' dualism, Freud's concept of the unconscious, Darwin's evolutionary epic, Pasteur's microbes, to mention but a few of the most salient examples, have all contributed to the development of the contemporary Western worldview. The distinctly historical quality of change in the modern Western worldview, its dialectical and directional quality, is the result of this post-print process of continuous interaction with philosophy.

Our concern in this book is with the Ojibwa worldview, the conceptual organization of experience characteristic of a group of people as a whole, and, more particularly, with the environmental ethic embedded in it. This represents an exercise in philosophy, nonetheless, because we shall be exploring and attempting to articulate the conceptual foundations of the shared Ojibwa world. David Bidney (1949, p. 337) has remarked that "to appreciate properly the philosophy of life and *Weltanschauung* (German for "worldview") which serve as leitmotifs for a given culture requires a measure of philosophical discipline and insight which necessitates that there be professionally trained philosophers working in the social sciences as well as philosophically minded social scientists." Bidney suggests, in other words, that a cross-fertilization of the peculiar interests and methods of both philosophers and anthropologists would be productive in the discovery and articulation of cultural worldviews.

Hallowell (1960, p. 20), even proposes a new subdiscipline of philosophy based on such a cross-fertilization—ethno-metaphysics, which we may think of as being to philosophy as ethno-botany is to biology:

> Human beings in whatever culture are provided with cognitive orientation in a cosmos; there is "order" and "reason" rather than chaos. There are basic premises and principles implied, even those that do not happen to be consciously formulated or articulated by the people themselves. We are confronted with the philosophical implications of their thought, the nature of the world of being as they conceive it. If we pursue the problem deeply enough, we come face to face with a relatively unexplored territory—ethno-metaphysics.

To attempt to bring to light a culture's worldview is an exercise in ethno-metaphysics. We should note that such an exercise should not be understood to focus exclusively on "exotic" non-Western cultures. An analysis of the Western worldview as it existed in the seventeenth century, the Middle Ages, the Roman Empire, would also be an exercise in ethno-metaphysics. Indeed, an analysis of contemporary Western worldviews is also an exercise in ethno-metaphysics, latterly known less formally as "culture studies."

B. Traditional American-Indian Philosophy

Whether anything analogous to Western philosophical history has existed among traditional American Indians is a matter of speculation because they did not leave a written record of philosophical reflection—at least not one that survived the genocidal post-Columbian conquest. The possibility of such philosophical activity has been postulated by Paul Radin (1927), who offers much evidence for the claim that among oral North American peoples (including the Ojibwa explicitly) there were in fact reflective individuals, an intellectual class, and a subcultural tradition of speculative inquiry. Such America-Indian philosophers as there may have been, of course, must have couched their speculative thought in a cultural worldview. In the Western philosophical tradition, the location of philosophy in worldview is most evident in Medieval philosophy, which is almost exclusively conducted within the parameters of the Christianity that dominated the Western worldview in the Middle Ages. Their ambient cultural worldview serves individual philosophers as not only a conceptual resource, but also a set of limitations. The Medieval Western philosopher, for example, was afforded a rich resource for speculation by the idea of God in the then-prevailing Christian worldview of the West, but apparently that idea also limited the Medieval philosopher, for none appears to have omitted the idea of God from their philosophies.

Clyde Kluckhohn agrees with Radin's overall thesis, but appends certain qualifications related to the fundamental difference between oral and written means of cultural transmission. "It remains true," Kluckhohn (1949, p. 356) writes, "that critical examination of basic premises and fully explicit systematization of philosophical concepts are seldom found at the nonliterate level. The printed word is an almost essential condition for free and extended discussion of fundamental issues. Where dependency on memory exists, there seems to be an inevitable tendency to emphasize the correct perpetuation of the precious oral tradition." While Kluckhohn acknowledges the existence of philosophy and philosophers in oral cultures, he insists that they differ both in degree and kind from the Western paradigm: they may be equally speculative, but less critical and systematic. Kluckhohn (1949, p. 356) further remarks that "folk societies [undisturbed by aggressive 'proselytizing religions'] do not possess competing philosophical systems." He certainly goes too far, however, in insisting that the *printed* word, in addition to the written, is required for free and extended discussion of fundamental issues, because that would exclude, by implication, the manifestly free and extended discussion of fundamental issues in the West among the ancient Greeks who could write, but not print their words. We might add a further caveat: that philosophy in the West emerged at the dawn of literacy in a cultural context that remained largely oral; and moreover, that one of the most renowned Western philosophers, Socrates, conducted his very critical, if not entirely systematic, philosophical inquiries exclusively in an oral mode.

C. Cultural Worldview and Personal Worldview

Still, Kluckhohn's intuition that the printed word alters the circumstances for the interaction between philosophy (or individual creative thinking) and worldview (or culturally constituted outlook) is, in view of the briefest reflection on post-print Western intellectual history, undeniable. Print clearly amplifies the intellectual opportunities made possible by literacy. Cultures, like those of the aboriginal American peoples, who had neither writing nor print and whose members were not geographically distributed around the globe, possess a more integrated, coherent, and consolidated cultural worldview than Western society today. Robert Redfield's field work supports this conclusion. His observations of the Central American Indians of the Yucatan peninsula, for example, indicate that in the city of Merida where the Western worldview is most pervasive, "the range of interest, knowledge, belief, and general sophistication is so wide that . . . it is necessary to deal with one social class or interest group at a time." There is, further, "a heterogeneity of mental worlds." On the other hand, in the remote villages where Western cultural influences have been resisted, "the ways of living exhibit to the greatest degree an interrelation of parts and inner consistency." And there exists within the folk culture "an organized body of conventional understandings" (Redfield 1941, p. 110).

If there was so much cognitive diversity and dissonance in the Merida, Mexico, of the 1930s and 1940s, one could only characterize the cognitive pluralism of the United States in the twenty-first century as a virtual supermarket of "mental worlds." Boylan (2000, p. 27) thus emphatically insists that—because in contemporary Western culture a person has a wide choice of competing worldviews—people committed to a moral way of life have the responsibility to "develop a single, comprehensive, and internally coherent worldview that is good and that we strive to act out in our daily lives." He calls this the "Personal Worldview Imperative."

As to "single," we agree with Boylan that—given the cognitive pluralism and freedom of choice that one finds in contemporary Western culture—if one puts on and takes off different worldviews just as one changes clothes then "there is really *no* abiding person at all," whom one can claim to be (Boylan 2000, p. 25, emphasis in original). More constraints on a moral person's freedom to select any old worldview are indicated by "comprehensive," and "internally coherent." A worldview that is not comprehensive (in the sense of taking account of everything) is unable to embrace all the facts of contemporary life and thus its subscriber cannot comprehend them (in the cognitive sense of the word; that is, understand them). The Malabranchian worldview, for example, in which animals are alleged to be wholly unconscious and insentient automata (or mechanisms) ignores an overwhelming amount of evidence to the contrary—from neurophysiology to ethology to common sense. Acting out such a worldview would lead one to commit unspeakable acts of cruelty to animals. Acting out a worldview that is not internally consistent would lead one to attempt to do contradictory things. An inconsistent married person may generally believe that one should be sexually faithful to one's spouse but, when presented with an opportunity to commit adultery, may think that to do so under the circumstances is all right. The untoward consequences of behavior based on such an inconsistent worldview are standard soap-opera fare.

Boylan (2000) recognizes another constraint on freedom of worldview choice emphasized here. Choice of a personal worldview is constrained by the habitus of one's cultural worldview. It is not possible for a contemporary Westerner to seriously subscribe to a geocentric worldview, to really believe that the sun, moon, stars, and planets literally circle the Earth every day. For a contemporary Westerner to seriously believe that the Earth is flat and that there is a danger of falling off the edge if one goes far enough in one direction is not possible. Nor is it possible for a contemporary Westerner to seriously believe that an epidemic disease, such as AIDS, is visited on a population by Apollo, although many contemporary Westerners seriously believe that AIDS is visited on sexual sinners by God. Worldviews that include belief in the biblical God are still viable in contemporary Western culture; those that include belief in Apollo and the other anthropomorphic gods of ancient Greece are not. To revisit a point already made, for a contemporary Westerner to adopt wholesale the traditional Ojibwa worldview found in the narratives included in this book is not possible. The way a Western person's whole life is structured by the Western worldview makes it impossible—without a complete change of location and lifestyle—to simply replace the Western worldview with some other. On the other hand, of course, one may enter another worldview in imagination and try to understand it on its own terms.

D. Worldview and Ethos

Boylan (2000) is also concerned that twentieth-century analytic philosophy has unnaturally divided the objective from the subjective and fact from value. Anthropologists, however, have not been persuaded that worldview and ethos can be so neatly segregated one from the other. According to Clifford Geertz (1957/1973, pp. 126, 127),

> In recent anthropological discussion the moral (and aesthetic) aspects of a given culture, the evaluative elements, have commonly been summed up in the term "ethos," while the cognitive, existential aspects have been designated by the term "worldview." A people's ethos is the tone, character, and quality of their life, its moral and aesthetic style and mode; it is the underlying attitude toward themselves and their world that life reflects. Their worldview is the picture of the way things in sheer actuality are, their concept of nature, of self, of society. It contains their most comprehensive ideas of order.

Geertz nevertheless draws attention to the fact that although ethos and worldview may be distinguished for purposes of analysis, in the living context of culture they are thoroughly blended together. "The powerfully coercive 'ought' is felt to grow out of a comprehensive factual 'is,' " he says, and by his choice of language indicates sensitivity to the analytic philosophical dogmas divorcing fact from value, which allege that the former is robustly objective, the latter merely subjective. "The tendency to synthesize worldview and ethos at some level, if not logically necessary, is at least empirically coercive—if it is not philosophically justified, it is at least pragmatically universal" (Geertz 1957/ 1973, pp. 126, 127). Hallowell (1960), in accordance with this anthropological and philosophical convention, distinguishes cognitive from normative orientation, but notes at the same time that they are "intimately associated." Because in practice they are so thoroughly entangled, the worldview concept may be understood to include normative orientation as well as cognitive; the ethos (ethics) of a people may thus be included as part of their total worldview.

The ambient and collective quality of the concept of a cultural worldview, together with its unconscious dimension, its unnoticed effect on such seemingly independent processes as perceiving and recognizing, and its subtle influence on conscious thought through unarticulated assumptions, premises, and principles, raises serious ontological and methodological questions, which we must now confront.

III. WHAT IS CULTURE?

We have conjoined the concept of "worldview" with the concept of "culture." Hence, we may not hope to get a real grip on what a cultural worldview is if we cannot attain an adequate working understanding of what a culture is. A systematic definition of "culture," of course, cannot be attempted here. Geertz (1973, p. 4) comments that in *Mirror for Man*, Kluckhohn did not manage both a fully coherent and comprehensive definition of "culture" in an entire chapter devoted to the concept, nor has Geertz himself in "Thick Description: Towards an Interpretive Theory of Culture" achieved anything like a crisp, clear, and concise formula to pin down this absolutely fundamental ethnometaphysical idea. Without saying exactly what culture is, we may nevertheless say a few things about it, mostly by way of analogy, so that we may at least point the way toward a solution of the ontological and methodological problems that we face at the outset of a cultural worldview study.

A. The Ontological Problem

"Though ideational," Geertz (1973, p. 10) remarks, culture "does not exist in someone's head; though unphysical it is not an occult entity. . . . " The ontological status of culture "is the same as that of rocks on the one hand and dreams on the other—they are things of this world." In this respect, "culture" is to some extent analogous to the concept of "species" in biology. The analogy, incidentally, between cultures and species is tacitly recognized by oral peoples, such as the traditional Ojibwa, through clan nomenclature—the bear clan, the crane clan, and so on. A tribe internally structures itself into clans by assimilating subgroups to various animal species.

Species are not physical, though they are quite real. Only the virtually Platonic Linneans, on the one hand, and the more contemporary Ghiselian philosophers of biology, on the other, are tempted to think of species as actual entities; the former think of them as eternal universals, the latter as individual organisms protracted in space and time. Like biological species, cultures are relatively discreet and persistent, though to a lesser degree. Cultures, like species, have discernible characteristics, some of which are borne severally by the specimens and members respectively, but which all individuals in either case do not manifest in equal degree. In species and cultures alike, there are also properties characteristic of the group that the respective individuals do not manifest at all. Density dependent demographic fluctuations are characteristic of some species, and some cultures exhibit matrilineal exogamic social structures—characteristics that could not conceivably be distributed among specimens or members, respectively. And, like species, cultures evolve, though not necessarily unilinearly. Our suggestion here is that the concept of "culture" and its correlative characteristics (one of which is a worldview) is ontologically no more (and, of course, no less) perplexing than the concept of "species" in biology. If we believe that species per se exist, then we should not feel reluctant to believe that cultures per se also exist.

B. The Methodological Problem

According to William H. Kelly (1972),

> It used to be that the way ethnographers got to understand [a culture's] worldview was to sit down with two or three informants and say, "Look, if you have got the time could you let me in your worldview this morning. I surely would appreciate it if you could explicitly tell me how things really work and let me in on the big picture." Consider what would happen if someone asked you that. You would have real difficulty and what you would learn might well be pretty trivial. . . . In addition, the ethnographer would get as many notions as there were informants.

The problem of finding some reliable method of discovering the elements of a culture's worldview—some of which may operate only at an unconscious level and all of which are shared, or collective—will require considerably more discussion and will involve for its solution a more roundabout approach. An extension of our analogy of the concept of culture to the concept of species may prove helpful.

C. Lamarckian Cultural Evolution

Theodosius Dobzhansky (1963, p. 138) suggests that "man receives and transmits . . . not one but two heredities, and is involved in two evolutions, the biological and the cultural." On this point Edward O. Wilson has more recently added an important insight. "Human social evolution," he writes, proceeds along a dual track of inheritance: cultural and biological. Cultural evolution is Lamarckian and very fast, whereas biological evolution is Darwinian and usually very slow. Lamarckian evolution would proceed by the inheritance of acquired characteristics, the transmission to offspring of traits acquired during the lifetime of the parent. . . . Lamarckism has been entirely discounted as the basis of biological evolution, but of course it is precisely what happens in the case of cultural evolution (Wilson 1978, pp. 78, 79).

This dual human evolutionary trajectory creates a paradox: Is *Homo sapiens* a part of nature, just one late-arriving, precocious species among many, many others; or is *Homo sapiens* set apart from nature, uniquely different from all other species? We are both. Biologically we evolve, as do all other species, in a Darwinian fashion, by random genetic mutation and natural selection; culturally we evolve in a Lamarckian fashion by transmitting acquired characteristics to future generations. The difference in temporal scale—the disparate rates of Darwinian biological and Lamarckian cultural evolutionary processes—creates the paradoxical boundary between the human and natural realms.

From the biological point of view, what Lumsden and Wilson (1981) call "euculture" is the defining characteristic of the human species. *Homo sapiens* is the cultural animal, par excellence. A biologist, whose professional perspective on human social phenomena is more distant than that of an anthropologist, might, therefore, simply define culture, in parallel to Darwinian genetic inheritance, as the body of "acquired characteristics" transmitted from one generation to the next, including physical objects and skills like tools and methods of tool making and tool use and also intellectual materials and means—mores, ethics, ideas, cognitive structures, and ways of thinking.

From the evolutionary biological point of view, "information" is the currency of both processes—Darwinian and Lamarckian—of transmission. The structure of the DNA molecule rigidly encodes genetic information. Significant changes in the inherited information content of genes must await a favorable mutation matched to fitting environmental conditions. In the more flexible, more rapidly changing processes of cultural evolution, information is inherited by means of social communication, which among animals may take many different forms. Predatory animals, for example, very often teach their young to hunt by demonstrative methods. Facial gestures, body language, and vocalization convey important "cultural" information among primates. *Homo sapiens* is by no means the only animal to possess something like culture in Wilson's sense of the term. But in the human species, culture has come to be developed to a degree, in comparison with other species, sufficient to constitute a difference in kind—to have become euculture. If human beings possess euculture, it might be more appropriate to say, in view of the hyperextension of the cultural phenomenon in the human species, that other animals possess "protoculture." For human beings, the primary means of adaptation to environments lying outside the climatic range of other primates, including those ancestral to *Homo sapiens,* is culture. It is the means as well for mankind's expanding ecological niche and intensive exploitation of virtually all the globe's environments.

A necessary condition for the luxuriant growth of culture and cultural evolution in the case of mankind is the sophistication of the communication process by means of which information is exchanged and transmitted. In addition to demonstration and symbolic gesturing, upon which other species largely depend for conveying protocultural information, human beings have also evolved language. "Cultural heredity, or simply culture, is transmitted by teaching, imitation, and learning, mainly by means of the symbolic process of human language" (Dobzhansky, 1963, p. 138). In sum, then, euculture—or hereafter simply culture—may be understood biosocially as a corpus of "information" exchanged among members and transmitted from one generation to the next largely by means of language and to a lesser extent by other modes of communication.

D. Biological Unity, Cultural Diversity

The analog of discreet speciation among cultures that we have already noted—their relative separateness and persistence—may be understood through Wilson's suggested Lamarckian evolutionary model. Populations of early *Homo sapiens,* during the Pleistocene, became geographically isolated from one another as they migrated, perhaps in response to prey migrations, to climatic fluctuations, to territorial competition with other human populations, or for any combination of these or other reasons. Cultural adaptation, material as well as ideational, to new environments proceeded rapidly and resulted in highly differentiated and diversified cultures, while genetic information remained relatively stable and uniform, partly due to the natural pace of Darwinian evolution and partly because the selective stress of new climates and ecosystems was largely absorbed through cultural adjustment, thereby relieving adaptive pressure on the gene pool. Thus, human beings remained essentially one species with a very slight tendency toward subspeciation (i.e., racial differentiation) and a very great tendency toward cultural diversity, because culture had taken over almost altogether the evolutionary or adaptive role.

Still, Geertz (1973, p. 22) wonders about the relationship between cultural variation and the unity of the human species. "The great natural variation of cultural forms," he writes, "is, of course, not only anthropology's great (and wasting) resource, but the ground of its deepest theoretical dilemma: how is such variation to be squared with the biological unity of the human species?" Dobzhansky (1963, p. 146) has at least pointed the way toward a resolution of this conundrum: "Mankind is a single species, *Homo sapiens,* which has become not only genetically adapted to, but in fact completely dependent on, culture acquired in every generation by learning mediated through a symbolic language." From the biological point of view, there are no necessarily universal cultural characteristics distributed species-wide. What is universal in human nature is the capacity for *a* culture and a genetic proclivity to learn *a* language. The remarkable unity of the species is a result, as Dobzhansky (1963, p. 147) clearly points out, of a genetic adaptation to cultural skills per se:

> Biological changes increase the fitness for, and the dependence of their carriers on culture, and therefore stimulate cultural developments; cultural developments in turn instigate further genetic changes. This amounts to a positive feedback relationship between the cultural and the biological evolutions. The positive feedback explains the great evolutionary change, so great that it creates the illusion of an unbridgeable gap between our animal ancestors and ourselves.

If this general model of cultural evolution is correct, populations of human beings isolated from one another for the longest period of time (as New World *vis-à-vis* Old World peoples) and occupying environments the most unlike would exhibit the greatest cultural differences. Isolated cultures would rapidly evolve in Lamarckian fashion, each along independent lines, while the carriers or custodians of these cultures remained genetically more or less the same, adaptive genetic evolution having been partially eclipsed by cultural adaptation. In all cases the environment in which genes are tried is primarily a linguistic and cultural environment. Hence, the slow genetic evolution of human populations completely isolated from one another for tens of thousands of years would nevertheless proceed along more or less parallel lines. It is possible to imagine the occurrence of genetic adaptation to a specific culture or language. According to Dobzhansky (1963, p. 146), however, the rapidity of the Lamarckian changes in culture have apparently precluded this possibility, and if such adaptation had occurred, he believes it would have been short-lived: "A genetically fixed capacity to acquire only a certain culture, or a certain role within a culture, would however be perilous; cultures and roles change too rapidly. To be able to learn a language is imperative, but a restriction on this ability to only a certain language would obviously be a drawback."

E. Drawing Cultural Boundaries

The biosocial perspective and our analogy of the social microcosm to the biological macrocosm suggests a method of identifying cultural units. A culture is constituted by a population of people among whom information of a verbal or more generally symbolic kind (in contradistinction to genetic information) is freely exchanged, just as a species, biologically, is constituted by a group of organisms in which genetic information may be freely exchanged. There are as many cultures, then, as there are distinct languages, because language differences inhibit the free exchange of symbolic information. Recent revolutionary modifications in linguistic phenomena, first writing, then print, and now electronic technology, have, however, complicated this otherwise simple relationship, which among oral peoples remains valid to the extent that their cultures remain intact. A further word of caution here is in order. In both the Old World and New, cultural boundaries are less impermeable than species boundaries. Ideas often cross cultural boundaries as easily as do trade goods. This phenomenon is called cultural diffusion.

From this point of view, cultures may be taxonomically grouped into genera or families, on the basis of linguistic kinship. The Ojibwa, for example, speak an Algonkian language and belong to the same cultural family as other Algonkian speakers like the Ottawa, Potawatomi, Micmac, etc. The Navaho speak an Athabaskan language and are thus related from the perspective of linguistic background to certain neighboring tribes (e.g., the Apache) but not to others (e.g., the Hopi). The Navaho are also linguistically related to peoples separated from them by considerable distance, such as the Koyukon who live in the interior of Alaska. As in biological species, other groupings are possible according to other principles of categorization. Species belonging to the same genus taxonomically may occupy very different ecological niches and play different roles in the natural economy, and the ecological similarities of taxonomically very different species may be of more interest and significance for comparative study than their phylogeny. And so with cultures, their economies—hunting and gathering, horticultural, pastoral, and so on—or their social institutions may be of more interest and significance for comparative studies than linguistic kinship.

F. The Methodological Problem Solved: The Analysis of Narratives

Now, let us return to the methodological problem of discovering and describing a worldview by a means more penetrating and reliable than, for example, the method of interviewing reflective old people and/or native philosophers caricatured by Kelly (1972). A people's language is a public property, like a style of shelter or a hunting territory. It is something necessarily common to a culture's members, because if everyone in a given society, to imagine what is in actuality impossible, spoke a different language (i.e., a private language in Wittgenstein's sense), communication would be frustrated and culture would be impossible. The forms of a people's speech, both semantic discriminations and syntactical relationships, contribute significantly to the cognitive orientation thus provided, as it were ready-made, for the culture's members. In each language there is also a public corpus of narrative material that is, especially in oral cultures, the common heritage of all the members. These materials, "narratives" as we call them—myths, legends, and tales, told and retold generation after generation—may serve as the primary resource for worldview analyses. The foundations of this method are stated concisely by Hallowell (1960, p. 28):

> When taken at their face value, myths provide a reliable source of prime value for making inferences about Ojibwa world outlook. They offer basic data about unarticulated, unformalized, and unanalyzed concepts regarding which informants cannot be expected to generalize. From this point of view, myths are broadly analogous to the concrete material of the texts on which the linguist depends for his derivation, by analysis and abstraction, of the grammatical categories and principles of language.

This approach (the narrative approach) is more or less the standard practice of classicists in the effort to recover the cognitive outlook at and just beyond the documentary horizon of Western traditions. What was the worldview of Helladic Greek culture just before and during the period when the Greek world was undergoing the revolutionary process of becoming literate? An analysis of Helladic Greek provides a foundation for answering this question. The subject/predicate syntactical structure, the economy, definiteness, tense stress, and semantic discriminations of their language provide a foundation for a description of the Greek outlook from say the twelfth to the seventh centuries B.C.E. But equally illuminating and complementary are the eventually transcribed and fortunately preserved oral narratives—especially epic and lyric poetry, and more especially still, the poetry of Homer and Hesiod—which supply resources that in comparison with the language alone are much more detailed and subtly shaded.

The profound degree to which the resonance of language and intricate interplay of meanings in the shared oral heritage of an oral culture shapes a people's worldview, the largely unarticulated premises of conscious belief and the cognitive foundations for recognition and perception, is clearly illustrated in the case of ancient Greek culture. Plato, among his other accomplishments, was something of an ethnographer, because he was interested, though hardly dispassionately, both in the semantic and syntactical discrimination and organization of experience in Helladic Greek and in the effect of the Homeric and Hesiodic epics, as well as other cycles of originally oral poetry, on the common perceptions, beliefs, and values of his still largely nonliterate contemporaries. Plato's notorious diatribes against the poets, most frequently against Homer, have been anachronistically misinterpreted as a conflict between reasoned philosophy and the emotive "fine arts." Eric Havelock (1963), however, convincingly argues that Plato's seemingly obsessive concerns about poetry have nothing whatever to do with poetry as fine art. The ethos and worldview conveyed and transmitted in the still living oral heritage provoked the reformer's hostility that Plato so often evinces. So effectively did the oral narrative heritage of preliterate Greek culture shape thought, value, and even perception itself that a person of Plato's utopian, literate, and progressive vision regarded it as the principal obstacle to the values and attitudes made possible by literacy, urbanity, and critical inquiry. On the other hand, Plato himself frequently appealed to a Homeric archetype, to Achilles or some other hero, when he wanted to commend a certain noble quality of character, drawing thus on the omnipresent, timeless, imaginative, mythic world in which he and his contemporaries still partly lived, one foot in and one foot out.

IV. LANGUAGE, WORLDVIEW, AND CULTURAL RELATIVISM

In American cultural studies, the notion that different cultures may provide their members with different cognitive orientations was first suggested, as now we might expect, by those ethnographers primarily interested in American Indian languages. Hoijer (1954, p. 92) credits Franz Boas with a seminal discussion in the introduction to *Handbook of American Indian Languages* (1911). It was Edward Sapir (1929/1964, p. 69), however, who much more deliberately and articulately than Boas proposed the theory that the language of a people unconsciously influences both their processes of thought and their perception in his now classic statement (emphasis added):

> Human beings do not live in the objective world alone, nor alone in the world of social activity as ordinarily understood, but are very much at the mercy of the particular language which has become the medium of expression for their society. It is quite an illusion to imagine that one adjusts to reality essentially without the use of language and that language is merely an incidental means of solving specific problems of communication or reflection. The fact of the matter is that the *"real world"* is to a large extent unconsciously built up on the language habits of the group. No two languages are ever sufficiently similar to be considered as representing the same social reality. *The worlds in which different societies live are distinct worlds, not merely the same world with different labels attached....* We see and hear and otherwise experience very largely as we do because *the language habits of our community predispose certain choices of interpretation.*

A. Linguistic-Cultural Relativism

Language habits, Sapir seems to suggest, arrange for the individual quite unconsciously what would, apart from their meditative function, be a structureless continuum of sensory information or "sense data," to borrow the jargon of his contemporaries, the Logical Positivists. They do so by providing a semantic taxonomy according to which experience is categorized and a syntactic relational scheme that unites the semantically divided items into a systemic whole. A "world" therefore comes into being that is divided into an array of separate entities all tied together and rendered whole by a system of relations that have their ultimate ground in grammar. While in the several Indo-European languages, the verbal tokens for this thing or that are, to be sure, usually different, the taxonomical schemata, possibly because of common origins and family relations among those languages, are so nearly the same that we may correctly suppose that the only difference is one of having "the same world with different labels attached." On the other hand, languages that are only very remotely, if at all, related may analyze, arrange, and connect experience along quite different lines.

Clyde Kluckhohn and Dorothea Leighton (1946/1962, p. 277) clearly express and forcefully illustrate the taxonomical function of language:

> Two languages may classify items of experience differently. The class corresponding to one word and one thought in Language A may be regarded by Language B as two or more classes corresponding to two or more words and thoughts. For instance, where in English one word "rough" (more pedantically "rough-surfaced") may equally well be used to describe a road, a rock, and the business surface of a file, Navaho finds a need for three different words which may not be used interchangeably. While the general tendency is for Navaho to make finer and more concrete distinctions, this is not invariably the case.

The semantic categories and grammatical forms are learned in infancy as the infant acquires skill in its mother tongue and are then, as it were, projected onto the continuum of otherwise undivided and inchoate experience. The native speakers of whatever language then uncritically assume that experience is "given" as so structured, and the "world" as thus mediated by language is naively taken to be real. This hypothetical relationship between language and experience is known as "linguistic relativism" and/or the "Sapir-Whorf hypothesis." It seems to be based upon a signal assumption: that experience as such has no natural divisions and arrangement. In Kluckhohn and Leighton's graphic if largely metaphorical statement, "the pie of experience can be sliced in all sorts of ways" (1946/1962, p. 254). The Western way is apparently not the only way of slicing the pie of experience; as Sapir and other ethnolinguists have insinuated, moreover, neither may it be the only true or correct way. According to Kluckhohn and Leighton (1946/1962, p. 254), "there are as many different worlds upon the earth as there are languages." This and other similar expressions betray more general philosophical and scientific affiliations.

B. Cultural Absolutism

Common sense seems to require belief in a public and independent physical reality. Especially the reflective scientist, however, is painfully aware that the nature of physical reality, the way things themselves in sheer actuality really are, is not directly presented to human consciousness. What exists for consciousness is rather a body of organized sensuous experience, which is naively taken to be reality itself, but which is in fact at best only a subjective image or analog of the objective world. The physical reality posited by common sense, maddeningly, cannot be directly apprehended as something fixed to which the psychological image may be compared, to see if it is true or not. The independently existing physical reality, upon critical reflection, must therefore be posited as an unknown "X," which is assumed to be a source—not to say "cause"—of experience. A subjective image of physical reality is all that we are directly aware of.

An instructive contrast to the relativism of twentieth-century cultural studies is provided by accounts touching on the cognitive culture of American peoples by Europeans adventuring in the New World centuries earlier. In the same decade that saw the publication of Descartes' *Discourse on Method*, a Recollect friar, Gabriel Sagard, described the Huron (like the Ojibwa, a Great Lakes people) in his *Le Grande Voyage et Histoire du Canada*. Among Sagard's remarks we find the following revealing anecdote:

> In each of the fishing lodges [which he had previously meticulously described] there is usually a preacher of fish whose practice it is to preach a sermon to the fish. If these are clever fellows they are much sought after, because the Indians believe that the exhortations of a clever man have great power to attract the fish into their nets. The one we had considered himself among the best, and it was a spectacle to see him gesticulating when he preached, using both tongue and hands, which he did every evening after supper, after having imposed silence and made each one take his place, like himself, lying flat on his back with his abdomen upward. His subject was that the Huron never burned fish-bones [a rule which Sagard earlier admits he had casually violated and had been scolded for so doing]; they, he went on with matchless sentimentalities, exhorted the fish, conjured them, begged and entreated them to come, to allow themselves to be caught, to take courage, to fear nothing, since it was to be of service to some of their friends, who respected them and did not burn their bones. He also made a special one for my benefit, by order of the chief, who said to me afterwards, "Well, my nephew, is that not fine?" "Yes, my uncle," I replied, "according to you, but you and all the rest of the Hurons have very little judgment to think that fish hear and understand your sermons and your talk" (Kinietz, 1965, p. 27).

Immediately preceding this, Sagard tells how he had in the course of trying to convey some idea to the Huron of the fauna of France

> showed them the shape of them with my fingers, the bright fire casting a shadow of them against the wall of the lodge. It happened by chance that next morning they caught far more fish than usual, and they believed that these shadow pictures had been the cause, so simple are they, and they

begged me, furthermore, to be so good as to make them every evening in the same way and to teach them how; this I would not do that I might not be responsible for this superstition, and to give no countenance to their folly (Kinietz, 1965, p. 27).

Sagard makes no attempt to enter sympathetically the Huron construction of experience, e.g., their relations of cause and effect. Not only is Sagard militantly skeptical and contemptuous of these savage "superstitions" and "follies," for him the European worldview is so firmly real and objective that he unconsciously forces Indian behavior and institutions into seventeenth century European categories. The native mediator between man and fish is called a "preacher" of fish, his words a "sermon," and so on. Throughout the writings of his contemporaries we read of Indian "jugglers" and "conjurors" who invoke "demons" whose ultimate origin is "Hell." For these pious Frenchmen there was but one world, and it corresponded exactly to their idea of it. That there may be a plurality of linguistically and culturally constituted worlds, each with a *prima facie* valid claim to be "reality," would have been a matter not so much for denial or disbelief in the seventeenth century as an unimaginable, even unintelligible proposition.

C. Descartes' Subject-Object Dualism

The cultural relativism characteristic of twentieth-century studies of cognitive culture (i.e., the conceptual matrices of various cultures) is rooted in broader developments in Western thought and philosophy that have evolved since the seventeenth century. The concept of worldview in current cultural studies might be better and more fully appreciated, especially its relativistic aspects, if located within this broader historico-intellectual context.

In "The Age of the World Picture" Martin Heidegger (1938/1977) traces the historical roots of the concept of worldview to the beginnings of modern philosophy. Descartes, the reputed "father" of modern philosophy, took the first step toward the notion of a plurality of worldviews, according to Heidegger, by insisting that human experience is fundamentally and unremittingly subjective or phenomenal. Descartes, of course, insisted that the subjective image of the world with which the mind is immediately acquainted might be exclusively true if it corresponded—element for element, relationship for relationship—with things as they actually are, with the real, objective world. Descartes further thought that a strict application of reason as a method of criticism of the subjective image would guarantee its truth, i.e., its correspondence to the objective. But this rational bridge from the manifest subjective domain to the now problematical objective domain was conspicuously flawed in Descartes' philosophy, and therefore skepticism concerning not only the exact nature but the very existence of an objective reality increasingly haunted Western intellectuals.

Experience has been the subject of criticism in Western thought since antiquity; Democritus, at the dawn of Western science, concluded that color, odor, taste, smell, tactile qualities and all other sensations, exist by "convention" (*nomos*) not by "nature" (*physis*). The clever empirical idealism of Berkeley and Hume proves moreover that even common sense is left largely undisturbed if we should do away altogether with the idea of an unperceived independently existing physical world and accept ambient experience as self-grounded. Not only is the hypothetical physical world a step removed by the veil of sensation from immediate consciousness, it is also, evidently, worked over by cognition, part of the function of which is to organize sensation into separate "objects," relationally united. Immanuel Kant was the first Western thinker to propose this idea.

D. Kant's Copernican Revolution in Philosophy

The putative independent physical reality was thus separated from immediate acquaintance by yet another interpretive gloss—cognition as well as sensation. Kant abandoned the dream of the ancient and early modern philosophers to penetrate the veil of sensation, which screens consciousness from the real itself, by means of critical reason. Instead he substituted the pragmatically equivalent idea of a common, indeed a universal, phenomenal reality for all human subjects. Less skeptically than Berkeley and Hume, he retained the unknown "X" (the "thing in itself") as a shared source of phenomenal excitation, but forbade any knowledge of it in principle. In Kant's metaphysic, "things in themselves" recede infinitely into the distance as unknowable sources of stimulation responsible for the involuntary, contingent character of subjective experience. The phenomenal world, the world as experienced, as emergent in consciousness, becomes, in effect, the only "world" or "reality" with which human beings can be acquainted. Phenomena, moreover, are presented to consciousness only insofar as they are conditioned by the forms of "intuition"—namely, space and time—which Kant claimed were *a priori* conditions of experience, because they are, he believed, universal and necessary. That is, all objects are extended in space and all events occur in time, without exception; thus space and time are essentially subjective *a priori* parameters of experience. The cognitive conditions, "the categories of the understanding," are equally basic. Such characteristics of objects as their "unity" or oneness and collectively their "plurality" and "totality," and such relations among objects as their causal connections are, according to Kant, necessary conditions of structured experience, and therefore are prior to the content of experience. Experience can be discriminated from its subjective *a priori* conditions as such because it is contingent. We know *a priori* that all objects are extended in space, that all events occur in time, and that all events have causes, but to know, say, when and why a given tree may fall is a matter of *a posteriori* experience.

This shift in perspective from an ultimately objective orientation to a subjective and phenomenal one Kant himself described as the "Copernican revolution of philosophy." Science could now proceed, undisturbed by the intractable ontological and epistemological problems that had bedeviled Descartes and the ancients. What the ultimate and naked realities were and how they could be known were questions dismissed as "dialectical" and in principle unanswerable. The empirical laws relating and connecting phenomena could, on the other hand, still be ascertained, and further, certain *a priori* or universal and necessary synthetic judgments could be affirmed (e.g., that space is described by Euclidian geometry, or that all events have causes) because they referred only to the structure of our *a priori* intuitive and cognitive mental apparatus per se, not to its emergent phenomenal content.

E. The Einsteinian Revolution in Philosophy

Historically, Kant is truly a watershed figure. Virtually all subsequent Western philosophy and science has felt his enormous influence. If Kant effected a self-styled Copernican revolution in philosophy, Sapir, in American anthropology, quietly added an Einsteinian revolution of his own. Kant held that although the "world" is phenomenal, it is in a certain sense nevertheless one and the same world for everyone, because *all* human beings are innately endowed with identical perceptual and cognitive orientations. By reason of our common humanity, he thought we all possess the same "forms of intuition" and "categories of understanding." The forms of intuition, according to Kant, are (Euclidian) space and (Newtonian) time in terms of which manifold phenomena are presented, while the categories provide a cognitive synthesis of the discreetly and sequentially presented given. Working in concert, the forms of intuition and categories of the understanding create an articulate, unified, and intelligible phenomenal world. Little more than a century after Kant's Copernican revolution in Western intellectual history, the universality and necessity (the *a priori* quality) of Kant's "aesthetic" and "logic" were shattered by a one-two combination punch. Einstein made time a fourth dimension of space and coherently applied a non-Euclidian formalism to his novel space-time continuum, thus demonstrating intraculturally that Kant's forms of intuition were not universal and necessary. And the dawning realization of ethnologists that non-Western oral peoples are not mentally incompletely evolved "primitives," but rather mentally sophisticated peoples who happen cognitively to arrange experience in ways quite different from persons of European heritage was equally fatal for Kant's universalism and absolutism.

The hypothesis that no culture's world is privileged in respect to truth is psychologically very difficult to accept. A particular cultural worldview may certainly be preferred to any other for pragmatic, moral, or aesthetic reasons, but of course assuming the theoretical posture of relativized phenomenalism, none has a corner on the truth-and-reality market. The modern

Western scientific worldview has been so spectacularly successful in its essentially mechanical mastery of the natural environment that its advocates sometimes claim that it is therefore both a better and truer representation of the real than any of the non-Western alternatives. However, despite the appeal of our unsophisticated desire for fixed belief and unshakable truth, the only thing for which technological success is evidence is that acting *as if* the Western worldview were true, the doing of certain things (propelling projectiles, creating large explosions, arranging concrete and metal on a vast scale, sending signals rapidly, transplanting organs from one body to another, etc.) is facilitated. These are not insignificant accomplishments, but they prove nothing beyond themselves.

Perhaps the only objective measure not of truth, but of the pragmatic value of various worldviews is biological. Which of the many cognitive orientations results in the greatest inclusive fitness of its carriers? At the turn of the twentieth century, the answer to this question seemed obvious—at least to those in the West (and North) who were benefiting from the industrial revolution. By the turn of the twenty-first century, serious doubts had emerged about the sustainability of Western memes—which may, it is feared, prove to be self-destructive and therefore, as faulty genes that destroy their carriers, fail the ultimate challenge of the principle of natural selection. Historical events in the twentieth century closely related to cognitive peculiarities of the current Western worldview, principally the development of nuclear technology and the general environmental degradation consequent upon the successful mechanical mastery of nature—all coupled with the increased disparity of material prosperity between the world's rich and poor—have contributed to the persuasiveness of cultural relativism.

F. The Connection Between Relativity in Physics and in Anthropology

The impact of Einsteinian relativity theory on the social sciences appears to have been historically direct and fully conscious. Sapir (1929/1964, p. 74; emphasis added) betrays such an influence in the following comment: "Of all students of human behavior, the linguist should by the very nature of his subject matter be *the most relativist in feeling*, the least taken in by the forms of his own speech." Sapir (1931, p. 578; emphasis added) alludes, more specifically, to Einstein's non-Euclidian geometry in this comment: "Inasmuch as languages differ very widely in their systematization of fundamental concepts, they tend to be only loosely equivalent to each other as symbolic devices and are, as a matter of fact, incommensurable in the sense in which two systems of points in a plane are, on the whole, *incommensurable to each other if they are plotted out with reference to differing systems of coordinates.*" And Joseph H. Greenberg (1977, pp. 80–81) notes that the term "linguistic relativity" [was] used by Whorf during a period when Einstein's theory of relativity had considerable influence on general patterns of thought. Our concepts are asserted to be "relative" to the particular language which we speak. The term "linguistic worldview" ("linguistic Weltanschauung") suggests another aspect of this theory. It is not only particular concepts that are derived from our language but also a coherent way of looking at the world, a philosophy, as it were, which will differ from language to language.

According to Benjamin Whorf, relativity theory in physics is not only a scientific paradigm to which linguistic-cultural relativism is analogous, it is also, and there is some merit to his claim, an alternate metaphysic, a distinct subcultural worldview. "The Hopi language and culture," he writes, "conceals a metaphysics, such as our so called naive view of space and time does, or as the Relativity theory does; yet it is a different metaphysics from either" (Whorf 1950/1956, p. 28). The impact of Einstein's theory of relativity on the study of the cognitive dimension of culture appears to be twofold: it serves as both a scientific paradigm to which linguistic-cultural relativism is a social-science analog and as a dramatic example of a fundamental and revolutionary change in the worldview of Western science, affording, therefore, an intracultural illustration of the possibility of mutually incompatible but more or less self-consistent conceptual schemata for the interpretation of the experiential raw materials.

G. The Basic Principle of Relativity in Physics

So far as the comparison of cultural relativism to relativity as a scientific paradigm is concerned, the basic principle of physical relativity appears to be that no "body of reference" is privileged in respect to measurements of motion and rest. Motion and rest are not "absolute," in other words, they are relative to some frame of reference that may be arbitrarily chosen. From the point of view of an observer on one "body of reference" an object may be judged to move along a certain path at a certain speed. From the point of view of a different observer on another "body of reference" the same object may be judged to move along a different path and/or at a different speed, or it may be judged not to move at all, to be at rest. The question then arises: Which observer makes the "correct" judgment about how the object is really moving?

The answer, according to the theory of relativity, is that neither judgment can be regarded as correct or true except in relation to a certain specified "system of co-ordinates" associated with an arbitrarily chosen "body of reference" and that questions regarding the real or absolute state of motion or rest, upon critical reflection, make no sense at all. At least they are not experimentally meaningful. If this fundamental idea is the principal paradigm provided by relativity theory in physics, then linguistic-cultural relativism appears to be rather obviously analogous. The cognitive system for the interpretation of experience that is mapped out in the semantic/syntactic morphology of a culture's language is, according to linguistic-cultural relativism, a qualitative and informal analog of Einstein's concept of a coordinate system or frame of reference. An event referred to two incongruent (not to say "incommensurable") cultural systems for the interpretation of experience may be differently judged or interpreted in each. In his (1916) popular exposition of relativity, Einstein illustrates the relativity of the temporal concept of "simultaneity" by means of imagined flashes of lightning striking a railroad track at two places, at once from the perspective of one observer at rest with respect to the track, but sequentially from the perspective of another whose coordinate system is established with respect to a moving (relatively speaking) train.

H. Analogous Relativity in Anthropology

To illustrate the analogy of anthropological linguistic-cultural relativism with physical relativity we may borrow an anecdote involving thunder from Hallowell's experiences with the Ojibwa, apropos of the Einsteinian lightning illustration. Hallowell (1960, p. 23) informs us "that the language of these people, like all their Algonkian relatives, formally express a distinction between 'animate' and 'inanimate'." Further, " 'Thunder' . . . is not only reified as an 'animate' entity, but has the attributes of a 'person' and may be referred to as such." Now, an old man and his wife together with Hallowell's informant were sitting in a tent one summer afternoon during a storm. "Suddenly the old man turned to his wife and asked, 'did you hear what was said?' 'No,' she replied, 'I didn't catch it' " (Hallowell 1960, p. 34). They referred to the thunder: "The old man had thought that the thunder birds had said something to him." Hallowell (1960, p. 31) also reports that on more than one occasion he had explained thunder and lightning according to "the white man's conception" of them. But, "of one thing I am sure: My explanations left their own beliefs completely unshaken."

According to the Ojibwa linguistic and conceptual arrangement of experience, thunder is animate and personal. Thus the old man heard a voice (albeit not very clearly) in the thunder, or, more exactly, he heard the voice of the thunder beings themselves. If we choose to say that he did not hear thunder birds speaking to him, our statement amounts to little more than a determination on our part to believe that things are as our language and beliefs interpret them, and would seem precisely analogous to Einstein's observer on the railroad embankment who might insist that the flashes of lightning were in fact simultaneous, though they were not so experienced by the observer riding the train because his perception was "distorted" by his state of (absolute) motion. Einstein's observer's claim, despite its intuitive appeal, is nevertheless quite indefensible, and so is Hallowell's typical "white man," who might have concluded that the old Ojibwa was merely deceived by the "superstitions" characteristic of his tribe.

If the argument is pressed and one claims that the scientific account of thunder permits its advocates to predict or anticipate future meteorological experiences (for example that hearing thunder will be accompanied by a drop in barometric pressure) and that this *proves* the "white man's conception" true, apart from pointing out the logical fallacy of "Affirming the Consequent" the Ojibwa could argue, by parity of reasoning, that their view also permits anticipation of future experience, because a message from the thunder birds may have significance of another phenomenal kind. The Ojibwa theory of the cause of thunder may make the Ojibwa less able to anticipate concomitant events of a certain sort, like barometer readings; on the other hand, the "white man's" theory may also lead its partisans to ignore subsequent events of a different sort to which the Ojibwa, because of their cognitive orientation, are more sensitive, e.g., changes in the attitude of game animals, which the thunder may announce, or the malevolent intentions of a sorcerer of which the thunder may warn, and so on. Now should subsequent experience confirm these expectations, as it might if—for example, a hunt were undertaken with successful results or an otherwise inexplicable illness suddenly appeared—then the Ojibwa prediction would be verified and the thunder-bird "hypothesis" and the general cognitive system into which it fits would be confirmed. It should be noted at this point that more than "linguistic facts," i.e., the semantic/syntactic structures of the Ojibwa language, are at play in the Ojibwa interpretation of thunder. The more detailed quirks of thunder-bird behavior is a matter not so much of linguistic structure as of narrative content.

I. Relativism in Postmodern Philosophy: Truth or Tenability?

The cultural-linguistic relativism characteristic of twentieth-century anthropology is complemented by the relativism of contemporary "postmodern" philosophy. In the Anglo-American analytic tradition, Richard Rorty (1979) points out the futility of the hope that the human mind eventually can perfectly mirror nature. Some Continental philosophers—among them Michel Foucault (1972), Jean-Francois Lyotard (1984), and Bruno Latour (1999)—variously argue that what we naively suppose to be unvarnished reality is actually "socially constructed." Arran Gare (1995) traces the "deconstruction" by contemporary postmodern philosophers of various aspects of the socially constructed reality of Western culture back through Heidegger and Nietzsche all the way to Giambattista Vico who lived approximately a century after Descartes. Vico thought that human knowledge could never penetrate nature because we did not create it, but that we could know human society because we did create that.

In general, contemporary postmodern philosophers agree with contemporary anthropologists that the subtleties of semantic discriminations in a culture's linguistic conventions are the principal means by which "reality" is socially constructed. Thus the power of naming is often the site of intense intracultural struggle. In an armed conflict, are the guerrillas who are battling an established government "terrorists" or "freedom fighters"? Women were once socially constructed as the "weaker sex" in Western culture. Feminist critics, fortified with the insights of postmodern philosophy, have successfully deconstructed and reformed, for the most part, the semantic-cognitive domain of gender-biased terms in English and other European languages.

Cultural-linguistic relativism in anthropology and deconstructive postmodern philosophy liberates non-Western worldviews from the tyranny of the globally dominant Western worldview. That is its virtue. The Western worldview is not exclusively true; nor are all the rest false and superstitious. Indeed, no worldview is true; and none is false. But cultural-linguistic relativism is also potentially vicious. How can we claim that, say, a racist worldview is wrong? It by no means follows, from the fact that no worldview is true, that we cannot prefer one worldview to another for sound epistemological reasons. Although no worldview is true, not all worldviews are equally *tenable*.

As noted, Boylan (2000) suggests criteria that a tenable worldview must meet. It must be self-consistent. A tenable worldview must also be comprehensive; it must take into account the full range of experience that its subscribers encounter. Living simply and in remote, isolated areas, some peoples may never encounter things like cell phones, computers, barometers, or Geiger counters. Therefore their worldviews need not comprehend such things in order to be tenable. Further, we have here suggested that a tenable worldview must meet a pragmatic criterion. It must enable its subscribers to survive and flourish—in the long run as well as short term. Boylan (2000) adds that a tenable worldview must also meet a moral criterion. It must be good. That would rule out the Nazi worldview propounded by Hitler. Finally, we might suggest that a tenable worldview meet an aesthetic criterion. It must be beautiful. Such a criterion is difficult to specify or even to illustrate and is far more elusive than the others, but its aesthetic quality is often a worldview's most endearing feature.

J. The Uncertainty Principle in Worldview Analysis

Mary B. Black (1974) has summarized the field of formal cognitive cultural research, which emerged after the more programmatic and less methodologically deliberate work of Sapir, Whorf, and their contemporaries. Ward Goodenough (1956) appears to have been a pivotal figure in this development, forthcoming under "more or less synonymous labels . . . : descriptive semantics, ethnographic semantics, ethnosemantics, ethnoscience," according to Black (1974, p. 522). She notes that in ethnographic semantics (etc.) an important distinction may be drawn between microsystems and macrosystems of belief as objects of study. The former have to do with separate cognitive "domains" (e.g., color discriminations, medicine classifications, taboo types, social roles and status, and so on), the latter with the interrelationship of several cognitive domains within the same culture. Such interrelationships include both lateral linkages between domains and hierarchical belief structures that subtend multiple ancillary domains. Formal studies of semantic discriminations and interrelations are foundational to a worldview analysis, but cannot capture the richer pattern of ideas playing on the surface of a symantic/syntactic infrastructure.

The narrative legacy of a culture transcends bare linguistic formalities and embodies its most fundamental ideas of how the world is organized and integrated at the most general level. The "ethno-metaphysics," as Hallowell called it, informing an Ojibwa environmental ethic is built on Ojibwa semantic and syntactic structures, to be sure, but is found as much, or more, in the substance of what is said in the language as in the linguistic organization of what is said. Indeed, one function of a culture's substantive narrative tradition is to school the young, remind the old, and reiterate to all members how things at large come together and what the meaning of it all is. The narratives of a culture, in other words, provide not only a most enjoyable diversion, they serve pedagogical and archival purposes as well. Thus, in addition to formal ethnoscientific research focused on linguistic structures, ethno-metaphysics requires the sort of qualitative analysis more characteristic of philosophy and literary criticism than of the social sciences. As we mentioned before, an analogous approach is typically used to arrive at some idea of the worldview characteristic of Western civilization at the dawn, and just beyond, of Western recorded history. Epic, lyric, mythic, and other originally oral narrative materials indeed are the principal resource for these traditionally less formal literary and philosophical analyses of the ancient preclassical Western worldview. The narrative approach to getting at a cultural worldview allows the culture to speak for itself and invites, by its very informality, alternative interpretations and analyses.

The idea that ethno-metaphysics is an essentially interpretive enterprise raises a fundamental question: Is cross-cultural interpretation possible? Even with the best and most complete cultural information available, there is an inherent uncertainty to the enterprise. Western science and philosophy represent in themselves specific cultural values, goals, and biases. They are indeed integral parts of the prevailing Western worldview. Any investigator of a non-Western worldview, to the extent that he or she remains an "investigator," must experience and report another culture's worldview through the semantics and syntax provided by English (and/or its sister tongues) and the cognitive orientation of the Western worldview. Of course contemporary postmodern philosophy and anthropology, as we have been at some pains to point out, maintain a relativist posture toward the worldviews of other cultures and place a premium value on objective and unbiased information gathering, theoretical organization, and reportage. Hence, the contemporary

Western investigator of another worldview will consistently try to compensate for the conceptual dispositions imposed by his or her own primary cultural outlook. But in the last analysis there is no purely neutral or objective place to stand, no acultural vantage point, and thus a measure of uncertainty must in principle be admitted.

V. THE OJIBWA NARRATIVES

When Europeans first made contact with them in the mid-seventeenth century, the people whom we today know as the Ojibwa—or Anishinabe, meaning "original man," as they call themselves (Warren 1970)—were living along the north shore of Lake Huron and around the east end of Lake Superior. During the summer, they gathered for the most part in villages at major fisheries, such as Sault Ste. Marie, and dispersed in the winter to live and hunt in smaller family groups. The rigid system of family hunting and trapping territories that came to characterize the Northern Ojibwa seems, however, to have developed in the post-contact period under the impetus of the fur trade (Bishop, 1970).

A. Four Segments of the Ojibwa People

There was and is no Ojibwa "tribe" in the sense of a unified sociopolitical entity. Deepening involvement in the fur trade stimulated migrations of various groups from their earlier homeland and by about 1800 there were four identifiable segments of the Ojibwa people. Those who moved westward through the region north of Lake Superior are commonly referred to as the Saulteaux (the name itself derived from their former residence at Sault Ste. Marie), or Northern Ojibwa. They lived mainly in small, isolated hunting bands, and, in contrast to their kin to the south, did not harvest wild rice or make maple sugar (Bishop, 1976; Hallowell, 1955,1976; Rogers, 1962). The Southwest Ojibwa—or Chippewa—migrated through what is today the Upper Peninsula of Michigan and westward into northern Wisconsin and eastern Minnesota, displacing the Sioux, who had previously inhabited large sections of that territory. Historically, they were hunters and gatherers preoccupied with the fur trade (Hickerson, 1956, 1962, 1970). Living far enough south for seasonal crops to ripen, they were also agriculturists (Ritzenthaler, 1978). The Southeastern Ojibwa inhabited portions of the Lower Peninsula of Michigan and adjoining areas of Ontario, where they hunted, fished, and engaged in horticulture (Rogers, 1978). The Bungee, or Plains Ojibwa, who integrated themselves into the bison-hunting economy of the Northern Plains, comprised the western-most group of the Ojibwa people.

Of these four divisions, the first two have historically been the most prominent. While there were important cultural differences between them—

for example, villages such as the one at Chequamegon on the southern shore of Lake Superior were more permanent and important in the south than in the north, while the system of family hunting and trapping territories was rigorously developed in the north, but not in the south—they shared a common language and participated in the broad patterns of the Woodland Algonkian culture (Quimby 1960, Ritzenthaler 1978, Ritzenthaler & Ritzenthaler 1970).

B. The Role of Narratives in Oral Education

It is regrettable, though hardly surprising, that early European travelers among the Indians overlooked much and misunderstood a lot of what they did see. Burdened as they were with chauvinistic attitudes toward their own worldview and the institutions of their own culture, they were apt to revile the natives as existing in an "uneducated and unimproved state." In the eyes of one of these sojourners, Indians in general appeared "to be the same every where, and to have nearly the same habits, and customs, and manners." He lists some of these—conjuring, decorating the body, and the like—and concludes: "I have not referred to the disgusting habits of these uninstructed and unfortunate People to disaffect you towards them, but rather to excite your pity" (McKenney 1827, p. 379). Several decades later another observer, Philander Prescott, commented on the existence of myths among the Sioux. Though he did not attribute to them any educational function he at least recognized that they were reflective of the native culture: "The Indians tell many tales about the departed spirits troubling them. . . . These tales do not give much, if any, insight to a future state, but they agree with the present manners and customs very well" (Schoolcraft 1851–1857, vol. 4, p. 70).

To imagine a culture in which no "educational" activities take place is quite impossible, but that the main modes of such activity might differ from society to society is not at all surprising. Among North American Indians we know that myths and tales were frequently important in this regard. Thus Skinner and Satterlee (1915, pp. 226, 232, 235) inform us that "the part that folklore has played in influencing Menomini [an Algonkian people living west of Lake Michigan] social life and vice versa, can scarcely be overestimated. Even today folklore forms an important factor in determining many usages." The tales themselves are employed to settle disputes, and are used as a basis for interpreting current events. "They keep alive many beliefs, and are a repository of obsolete customs." They are used to inculcate "the principles of honor, virtue, and bravery among the children," and many "apparently trivial stories" are transmitted "presumably for no other reason than that they contain practical information." A similar point is made by McTaggart (1976) about the Mesquakie (Fox) Indians of Iowa. In a series of footnotes in his collection of Tlingit myths, Swanton (1909) records remarks by his informant—a chief from

Wrangell, Alaska—on how specific episodes were cited when people wished to give their children (or other persons in need of admonition) advice. To give one further example, after summarizing two Eskimo stories upholding the custom of providing for destitute children and orphans, Hambly (1926, p. 359) comments: "With regard to this particular point, juveniles are educated in two ways, namely, by the examples of their elders and the grafting of ideas by means of attractive narratives."

George Copway was an acculturated Ojibwa Indian who saw the Christianization of his people as having been, on the whole, a good thing. And he encouraged the education of Indians in the white man's schools. But for all that, he did not lose his appreciation of the traditional narratives. "The Ojibways," Copway (1850, p. 95) wrote, "have a great fund of legends, stories, and historical tales, the relating and hearing of which form a vast fund of winter evening instruction and amusement." Many people could tell such stories every evening from October to May without repeating themselves.

> Some of these stories are most exciting and so intensely interesting, that I have seen children during their relation, whose tears would flow most plentifully, and their breasts heave with thoughts too big for utterance. Night after night for weeks have I sat and eagerly listened to these stories. The days following, the characters would haunt me at every step, and every moving leaf would seem to be a voice of a spirit. These legends have an important bearing on the character of the children of our nation. The fire-blaze is endeared to them in after years by a thousand happy recollections. By mingling thus, social habits are formed and strengthened (Copway 1850, p. 97).

C. The Provenance of These Narratives

The narratives constituting the core materials of this book were collected by William Jones under the auspices of the Carnegie Foundation during the years 1903–1905. He did his fieldwork west and north of Lake Superior. Jones was an especially well qualified and gifted collector of Ojibwa myth and story. He was an American Indian with an extensive knowledge and command of native languages. And he was an academically trained and highly skilled ethnographer, the first American Indian to earn a Ph.D. in anthropology. In 1906 Jones accepted a position with the Field Museum of Natural History, and, strangely, was sent immediately on an anthropological mission to the Philippine Islands! Unfortunately, the natives there with whom he was working murdered him in 1909. He took his Ojibwa materials with him to the Philippines, but died before he had an opportunity to revise and send them back for publication. His collection of Ojibwa tales was eventually rescued and found its way into print under the title *Ojibwa Texts* (vol. 1, 1917; vol. 2, 1919), edited by Truman Michelson. Jones's Ojibwa materials were published as he had transcribed them with his rough, unadorned English translations on facing pages. The translations have a particular charm; they are direct and literal and thus they preserve much of the flavor, inflection, and syntactical patterning of the native language. Even then, in the first decade of the twentieth century, prior to the Sapir-Whorf hypothesis and long before the emergence of "ethnosemantics," Jones (1917, p. x) presciently planned to provide "a linguistic introduction dealing with the phonetics, morphology, and syntax of the Ojibwa language, together with a dictionary of stems to the same" as a foundation for understanding the narratives.

We cannot, of course, assume that these narratives have come down to us unchanged from aboriginal times. Culture is inherently dynamic and cultural change occurs with or without radical foreign influence. By the time Jones made his collection, the Ojibwa had been in contact with Europeans and European Americans for some two and a half centuries, had migrated hundreds of miles from their pre-Columbian homeland, and had suffered the cultural disruptions of Old World diseases, war, the fur trade, and Christianity. Quimby goes so far as to suggest that the fur trade brought about profound changes in native economic systems and caused the appearance of "a uniformity of tribal culture" in the Upper Great Lakes region. Quimby (1960, pp. 147–48) does, however, note that "the fur trade seems to have most favored the aboriginal mode of life of the Chippewa [i.e., Ojibwa] who lived by hunting and fishing. Consequently, as the Pan-Indian culture developed in response to the fur trade, it developed in the direction of the Chippewa culture type." Certainly the Ojibwa were influenced by their contacts with whites (and vice versa). This is particularly obvious in the realm of material culture, such as modes of transportation, weapons, dress, diet, and the like. Some European influence may also be detected in Ojibwa cognitive culture. For example in one story reprinted here, "The Birth of Nanabushu," the hero appears to have been immaculately conceived. Nanbushu (as we explain in the "Interpretive Essay") is, among other things, the Ojibwa's principal culture hero and—in some narratives—a kind of savior of the people. Hence it is possible that his birth to a virgin may reflect some borrowing from the European Catholic worldview to which the Ojibwa were exposed by missionaries. As to European influence in the domain of material culture, in "Nanabushu Swallowed by the Sturgeon," Nanabushu sharpens his (talking) axe on a whetstone—thus evidently the axe is metal, of ultimately Western origin. On the other hand, the axe used by the Foolish Maidens in "Clothed-in-Fur" breaks at the edge—therefore evidently that axe is made of stone and not of ultimately Western origin.

D. The Authenticity of These Narratives

Stories, in any case, have a life of their own. The Ojibwa in fact regarded the stories themselves—in addition to some of the characters in them—as "other-than-human persons" (Hallowell 1960). The characters, the plot, the action of stories are bound together into a coherent whole. Thus core themes of oral narratives such as these remain relatively unchanged in the midst of radical change in other dimensions of culture, such as technology, economy, and religion. For example, if Nanabushu's immaculate conception in "The Birth of Nanabushu" is a borrowed detail, the essential Nanabushu personality and character remains un-Christianized (and unsanitized) in this and the other stories about him. By way of comparison, consider so-called fairy tales in Western culture. They are about forlorn princesses sequestered in castles and princes who have been turned by witches into frogs, about ogres, fairy godmothers, and magic mirrors. They are passed down, largely still orally, from generation to generation, even though most modern Western countries have no royalty living in castles; and sincere belief in witches, fairies, ogres, and magic is rare in the West. The Ojibwa stories reprinted here are still alive and intact in Ojibwa culture today. According to Rabb and McPherson (1994, p. 10), directors of the Native Philosophy Project at Lakehead University in Ontario, Canada, located in Thunder Bay on the north shore of Lake Superior in the heart of Ojibwa territory, "Many of our students have found these [Jones] narratives very familiar and are able to tell the entire story with astonishing accuracy after reading only the first few sentences."

Because Jones did not have a chance to polish his translations, their rough form preserves something of the character of the original Ojibwa language in its word order, pacing, and rhythm. As Jones (1917, p. xi) himself put it, "Simplicity is a characteristic mark of the narratives throughout: they run along with . . . an even, quiet pace." He also notes that

> The language of most of the material is conversational; the periods are short. . . . Vagueness of reference is [also] common. The unconscious assumption on the part of the narrator that one is familiar with the background of a narrative is one cause why. . . . This vagueness of reference has been helped along by the tendency to abbreviated expression—such as the frequent occurrence of a quotation without mention of the speaker, and the presence of subjects and objects without verbs—thus rendering sentences often extremely eliptical (Jones 1917, pp. ix–x).

To make the stories intelligible to an anglophone audience, Jones added in parentheses the missing identity of speakers and elements of diction necessary to complete sentences. He seems to have kept these additions to the minimum required to make them coherent without compromising the accuracy of his English rendition. (We have supplied an example of the Jones texts with the Ojibwa and English on facing pages.)

At the time Jones recorded these narratives, the people from whom he got them were living in a very remote and isolated area by largely traditional means of subsistence in an era before automobiles, snowmobiles, and airplanes and before radio and television. As an American Indian himself, Jones was trusted by his informants. And he recorded their stories in their own language. Jones's untimely death—tragic though it may be—bequeaths to us one happenstance that is of advantage for our enterprise of worldview analysis. He had planned to polish his translations and thus make them more accessible and palatable to readers of English. But his death prevented him from doing so. Here then we find no glosses, reworkings, embellishments, or paraphrases. These narratives are as rawly authentic and unredacted as any available in English. In short, Western cultural influence—both on the storytellers and on the stories themselves as the ethnographer presents them—is minimal. And if our surmise—that stories remain relatively constant in the midst of radical change in other domains of culture—is correct, they are a window on a socially constructed reality that evolved independently for at least ten thousand years. We hope that, in these tales, a traditional Ojibwa way of perceiving the world and associated environmental ethic will come through to the reader with some clarity and vigor. And that reality is as different from the one socially constructed in Western cultures as any that can be imagined.

chapter two

narratives

1. The Orphans and Mashōs

A. The Brothers' Escape

Once on a time they say there lived a man and his wife, and two they say was the number of their children; one was very small. And it is said that they continued there. The man, as often as the days came round, hunted for game; and the woman, on her part, gathered fire-wood and cooked the meals. And their two children were boys. And the boy that was older had the care of his tiny brother while his mother went to gather fire-wood and while she was busy at her work.

Once on a time, so they say, while they were living at home, the man was every day away on a hunt for game. When the man came home, his wife would that moment go for fire-wood, that she might make ready to cook the meal. The children were also very much neglected. And once they say the man felt as if he would give reproof, (and) thought: "I wonder what is going on!" he thought. That was the way it always was, he would find his wife in the act of getting ready to cook the meal. Nothing did the man say. And then they say he thought: "Now, I will ask my son that is older what is going on here at our home." Thereupon truly he asked his son in secret: "My son," he said to him, "come, and truly tell me, what is your mother doing? Straightway does she go to work as soon as I come home. And both you and your little brother look as if you were weeping all the time."

And the little boy did not wish to say anything. Then at last the man, after he had spoken much to him, was told: "Well, I really will tell you, yet I am not anxious to tell you anything; and I will tell you, simply for the reason that very sad am I all the time, that my little brother should cry during the whole of every day," he (thus) said to his father. "For just as soon as you are gone in the morning, then later does our mother also make ready and adorn herself and carefully comb her hair. Thereupon she too goes away, and you almost precede her on the way home. She comes and takes off her clothes, and then gives suck to my little brother," he (thus) said to his father.

And the man said: "That is just what I wanted to know," he said. And then the man, so they say, on the morrow lay in wait for his wife. In fact, the man, on the morning of the next day, pretended that he was going away; and near the place from whence he could barely see the lodge, he remained in hiding. He thought: "I will now see what she is going to do." And so truly now was he gone.

Now, afterwards, when he was clearly gone, then truly did his wife come out of the lodge. Gracious, but she was in gay attire! Very beautiful was she. Right over there by a straight course she went, by way of the path used in going after the fire-wood. And not exactly did he make out just what his wife was up to. And then again, they say, on the next day he did the same thing, he went over to the place where he had barely lost sight of her on the day before. And then he found standing alone a great tree, which was very red by reason of the bark being peeled off on account of much travel upon it. And then, "It is perhaps here that she goes," he thought. And very plain was the beaten path (to the tree). And then he thought: "It is near by this place that I will hide myself," he thought.

Thereupon, of a truth, coming hither into view was his wife. Oh, but she was truly arrayed in fine attire! Now close by she came to where the tree was standing. Whereupon the woman pounded upon the tree, at the same time she said: "O my husbands! I am come once again," she said.

Without ceasing, they say, out came crawling the snakes. In a little while she was coiled about by them, and made use of as a wife.

And the man saw what his wife was doing. He went speedily away; around he turned (and) went home. And then he spoke to his children, he said to them: "I've seen what your mother is doing. I've made up my mind to kill her. —And you, my son," he said to him, "your wee little brother would I have you take away, I would that you carry him on your back," he said to him. "And I here will remain until the arrival of your mother," he said to him. "Do as well as you can, my son," he said to him; "so that you may live, and also save the life of your wee little brother. Straight in yonder direction shall you go," he said to them; "straight toward the west, for over by that way will you go and see your grandmothers," he said to his little son.

"And yet I say to you, she will pursue you; in spite of all, will your mother (follow you). And don't ever under any condition look behind you!" he said to him. "And also don't ever stop running!" he said to him. "And by and by at that place will your grandmothers give you words of advice," he said to him. And then they say he took up the cradle-board on which was tied his little son. He lifted it upon the back of his son who was older.

And with that cradle-board the boy almost touched the ground. And as he started away, "Go fast, my son! at full speed must you go," said the man to him. "As for me, here will I remain."

44

3. The Orphans and Mashōs.

I.

Ningutinga kīⁿwäⁿ anicinābä aˑïˑndā wīdigämāgąnąn gayä nīji-
wąn kīwäⁿ unīdcānisiwān; päjik āˈpidci agāⁿcīwąn. Mīdec kīwäⁿ
aˑïˑndāwąg. Inini ändasogījik ąndawändcigä; awädec iˈkwä kayä
wīn mąnisä tcībāˈkwä gayä. Īni'ᵘ dec unīdcānisiwā mądcinīⁿj
5 kwīwisänsąg. Mīdec awä zäzīˈkizit kwīwisäns känawänimāt ucī-
mäyänsąn ugīn mąnisänit tąnamaˈkąmigizinitsagu gayä.

Ningudingdąc kīwäⁿ aˑïˑndāwāt awä inini kayä wīn ändasogījiˈk
mādcāt papāndowändcigät. Awinini patagwicing umiˈkawān
wīwąn pîtcinag wīmanisät kayä wītcībāˈkwät. Ąbinōdcīyąg gayä
10 āˈpitci nicīwunātisiwąg. Nīguting dąc kīwäⁿ awinini māminō-
nändąm, inändąnk: "Ąmantcisa äjiwäbątogwän?" inändąm. Mīgu tąsing äjimiˈkawāt īni'ᵘ wīwąn pitcīnąg mādciˈtānit tcībāˈkwä-
nit. Kāwīn kägō iˈkitosī inini. Mīdec kīⁿwäⁿ änändąnk: "Taga,
nīngągagwätcimā ningwisis zäzīˈkisit ānīn äjiwäbaˈk ändāwāt."
15 Mīdąc kägäˈt äjigagwädcimāt ogwisisänsąn kīmōtc: "Ningwisis,"
udinān, "ambäsanōnā wīndąmawicîn, ānīn änaˈkąmigisit kīga?
Pîtcīnąg kimādciˈtād tägwicinānin. Kayä gīn kecīmäⁿyäns kayä
ijināgusi mawit panä."

Kwīwizänsidac kāwīn kägō wīˑiˑˈkitusī. Gägaˈpīdąc aˑiˑnini
20 āˑïˑndącimāt udigōn: "Ānīc kigawīndamōnsa, ānawi kāwin kägō
kïwiwīndamōsīnūninābąn; kīgawīndamōnidacigu äˈpītci kaskändą-
mān aˈpanä nicīmäⁿyäns mawit kākabägījiˈk," udinān ōsąn. "Mīgu'
kāˑaˑnimādcāyąnini kigicäp nānāge kayä wīn ninganān mīga'yä wīn
ujīˈtād zazägāwąt wäwäni gayä pināˈkwäˑuˑ. Mīdec äjimādcāt
25 kayä wīn, mīdec kägā kīgäsiˈkawā pitągwicing. Pīˑāˑntcikwąn-
ayät kayädec pinūnāt nicīmäⁿyänsąn," udinān ōsąn.

Original transcription of Ojibwa narrative.

45

3. The Orphans and Mashōs.

I.

Once on a time they say there lived a man and his wife, and two they say was the number of their children; one was very small. And it is said that they continued there. The man, as often as the days came round, hunted for game; and the woman, on her part, gathered fire-wood and cooked the meals. And their two children were boys. And the boy that was older had the care of his tiny brother while his mother went to gather fire-wood and while she was busy at her work.

Once on a time, so they say, while they were living at home, the man was every day away on a hunt for game. When the man came home, his wife would that moment go for fire-wood, that she might make ready to cook the meal. The children were also very much neglected. And once they say the man felt as if he would give reproof, (and) thought: "I wonder whăt is going on!" he thought. That was the way it always was, he would find his wife in the act of getting ready to cook the meal. Nothing did the man say. And then they say he thought: "Now, I will ask my son that is older what is going on here at our home." Thereupon truly he asked his son in secret: "My son," he said to him, "come, and truly tell me, what is your mother doing? Straightway does she go to work as soon as I come home. And both you and your little brother look as if you were weeping all the time."

And the little boy did not wish to say anything. Then at last the man, after he had spoken much to him, was told: "Well, I really will tell you, yet I am not anxious to tell you anything; and I will tell you, simply for the reason that very sad am I all the time, that my little brother should cry during the whole of every day," he (thus) said to his father. "For just as soon as you are gone in the morning, then later does our mother also make ready and adorn herself and carefully comb her hair. Thereupon she too goes away, and you almost precede her on the way home. She comes and takes off her clothes, and then gives suck to my little brother," he (thus) said to his father.

Translation of Ojibwa narrative.

And truly the man remained. He put things in order, much fire-wood he gathered. And when he had finished work, then he went inside. He was prepared to kill his wife. Now, in truth, he suspected that she was coming. And he was ready with bow and arrow to shoot her as she came entering in. As soon as she lifted the flap of the doorway, then he shot her, at the very centre of her heart he shot her.

And then he was asked by her: "Why do you do it?"

But the man made no remark.

And the woman came over there by the edge of the fire and fell.

And the man dragged her, and closer to the centre of the fire he placed her. Thereupon he built a great fire, and then he burned her; and while she was burning up, he gazed upon his wife.

He was addressed by her saying: "Now, why do you treat me thus? You have brought woe upon our children by making orphans of them."

The man did not say anything; for in truth he had seen what his wife had done, and very much was he angered by her. And the woman said all sorts of things, that she might be pitied by her husband.

But the man had not a single word to say to her; he simply worked with all his might to burn her up. And when a little way the fire went down, then again would he be addressed by her, till finally the woman wept. In vain she tried to appease the wrath of her husband. Yet no pity did she get from him.

Consequently they say the man became very tired with keeping up the fire all night long, (and) he wanted sleep. And all the time did his wife have the same power of voice. And then once more he built up a great fire. And when it was nearly morning, they say that then was when he burned her up; and he no longer heard her voice. And then truly in good earnest he built up the fire. And then they say by morning he had her all burned up.

Accordingly he covered up his fire. Whereupon he too went away, but in another direction he went.

And now once more the children are taken up in the story. It is said that one evening, when the boy was travelling along and carrying his little brother on his back, very weary did he become. As he looked ahead, he saw that straight in the way where he was going was a little lodge standing. And then he directed his way to it. They say that as soon as he was come near by, he heard somebody speak, saying: "Oh, dear me! my grandchildren, both of you are to be pitied," they (thus) were told. And then they say that the boy wept bitterly, likewise he that was carried in the cradle-board.

"Come in!" they were told by their grandmother.

And then truly went they in. They were fed by her, and by her were they put to bed. And in the morning it is said that they were told by their grandmother: "Now, then, come, and rise from your sleep! you need to be on your way again," they were told. And then it is said that he was given by his grandmother an awl and a comb. And he was told: "Presently will you be pursued by your mother. Do as well as you can, my grandchild. And the reason why I have given you these things is that you may use them, if, when she follows after you, you think her to be near by; then you shall fling them behind you. You shall throw the awl," he was told. "And be sure not to look. The same also shall you do with the other thing," he was told. "And then you will be able to reach another grandmother of yours."

And then was his little brother helped upon his back by her. And then he set out after they had been kissed by their grandmother.

"Now, then, go fast!" they were told.

And then truly away they went. And once they say, that, as he went running along, he now heard the sound of somebody behind, saying: "Do stay there! I wish to suckle your little brother."

And then they say that the boy became mindful of what he had been told by his father and his grandmother. And then he was greatly afraid. And then he started to run; not very well was he able to run, for with the cradle-board he would hit his heels. And then again he heard his mother saying: "Do stay there! I want to suckle your little brother."

And then all the more did they weep when they heard their mother, and they did not want to listen to her. And then the same thing as before were they told by their mother: "Do remain there, I tell you! I really want to suckle your little brother, I tell you! You are surely doing him injury," he was told.

And then truly at full speed he ran, (and) nearer still could be heard the sound of her voice. Upon that he flung the awl, and then a great mountain came to be; everywhere over it were awls. And then far away they heard the faint sound of the voice of their mother.

Thereupon a skeleton caught fast its bones in among the awls. Accordingly they say that it said to the awl: "Make way for me, I am following my children!" But not in the least did (the awls) listen to her. And so once again she said to them: "Oh, do (let me pass)!" said she to them; "and as a reward I will be a wife to you all," she said to them. But not the least faith was placed in her word. And it was a long time before she was able to pass over the mountain of awls. And so once more she was in pursuit of her children.

And then again did the children hear their mother, faintly they heard the sound of her voice coming hither. In the same way as before it came, saying: "Bring him to me! I want to suckle your little brother!"

And then again the boy wept aloud, all the harder did he begin to run; whereupon again he bumped his heels (against the cradle-board). And now again they heard their mother, ever nearer kept coming the sound of her voice. And then again he began running, and once more he heard his mother. Very close came the sound of her voice, saying: "Bring me your little brother! I want to suckle him!"

Thereupon all the harder did he start to run, and this time he flung the comb behind, whereupon a mountain-range of combs strung out over the country at the rear. And then he began running at full speed; and after a while they again heard her, feebly could she be heard.

It was a long time before the woman was able to pass the place. And the same thing (she had said) before, she now said to the mountain, but no heed was given her; and it was a long while before she was able to pass. And so again she called after them, and she said: "Give me your little brother! I want to suckle your little brother!"

And only once they heard the sound of her voice. And then the boy walked with hurried step, very tired was he becoming; and it was now growing very dark. Once, as he was walking along, he raised his head to look, and saw a little wigwam; it was the home of another grandmother of his. Very much was he pitied by her. And he was told: "You are in distress, my grandchild. Come in!" he was told.

And so, after they were fed, then by her were they also put to bed. And in the morning they were again told by their grandmother: "Come, my grandchild, rise up! Come! for soon again must you be going." Thereupon again he was given by his grandmother, as a means of protection, a flint and some punk. And then with her help was his little brother lifted upon his back, and he was told: "Still yet will you be followed by your mother. And now, my grandson, this punk which I have given you is the last thing for you to throw; thereupon you will be able to come out upon a great river. And there you will see a great horn-grebe that will be moving about over the water in the river there. And it shall be your duty to address it. You shall say to it: 'O my grandfather! do please carry us across the water, for a manitou is pursuing after us,'" he was (thus) told by his grandmother. "That is what you shall say to it," she said to him. "And after you have crossed over the river, then no longer will you be pursued. Carefully, my grandson, do you give heed to what I have instructed you," she said to him.

And so off started the boy again. And once more, as he went running along, he heard again the sound of her coming behind with the clank of bones striking together. At the same time she was calling after him, and saying: "Remain there! I want to suckle your little brother!"

And then, in truth, with great speed did the boy start running; and loud was he crying, for he knew that it was his mother who was pursuing him; and he was mindful too that their mother had been killed, and they were afraid of her. Once more he heard her. Still nearer came the sound of her voice, saying to them: "Give me your little brother! I want to suckle your little brother," (thus) they were told.

And then with speed he started running. Again he heard her, very near came the sound of her voice. The same thing as before she was saying: "Bring me your little brother! I want to suckle your little brother!"

And then the boy, in truth, was greatly afraid. Almost forgot he what had been told him by his grandmother, which (of the objects) he should first fling away. It was a long while before he recalled (which) it (was). Very close behind suspected he the presence of her by whom he was pursued. Thereupon he flung the flint, and of a sudden there happened a range of mountains, —mountains of flint. And when some distance farther on, he then felt secure in having gotten so far away.

Now, the woman slipped on the flint. And even though she reached the top, yet back again she slipped. And so again she said to (the mountains): "Do, please, let me pass over you! In return I will be a wife to you," she said to them. And it was a long time before she succeeded. And from the place up there came she sliding down. And then again she went in pursuit of her children.

And so again the boy went running along the way. Soon again somebody could be heard coming behind, saying to them the same thing that in the past they had heard: "Give me your little brother! I want to suckle your little brother!" Thereupon the boy with even greater speed did run. Again he heard her: "Give me your little brother! I want to suckle your little brother!" Still nearer was coming the sound of her voice. And the little brother whom he bore on his back had been crying, till now he could cry no more. And so now again he heard her, ever so close came the sound of her voice: "Give me your little brother! I want to suckle your little brother!" And while he was hearing the sound of her voice, he hurled away as the last thing the punk, saying: "This is the last, O my grandmother! that you gave to me. Set it afire!"

And verily there was a great mountain of fire everywhere, stretching from one end of the world to the other at their rear. And then they went on again with speed. And now the boy heard his mother wailing in a loud voice. All the faster then he went, he too was weeping aloud. Once more he heard her, barely could the sound of her voice be heard as she wailed in deep grief. And then again they also wept for bitter grief. And then they say that the woman passed round the boundaries of the fire till she came to the path of her children.

Now, the children came out upon a river. Thereupon truly did they see what had been told them by their grandmother. And then in truth the boy spoke to Horn-Grebe: "Oh, please, my grandfather, carry us over the water to the other side! A manitou is pursuing us," he said to him.

Then of a truth was he told what had been told him by his grandmother. "If you will only do what I tell you, then will I carry you both across the water," they were told.

"We will," he said to him.

"You yourself only will I take across the water, but not your little brother," he was told.

And then he said to him: "Not to that sort of thing will I listen from you. Very fond am I of my little brother," he said to him.

"All right, then!" he was told; "you first will I carry across the water."

And then he said to him: "How shall I be able to put my little brother upon my back if I put him down?" he said to him.

"Oh, you will be able to do it," he said to him. "Let him down!" he was told by his grandfather.

And then truly was he in the act of letting him down, when, "Now he might fall," he thought; so again he hesitated.

"Let him down!" he was told by his grandfather. "He will not fall," he was told.

And then truly at last he let him down in a careful manner.

"Therefore first you will I carry across the water," he was told.

And then the older boy drew a deep sigh. At the same time he said to his grandfather: "O my grandfather! do please carry my little brother first over to the other side!" he said to him.

And it was so that his grandfather did what was asked of him. It was truly observed how so very fond he was of his wee little brother, and how careful he was not to lose him. Therefore was he told: "All right! put him on, but don't you touch me on the back!" he said to him. And then he carried him over on the other side and put him on the other shore. And then was the other afterwards taken across. Therefore now were both on the other shore.

And then was he told by his grandfather: "Now, then! put your little brother upon your back!" he was told.

Whereupon he found it easier than before to lift his little brother upon his back, as easy he found it as when he first wanted to put him down. And then again they continued on their way.

And so next was the woman herself to arrive there at the river. And she too saw Horn-Grebe, and said to him: "Do, please, carry me over to the other side, my little brother!"

"Oh, bother!"

"Oh, do!" she said to him. "After my children am I anxious to pursue," she said to him.

"Oh, pshaw! No!" she was told.

"Come!" she said to him; "and in return you may have your desires with me."

"I don't wish to," he said to her.

"Come, hurry up!"

"Well, all right!" he said to her. "But don't step over me," he said to her.

Whereupon of a truth was she then being conveyed over to the other side. And so, as she was about to land, then the woman thought: "Therefore shall I now be able to leap ashore," she thought. Whereupon she stepped over Horn-Grebe at the same time that she leaped. And then down fell the woman into the middle of the sea. And at this point ends the story of the woman.

B. *The Contest With Mashōs*

Once on a time, they say, as the boy was journeying along with his little brother upon his back, he marvelled at the sight of things, and the trees looked unfamiliar. And then they say that he thought: "So strange is the look of these trees!" And in a little while he came out upon the sea. And over there on the sandy beach was also a place of pebbles. And then thought the boy: "I am going to put my little brother down at this place. I will play with him to amuse him," was his thought, so they say. And it was true that he let him down; and there he set him (in his cradle-board) against a tree, and set free his little arms. He gathered pebbles for his little brother to keep him quiet. And there they remained, (and) he entertained his little brother.

Once while they were continuing there, and he was keeping company with his little brother to prevent him from crying, of a sudden somebody slid inshore with his canoe directly opposite to where they were; it was an old man. Thereupon it is said that they were asked: "What are you doing there?" they (thus) were asked.

Whereupon the boy answered him: "Nothing, I am amusing my little brother when he cries," he (thus) said to him.

And then they say that the old man said to him: "Just you look at these pebbles, they are pretty!" he said to him.

And it is said that the boy was not willing to go. "That is all right, for of sufficient pleasure are these little stones which he fondles in his hands," (thus) said he to him.

"But these are prettier," he was told.

Now, they say that the boy was not anxious to go over there.

"Just look at these, come get them!" he was told.

"No," said the boy to him; "to crying will go my little brother if I rise to my feet," said he to him.

"Oh, no!" he said to him; "he will not cry," he was told by that hateful old man. Again was he urged by the other: "Come and get them!" he was told.

And then at last, when the boy rose to his feet, with a fearful scream his little brother gave vent. And then down again he sat.

At that the old man laughed aloud; he made fun of the children, saying at the same time to the boy: "Just for nothing is he crying. Come get these little stones, pretty are they for your little brother to play with!" (thus) he said to him.

And then up he rose to his feet again, and once more cried the little baby. Yet nevertheless he went over to where the old man was. And they say that to him said the boy: "Not any prettier are these stones," he said to him.

"But these are," was he told by the malicious old man. "These here, these will I place upon my paddle," he was told. "Do come and take them!" he was told, so they say.

"No, my little brother is crying," said the boy.

But in spite of all, the devilish old man kept on insisting with the boy to take them, saying: "Anyway, come and take them! I will put them upon my paddle."

And then at last once more he started, and so finally over he went to take the pebbles. Thereupon they say the ruthless old man scooped the boy up with the paddle, and landed him in the canoe; at the same instant he struck his canoe. And then they say that the boy heard his dear little brother begin to cry, loud he heard him cry. Again the mean old man struck his canoe. And at that the boy was barely able to hear his fond little brother, still yet he heard him crying bitterly; he himself also cried aloud. Though he pleaded with the wicked old man to go to his wee little brother, yet, in spite of all, was he made fun of; and at the same time he struck his detestable old canoe. And then the boy at last (could) not hear his poor little brother. And then they say he was told by the hateful old man: "Over at this place whither I am taking you, my daughters abide; and one will I give to you for a wife," he said to the boy. And as for the boy, barely was he alive, so grieved was he at the thought of his dear little brother.

And then truly now they slid inshore with their canoe by the dwelling-place of the old man. "At yonder place is where I dwell," he was told. "In a little while somebody will come after you," he was told. And they say on, up from the shore, went the old man. And so it is told that he said to his daughters: "O my daughters! a man have I fetched home. Now whichever runs to and first reaches the place of my canoe will be the one to have him."

"Maybe upon some other person has our father again inflicted sorrow," they said, as at the same time they sprang to their feet and ran out of doors together; hither came the maidens, racing to the canoe. And both in running got there at the same time. And then it is said that they saw the boy lying asleep in the peak of the bow. Whereupon they said: "Oh, pshaw! that really he was a sure-enough man was what I thought he was," (thus) they said. Back from the shore then they went.

And then it is said that the younger sister turned, swinging quickly round as she went back there to the canoe. Thereupon she took the boy up in her arms, for she pitied him. And then she took him up from the shore to where they lived; she fetched him inside to the place where she sat, and there put down the boy.

And by and by they say, while they were living (there), so the story goes, large grew the boy. And once on a time they say the old man said to his son-in-law: "It is a good time now for us to go hunting for ducks," (thus) he said to him. And then they say that in truth away they went by canoe to hunt for ducks. And now the man recognized the place where he had left his dear little brother. Whereupon it is said that he heard the sound of somebody's voice saying: "O my big brother! already have I now become half a wolf!" Three times, indeed, did his younger brother say the same thing. And then truly was the man sad. But he made no remark. And then they went back home again.

And then once upon a time, while they were dwelling (there), the man said to his wife: "Come, let us go out in the canoe!" he (thus) said to her. And so it is said that truly did they go.

And it is told that the old man was not pleased about it. (And) he said to his daughter: "I myself should have gone along with the son-in-law," he (thus) said to her.

"Oh, dear!" said the woman. "So was I myself eager to go with him," she said to her father.

And so another time they went canoeing about along the shore. And then it is said, while speaking to his wife, he was telling her about his little brother. Whereupon they say, while going on with his story, they were then passing the place opposite to where he had been scooped up into the canoe. And then, "Oh, look!" she said to her husband. Whereupon it is said that the man looked, and saw three wolves running up from the shore. Thereupon he thought: "One of them may be my little brother." And then at some distance off in the forest he once more heard his little brother say: "O my big brother! wholly now have I become a wolf. Never again shall I bother you," he said to his elder brother. "As often as you see the wolves, 'My little brother do I see,' shall you think," (thus) was he told.

And that was the last he ever saw of him. Whereupon the man also felt at ease in his mind. And then the man bade his wife not to say anything (about it) at home. And so truly the woman did (as she was told).

Now, once, it is said, while they were living (at that place), the old man became troubled in his heart to see that his son-in-law was growing into the full stature of a man. And then they say that he began to lay plans to find out how he might kill him; and yet, too, he feared that his daughter would know that he had done it. Very much was he bothered, all the time was he watching his son-in-law.

Now, once, they say, by the glance of an eye was he caught by his daughter at a time when he was looking at him. Whereupon it is said that he was asked (by her): "Why are you always looking at him whom you are gazing at?" (thus) said the woman to her father.

"Oh, for nothing in particular have I him in mind, that I should be gazing at him," he said. "I was only thinking where we might go hunting for game to-morrow," (thus) by way of an excuse replied that malicious old man. And then truly they say that he said to his son-in-law: "To-morrow let us go hunting for game!" he said to him. "Let us go to get sturgeon!" he said to him.

"All right!" he was told.

And then they say the woman said to her husband: "Be careful! for he wants to kill you; he is such an awfully bad man. That is what he is always doing, he is murdering somebody. And now do be careful! For surely will he kill you if you have not been blessed with the possession of some miraculous power," (so) said the woman to her husband.

And then truly in the morning they set out, they embarked in their canoe (and) went away to hunt sturgeon. When the hateful old man struck his canoe, at once far off were they come; when again he struck his old canoe, then the sight of land went out of view; when once more he struck his canoe, then they arrived at the place where they went to get the sturgeons. Thereupon they say that the mean old man said to him: "This is the place where we will hunt for sturgeon. It was at this place where the fishermen of old always used to hunt for sturgeon," (so) he said to his son-in-law. But not the truth was the old man telling, for never had anybody hunted for that evil sturgeon.

And it is told that the man said to him: "It is strange that there are no signs at all of habitation."

"Long ago it happened, as far back as I can remember."

"Really!" to him said the man.

And then they say that the old man said: "Come, let us now hunt for them! Exactly at noon is the time we shall see them. Very big are the sturgeons," he said to his son-in-law. And then they started for the rapids. "Over there you go at the middle of the rapids," he said to him. "And here will I remain in the canoe," he said to him.

And then truly the man went ashore, he went yonder to the middle of the rapids. And as soon, they say, as he was come at the place where he was told to go, then he heard his father-in-law calling aloud, saying: "O ye Great-Sturgeons! I feed you a man," (thus) he said to them. And then he also struck his canoe.

Thereupon the man looked; and there, with wide-open mouth, was a Great-Sturgeon ready to swallow him. And they say the man spoke to him, saying: "Wait, wait, wait, O my grandfather! You have taken pity upon me in times past," he said to him.

Whereupon the Great-Sturgeons withdrew (into the deep), for he was pitied by them.

And then again, so they say, did he speak to one, saying: "O my grandfather! carry me back to my home," (thus) he said to him; "and I will give you whatever choice food that I may have to take home to my children," he said to him.

At the time two were the children the man had.

And then they say that he was told by the Great-Sturgeon: "All right!" (thus) he was told; "I will swallow you."

"All right!" likewise said the man, on his part; "for such indeed is my fate," (so) thought the man. And then truly was he swallowed. And now he was mindful that at home was he truly arriving. And then he was addressed by his grandfather saying: "Seize that sturgeon by the tail!" he was told.

Thereupon the man truly took hold of the tail with his hand, and then was he cast up from the belly of the Great-Sturgeon; and so there upon the shore he fell. He was not wet, and his sturgeon he held by the tail. Thereupon he gave thanks to his grandfather. And when the Great-Sturgeon departed, then he too went up from the shore. He was proud for that he had been saved. And when he entered into the place where they lived, he surprised his wife. And he was addressed by her saying: "What!" he was told. "Where is your companion?"

And the man said: "Why!" he said to her. "Is it possible that he has not yet arrived? Long ago was it since he himself started on his way back," he said to his wife. And then he said to her: "Cook some food!" he said to his wife. "Down by the water have I left a sturgeon."

And then up leaped the woman. She went, taking her kettle. And when she reached the shore, she looked at the place where her husband had put the sturgeon, and what a huge pile of sturgeons there was! Very happy was the woman. Running back up from the shore, the woman went, and said to her elder sister: "Come! he has fetched us a bountiful supply of food."

Then up must have leaped also her elder sister, for down the path to the water she went running. And she also saw the many sturgeons. Both were pleased.

And now they say that the man thought: "Why are they so very happy?" he thought. He had in mind only the one sturgeon that he had fetched; for he did not know about (the vast quantity of fish), and he also did not wish to say anything (about his adventure).

And then they say that the women quickly prepared the sturgeons for use; they smoked them upon drying-frames; they hung them up out of doors and inside of where they dwelt. And then they had a great deal to eat, and of sturgeon they ate. And the children went about outside, eating the spinal cord.

And they say, when the old man returned, he came riding his canoe upon the shore. Thereupon the children ran racing down the path to the water, at the same time holding in their hands the spinal cord.

And then they say that he said to his grandchildren: "Where did you get what you are eating?"

"Why our father fetched it."

"What is it?" he said to them.

"Why, sturgeon," he was told.

"Pshaw! what foolishness are they saying!" (so) said the old man. " 'Oh, it was our father!' Why, it is some time since that by a big sturgeon was your father swallowed. In fact, by this time is your father digested," (so) he said to his grandchildren.

"Why, our father has already come home."

Now, the old man was late in the evening arriving home. Not a single thing did he fetch. And then he went ashore; and as he looked, everywhere he saw something hanging, pendant pieces hanging out of doors. And when he went indoors, brimful of things hanging was the space inside. And then it is said that the old man knew not where to look. When he saw his son-in-law reclining at his sitting-place, nothing had he to say.

And now they say that on another occasion, according to the story, he said to his son-in-law: "Let us go hunting for gull-eggs!"

Whereupon they say that he said to him: "Well, all right!"

"Then to-morrow will we go," he was told by his father-in-law. "I know where there is a fine place for gull-eggs," he said to his son-in-law.

And then it is said that the man was again told by his wife to be ever so careful.

Thereupon they started away, embarking again in the canoe. And so the same thing as before the hateful old man did; he struck his old canoe, and soon they were suddenly a long distance away; again he struck his canoe, whereupon they arrived at a great island of rock; (it was) a great island of rock. "Here is the place," the other was told; "here is just the place where we will go ashore," the other was told.

And then truly they went ashore. And then the other was guided round to the top. Sure enough, many (eggs) they found. And as for himself, the man soon obtained many; he gathered the eggs, loaded them in the canoe, (and) kept on going after more.

And then the old man again said to him: "Do go yonder, son-in-law, (and) get those eggs!"

"Go yourself (and) get them!" he said to him.

"Go on, go on! Go get them, I tell you!"

And then truly against his wish he went. "Perhaps I can overtake him," he thought, "before he gets to the canoe." Slow indeed was (the old man) coming when he met him on the way. And that was why he thought, "I will overtake him." But when he turned round to look, already far out at sea was the other in the canoe. And then the man heard him saying: "O ye Great-Gulls! I feed you a man; long have you wished him of me."

Thereupon truly was there a great host of Great-Gulls.

And now they say the man said to them the same thing that he had said before: "Hold on, hold on, hold on!" he said to them. "Why, you have taken pity upon me in the past," he said to them.

Thereupon they withdrew.

And then again he said to (one): "O my grandfather! carry me back to where I live," he said to him.

"All right!" he was told.

And then the man took along a few of the eggs.

Thereupon it is said that now came and alighted Great-Gull, by whom he was to be taken home. "All right!" he was told; "upon my back shall you sit."

And truly, when he was seated, then away went Great-Gull flying. And as he went through the air, he beheld that contemptible old man in the middle of his canoe, lying there upon his back, singing as he went along, at the same time beating time against the canoe. And then they say Great-Gull muted upon his chest.

And then they say that afterwards, when he rubbed his finger in it, he smelled of it. Whereupon they say he said: "Phew! such is the smell of the mute of the one by whom (my) son-in-law was devoured."

And so it is said that the man was conveyed home by Great-Gull. And then he was let down over there at the shore. Thereupon he went on up from the water, and passed on into where he and the others lived.

And very pleased, so they say, were his wife and children. Always was the woman (thinking), "I wonder how my husband is, and when again he will be home!" thought the woman.

Thereupon again was she told by her husband: "I wish to eat," (so) she was told. And then he gave to his wife the few eggs that he had fetched. And he said to her: "In the canoe are many eggs I put in," he said to her.

"Oh!" said the woman. And then they say that she cooked the few that her husband had fetched. Thereupon they ate.

And then it is said that the children were sitting out of doors, when again they saw their grandfather coming home. Thereupon they were asked: "What are you eating?"

"Eggs," they said to him.

"What kind of eggs?" he said to them.

"Gull-eggs, to be sure," they said to him.

"Where did you get them?"

"Why, our father fetched them," they said to him.

"Fie!" he said to them. " 'Oh, it was our father!' Why, it has been some time since that your father was digested by Great-Gull," he (thus) said to them.

Thereupon they say that back sped the children, racing home.

And now it is said that the old man went on up from the shore; and when he passed on inside, truly, there he saw his son-in-law, who was within. And it was true that he knew not where to look; and he began to wonder what manner of person the other was, so very much was he puzzled in thought concerning him. But he had nothing further to say.

And so once on a time they say that he said to his son-in-law: "Son-in-law, it is now time for us again to go hunting for game. Let us go hunting for caribou!"

"Well, all right!" to him (thus) said the man. Thereupon he said to his wife: "Make some moccasins."

Whereupon in truth the woman made them.

And the mean old man likewise had some moccasins made.

Thereupon they set out; it was in the winter-time. And when a long way off they were come, "Now this is the place, son-in-law, where we are to camp," (thus) to his son-in-law said the old man. And then they say that truly there they made camp, a great shelter-camp they put up. And also a huge fire at one side (was kindled). And now it is said that the contemptible old man had already, by this time, made up his mind as to what he would do to his son-in-law. Therefore they say that he said to him, after they had eaten in the evening: "Son-in-law," he (thus) said to him, "build up a great fire," he said to him. "And after you have kindled a big fire, then let us remove our moccasins, so that we can dry them; our clothes will we hang up, and likewise our moccasins," he (thus) said to him.

Thereupon they say that truly the man rose to his feet; in truth, a great fire he built.

After he had the fire going, then said the old man to his son-in-law: "Here in this place come you, and throw some of the fire-wood, near here where I am. I will put it on when the fire gets to burning low," he said to him.

Thereupon truly did the man heap up a pile near by where the mean old man was. And then the man, in turn, likewise made ready to go to bed. Accordingly he took off his moccasins and hung them up, for of nothing at all was he suspicious that should lead him to think, "Perhaps some evil will be done to me."

And while he was making his pallet ready, the hateful old man was himself lying close to the fire; not yet had he taken off his moccasins. And then truly the man said to him: "Why come! Why are you not taking off your moccasins (and) hanging them up to dry while yet the fire blazes high?" he (thus) said to him.

Now, they say that the old man acted as if he were asleep. Some time afterwards he rose (from his pallet). And while the man was lying down at rest, then the old man later hung up his miserable moccasins, at the same time he kept on talking. And now they say that the youth, in all this while, was not very eager about going to sleep. But the old man nevertheless kept on talking, he was spinning stories; for a purpose of course was he doing it (which was) to the end that he might tire out his son-in-law. And when the other fell asleep, into a very deep slumber did he fall. And they say it is true that what the man had done to him happened while he was asleep. And the old man now and then was addressing him to find out if he were asleep. At last the man had fallen asleep, for he did not hear the other when he was spoken to.

And then they say that after the hateful old man had risen from his pallet, he then later took down the moccasins of his son-in-law (and) put them into the fire. And when they were nearly burned completely up, then spoke the base old man, saying: "Phew! something is burning up! O son-in-law! your moccasins are burning up," he (thus) said to him.

Slowly rose the man from his pallet. And then he saw that his moccasins were burned up, for in fact the evil old man had by that time thrown them out (of the fire). And then, after the man had taken a look at his moccasins, he lay down on his pallet again. And then they say that in the morning the hateful old man built the fire. Whereupon he said to his son-in-law: "What are you going to do about getting back home, now that you have no moccasins? And a long way off are we, too," he said to him. "Did you not fetch yourself two pairs of moccasins?"

"No," he said to him.

"I will tell you, son-in-law, what I will do. I will go back home," he said to him. "I will go fetch you your moccasins," he said to him.

Scarcely even an answer, so they say, did the man give him. Thereupon the mean old man started away; while the man himself remained there at the place, for nowhere at all could he go. And then he pondered what to do, for he knew that his father-in-law would surely not fetch his moccasins. And then they say that accordingly he began getting ready to go back home. And so they say that after he had taken the three great stones (and) after he had heated them, he then said: "Now, my grandfather, come and help me to return home again! I long to see my children," he said. And then truly he took these stones out (of the fire) red-hot; and directly (in the path) whither he wanted to go, along that course straight (ahead) did he roll them. Thereupon the stone truly started going, more than half the distance home it went before it stopped. And in the path where the stone had moved, along that course was the snow melted; accordingly by that way did the man travel. And while he was walking along, he began to feel the presence of somebody at his side; and as he looked, he beheld a Wolf walking along. And by him, from his place over there, he was addressed: "What," he was told, "my elder brother?"

And to him said the man: "Nothing."

"Where are you going?" he was asked.

"I am going home," he said to him.

And then, as he and the Wolf went along together, they kept up a talk. Now, the man walked along where the stone had rolled; and the Wolf passed along at the side, on the snow.

And they say that when the mean old man arrived at home, for he was a long time reaching home, he had nothing whatever to say.

Thereupon the woman herself asked her father: "And where is that companion of yours?" she said to him.

"Oh, I don't know where. He parted company with me, and also went his way hunting for game. I grew very tired of waiting for him," he (thus) said to her. "And that is why I came home," he said to his daughter. "Anon will he be home," he said to her.

And now they say that while the man, and his younger brother the Wolf, were coming hitherward together, very happy were they as they walked along in each other's company; at the same time they went singing on their way in the same manner as one does when in a joyful frame of mind. And the man by no means forgot that he was in bare feet, yet in spite of that he kept on laughing. And then by this time he was come at the place which was as far as the path, had been made for him by his grandfather. And when they were about to arrive, he was asked by his younger brother: "Why are you going to remain in this place?"

But nothing did the man say.

"Come!" he was told; "I am going to accompany you," he was told by his younger brother.

But the man did not speak. And as he smiled at him, he felt ashamed to tell him about what had happened to himself.

Thereupon was he told by his younger brother, the Wolf: "Come!" he was told, "walk along in my footsteps!" And the Wolf also had nothing more to say to his elder brother.

It is true that then they started on. Whereupon truly did he follow in the footsteps of the other. In a little while, as he went along, he caught the smell of fire. It meant that now he was arriving at home. And then to the place where their path for fire-wood forked off was he led by his younger brother. Thereupon he was told: "It is here that I shall part from you," he said to him.

"All right!" he said to him.

And then he was told: "Rub your feet here on my hand!"

Whereupon in truth the man did as he was told by his younger brother, Wolf.

And then truly: "Go with speed!" he was told. Thereupon truly the man started running. And when he arrived at home, he passed on into the lodge. It was at a time when the hateful old man was in the act of taking off his moccasins. "And have you just come, too?" he said to his son-in-law.

But the son-in-law said nothing at all. He simply said to him: "Yes," he (thus) said.

And then they say that after the contemptible old man had eaten, it was then evening. And so they say that the old man kept gazing constantly at his son-in-law, not knowing what to make of him. "What in the world can I do to kill him?" was his thought of him. All the time he was gazing at him in the face. Thereupon he was addressed by his daughter saying: "Why on earth are you always gazing at him?"

"Oh, for nothing!" he said. "I was only watching the dragonfly that was flying close about his face," he said to his daughter.

But nothing more said she to him, for though she knew what her father had done to her husband.

And now they say, on another occasion during the time that they were dwelling there, the old man said to his son-in-law, so the story goes: "It is now time for us again to go hunting for game," he (thus) said to him.

"That is true," (thus) to him said the man. Thereupon again to his wife said the man: "Make two pairs of moccasins for me," he said to her.

And it was true that when the woman had finished his moccasins, very nice was the work she did on them, she did one pair with porcupine-quills.

Thereupon they set out again. And so in a little while a long way off they were come. By and by again he was addressed by his father-in-law after they had come afar. And this the old man said to his son-in-law: "Now, here is a place for us to make a camp. And also from this place will we go to hunt for game."

And it was true that they pitched camp, they made a shelter-camp. And the man worked away gathering fire-wood, while the old man himself lay close by the fire. Thereupon in the evening, after they had finished eating, then in the same way as before behaved the malicious old man. Again was the man not mindful of the wrong that had been done to him, and that was the very reason why he paid no heed to him. Thereupon again the old man began relating stories. After the man had gone to sleep, and while he was slumbering, then again (the old man) addressed his son-in-law, saying to him: "Hey, son-in-law! something smells, something is burning up again!"

But the man did not speak to him; for he already knew that his moccasins had been burned up by the other. The man knew that he still had one pair of moccasins which were quilled. And so in the morning, after they had risen, he was told by his father-in-law: "Truly are you exceedingly unfortunate to have your moccasins always burning up," he (thus) was told.

The man did not speak; he went on making preparations, putting on his other moccasins.

Thereupon again they wandered about, looking for game. And so, when it was evening, in the same manner as before acted the old man; again they made ready to go to sleep; and so again they hung up their moccasins to dry. Then at the place over there, the instant that his father-in-law had turned his back, he changed the place of his moccasins; the moccasins of his father-in-law were now hanging where he had hung his own moccasins; in the place where his own moccasins had been hanging he now hung the moccasins of the other. And then they went to bed. And then for some time afterwards, so they say, did the man wait to see what the other would do.

And then truly by now, they say, was he risen from his pallet. "He is asleep," the (youth) was thought to be. And then he took down the other moccasins (and) he laid them in the fire. Whereupon the hateful old man at once lay down, and then said: "Phew! a smell of something comes this way. —Son-in-law, your moccasins!" he said to him.

Quickly springing to his feet, the man went and grabbed his moccasins, which he had hung up in a different place, and then said to the other: "Here are my moccasins. It is your moccasins that have been burned up," he said to him.

"No," he said, "it is your moccasins," he said to him.

"No," to him said the man. "Look! worked in quill are my moccasins," he said to him. "And not quilled are your moccasins," he said to the disagreeable old man.

And then they say not till now did the mean old man realize that his own moccasins had been consumed in the fire. Whereupon they say that the man at once made ready to go back home. And then he said to the other: "Now, then, I am going to leave you," he said to him.

Thereupon said the old man: "Tell my daughter to fetch my moccasins."

"All right!" he said to him. And then back home went the man.

Thereupon they say that after the departure of his son-in-law, the old man likewise did all sorts of things. He too tried in vain heating a rock, but soon would the rock become cool. And again he tried heating it, and another time it would quickly become cool. Truly he worked hard to get back home.

And now they say that the man kept on till he arrived at home. Whereupon he said to one (of the women): "Back at yonder place have I left your father. All burned were his moccasins," he (thus) said to his sister-in-law.

"Really!" she said to him. "And so at last he brought it on himself. Very persistent is he always in the doing of some sort of mischief," said the woman. And then they say that she said again: "Just for a while, now, let him be there. He will then realize the consequence of his repeated efforts at doing all kinds of things," she said. Thereupon they say that truly on the morrow she then made the moccasins. And now they say, so goes the story, the woman who was older than the other, who bore the name of Coming-Dawn, was the woman who tied the moccasins into a bundle, as if she meant to take them. Thereupon, when the woman had risen from her couch at nearly the time of the break of day, then accordingly out she went from the lodge, after she had arrayed herself in fine garments. And so, after she had spoken, she flung the moccasins: "These moccasins does your daughter Coming-Dawn bring." Thereupon, at the moment when the light of day was breaking, then to yonder place at the same time went the moccasins, going to the place where the old man was.

"Good for you, O my daughter Coming-Dawn!" And then was the old man going to put them on. After he was ready, he then started on his way back home; hardly was he able to walk. His feet had frozen on account of his attempt at walking on the snow in bare feet. And now he kept on until he arrived at home. Not a single word had any one for him. What he did again was to keep a constant eye upon his son-in-law; his thought of him was to know how he ever succeeded in getting back home, such was his thought. And while he was watching him, then by his daughter was he caught looking (at him). Whereupon he was told by her again: "Why are you always looking at him whom you are gazing upon?" she said to him.

"Oh, nothing! I was merely looking at the whirligig-beetle that was crawling about inside of his eye," he said to her. And still again he wished to contend with his son-in-law. And then he thought of that great steep cliff yonder. And this he thought: "Over there will I bring him," was his thought. And now they say that again, while they were continuing (there), the old man said: "I tell you what, son-in-law, let us go tobogganing at yonder place!" he (thus) said to him. "Down the hill long ago used to slide the men of times gone by," he thus said to him. "I know where there is a fine place," he said to him.

And then said the woman: "There you go again!" she (thus) said to her father.

"Why, only in jest am I saying it to him. So quietly are we continuing in the same place, and, too, the days are so long. And over there we can go and have a contest," he said to his daughter.

But there was not a word for him from any one, for well they knew what their father wanted to do and what his thoughts were.

And then again he addressed his son-in-law, saying: "Why, son-in-law, do you want to go?" he said to him.

"Well, all right!" he said.

"Then come on!" he said to him.

And then they set out, taking along their toboggan. And then he took his son-in-law to the place where they were to coast down the slope. And now they say, on the occasion of their arrival, what did the man behold but a steep cliff! "Now, then, son-in-law, you are the first to go coasting down," (the mean old man) said to him.

"And why not you?" (the son-in-law) said to him.

"Why, not till (you are) done, (then will) I (go)," (the man) said to (his son-in-law). "Come on, now!" said (the son-in-law) to him.

"Very well," to him said the man.

And now they say that already had (the father-in-law) fixed in place his toboggan, whereupon he said to his son-in-law: "This is what the men of yore used to do, on (the toboggan) was tied the one who was to go coasting down," he said to him. "Therefore will you too have to be bound on," he said to him; "lest perhaps you bounce off," he said to him.

Well, and so that truly the man did; and so he was bound (with cords) to his toboggan by his father-in-law. "All ready, now I am, to push you off," he said to him. Now, then, now it was that already was the old man standing in place, thinking in what direction (the youth) would be going with such awful speed. With great eagerness did the malicious old man dig his feet (into the snow for a purchase to push), and now he began heaving against his toboggan. But not at all would the toboggan move even though the cliff was as smooth as ice, for such was the look of the rock down which (the youth) was to slide, (but the toboggan would not go). Again with his might he heaved against it.

And now willed the man: "Only let me slide but a little way!" And so he did. And then he thought: "The cedar took pity upon me once in times past." Thereupon the toboggan stopped in its downward flight.

Therefore now look you! wherever you behold a high cliff, there you will see a cedar standing near the edge of the rock. That was the one by whom was blessed the son-in-law of Mashōs.

And then they say, after (the old man) could not start him coasting down, then did the man get up (and) untie himself. Thereupon back to the top he fetched his toboggan, (and) said to the other: "Now, then, it is your turn," he (thus) said to him.

"All right!" said the old man. "Naturally the same thing will also happen to me," (so) he thought, (believing he would be blessed) in the same way as his son-in-law was blessed.

Thereupon the man bound him to the toboggan in the way that he himself had been tied. And now they say that while he was busy with him, eager was the toboggan to coast away. "All right, now!" he said to him. "Go ahead!" He shoved off the toboggan.

And then old Mashōs started sliding off, forever away went coasting the old man. After a time, they say, then with a loud voice the old man began calling: "O my canoe!" Again, "O my canoe!" Again, "O my canoe!"

Thereupon it is said that the women knew that now was their father being vanquished in the contest. And then was his canoe eager to go. Whereupon the women tried with great efforts to hold it back, (but) it was eager to go where it was thought (the master) was. They tried in vain to tie it down; but they say that the miserable boat got to creaking, so anxious was it to be off.

And now they say that after the man had become tired waiting for the other's return, "Therefore at last has he done harm to himself," was his thought of him. And then on his way back home he went. And on his arrival there at home, he saw how it looked about the place where the women had striven to hold the canoe. And there they lived, and perhaps even to this day they may be there.

The gizzard of the ruffed grouse now hangs aloft for the story of Mashōs.

2. Clothed-in-Fur

Once on a time there lived a boy and his elder sister, by whom he was reared; Clothed-in-Fur was the name of the boy. He was a very good hunter of game; and when he was growing up, he killed a deer, and he shot caribou also. Accordingly he had his elder sister make a coat, —a coat of fur, —that he might have it to wear. It was true that the maiden made the coat.

Now once, after they had been continuing there for a long while, he spoke to his elder sister, saying: "I say, my elder sister! I am going off on a journey." Whereupon truly he was granted leave by his elder sister. So away went Clothed-in-Fur.

Now, once he came to a town, whereupon he entered into a small wigwam where an old woman was abiding. And this was what he was informed: "These people are often playing at games. You too will be asked (to join in play). All kinds of things they do: they play ball, and the women play the double-ball game; sometimes all play together."

And on the morrow by two youths who came over he was addressed: "Come hither, my friend! Join with us in the games we play!"

Whereupon truly he went, joining in with them; he too went to where the play was going on. All day long they played. Now, by two maidens was he annoyed, —by the Foolish Maidens; and he did not like them. Thereupon back he went in the evening to where his grandmother lived. "I say, my grandmother!

coil your net about this place where you live! for perhaps hither may come the Foolish Maidens; I was annoyed by them," said Clothed-in-Fur. When it was night, then hither came the maidens. Very handsome was Clothed-in-Fur. They were not able to enter, for the net was in their way; and when it was nearly morning, back home went the maidens.

And on the morrow they came again to invite the youth; all day long again they played at games. Thereupon again he was annoyed by the Foolish Maidens. Again back he went in the evening to where his grandmother lived. He repeated to his grandmother: "Coil your net about this place where you live!"

That truly was what the old woman did.

Again hither came the women; all night long were the women bothered with the net. When it was nearly morning, they could be heard going away.

Thereupon he said to his grandmother: "Confound it! I am going (back home)," said Clothed-in-Fur.

Whereupon he was told by his grandmother: "You are to be pitied, my grandson. You could not leave them behind, so exceedingly fast do they walk."

"But nevertheless I am going," said the youth. It was true that away started the man, all day long he went running. Suddenly he heard the approaching sound of somebody talking behind him. It was the Foolish Maidens who came talking about him. "To be pitied is Clothed-in-Fur if 'I can leave them behind' he thinks. Not large is this earth."

All the faster he then tried to run; yet nearer still they came talking. Thereupon he climbed a tall birch which was very thick with foliage. Now a single leaf he took; whereupon away he went clinging to the leaf, and a long way off was the leaf wafted by the wind. Thereupon from there he again started on his way.

And as for the Foolish Maidens, when they came to the place where the birch was standing, they said: "It is up here where our husband has climbed and disappeared." Whereupon they said: "Let us cut down this birch!" Each had a small axe. So then they cut down the birch. And when down the birch fell, they ran to it at the same time, but they did not find him. And then they looked to see if he had left any tracks, but they did not find any trace of him. And then (the elder) said to her younger sister: "Come, my little sister! let us count how many leaves there are upon this birch!" And truly, after they had counted them, there was one leaf missing. Whereupon they started looking for that leaf; farther on the way was where they found the leaf. Thereupon from there was where Clothed-in-Fur began leaving the sign of his trail. Whereupon once more they pursued him.

Once more he heard the sound of them as they came talking, with all his speed he tried to run; closer were they coming. So then next he climbed a tall spruce.

Thereupon said the woman who was older: "My little sister, up here is where our husband climbed and disappeared."

And as for Clothed-in-Fur, after he had taken the stem of a spruce-leaf, he pulled it off; thereupon he blew upon it. Yonder he went clinging to it; and far away by the wind wafted the stem of the spruce-leaf.

Now, as for the Foolish Maidens, they said: "Let us cut down this spruce!" And when down fell the tree, they ran to it, they looked to see where he was; but no one was there. Again they counted the number of (leaves) it had. Truly, there was missing one spruce-leaf. Thereupon again they sought (everywhere), a long way off they found the spruce-leaf. So then again they saw the sign of his footprints, whereupon they continued their pursuit after him.

And another time he heard them as they came talking at his back. Now, by this time he was very tired. Next he climbed a tall poplar; and he did the same as he had done before, a single leaf he plucked; and as he went clinging to it, a long way off was it wafted by the wind. Still farther away it alighted; thereupon again he started running as he went.

So again the Foolish Maidens felled the poplar; again they made a wide search, but they did not find him there among the leaves. Again they counted the number of the leaves (of the tree); one leaf was not there. Again they made an extended search; very far away they found the leaf, whereupon again they saw the footprints of the youth. Accordingly they continued their pursuit after him.

Another time he heard them as they came talking, they came talking about him. "To be pitied is Clothed-in-Fur if 'I can flee away' he thinks. Where is the earth so large as to make it possible for him to get away?" (thus) they came saying.

Very tired now was Clothed-in-Fur. When near by they were come, he saw a ball straight where he was going. And this thought Clothed-in-Fur: "In that very ball will I hide myself." He shot at the ball with his arrow, whereupon he then flew into it, in the ball he concealed himself.

And when the Foolish Maidens arrived, "Up here must be the place where our husband has climbed," said she that was the older. Thereupon again they felled (the tree); up over the top of the ball they had cut it, and that was where it fell. After the little birch had fallen, they went to where the leaves were; but there was no one there. And again they counted the leaves, and they were all there. Whereupon they said: "Perhaps here in this ball he may be." Thereupon they carefully hewed the ball. Now, when the little axe had cleaved into it, then upon it breathed Clothed-in-Fur. Whereupon broken was the little axe at the edge. "Ah, me! my little sister, broken is my axe! Do fetch your little axe!" she said to her younger sister. And so, after it was given her, she thereupon continued hewing the ball. Again upon it breathed Clothed-in-Fur, so again was (the axe) broken at the edge.

Thereupon aloud began the women to cry. And then they began rubbing themselves upon the ball, till at last they were bleeding. And then finally back home went the woman who was younger, but she that was older did not go back till a long while afterwards.

Now, blood filled up the place in which was Clothed-in-Fur. Thereupon out he came from the place in the ball, very bloody was his coat. Therefore, as he started on his way, he went seeking for a little lake; and when he came out upon a little lake, he washed his coat. Then bloody became the pond. For another lake he went seeking, and there again he washed his coat. Thereupon it became clean, and he dried it. Whereupon he started on his way again.

And when he was on his journey again, he once put down his pack to go into camp. At the time, snow was on the ground; whereupon some one arrived there where he was going to camp, (it was) a woman. Already had the woman put up the wigwam. "Who is she?" thought Clothed-in-Fur. And when he went into the wigwam, a woman he saw seated (there). Accordingly he went and sat beside her; she was a handsome woman. A beaver he had fetched home. Accordingly the woman took the beaver (and) skinned it; thereupon she cooked a meal. And when she had finished cooking, they ate. So when it came time for them to go to bed, Clothed-in-Fur thought that he might just as well marry her. And after they had gone to bed, he was asked by her: "Do we, then, on the morrow move away?" he was told.

"Yes," she was told, "it is on the morrow that we move camp."

"When you have gone, you will hear me speaking to you; you shall speak to me when I speak to you."

At that he said to his wife: "Yes, I will speak to you when you speak to me."

So in the morning on his way started Clothed-in-Fur. Some time afterwards, when he had come afar, he heard the voice of his wife calling to him: "Halloo!" But he did not answer her. For a long while she tried in vain to call to him with a loud voice, but he did not answer her. On his way went the man, carrying his bag upon his back. And now he sought for a place where they would camp, and so there he put down his pack. "Here is where my wife will put up the camp," he thought. Thereupon he wandered about, hunting for game. Now, when he came back to the place where he had put his bag, nothing of his wife was there. Accordingly he started out to look for his wife; and when he came to the place where they had previously camped, he saw that his wife was there. Still yet was she trying to lift her pack upon her back; but she was not succeeding. Whereupon Clothed-in-Fur took up a stick with the intention of beating her. "Really, in very truth, a woman I took her at the time to be!" And the moment that he struck her a wolf leaped up from the place. "Behold, a wolf shall you be called till the end of the world!"

Thereupon again on his way started Clothed-in-Fur, alone. Now, another time he had left his bag at the place where he was going to camp. And when he came back, another woman was already there where he was to camp. The woman had put up the wigwam. Very large was the netting of her large, netted snowshoes. And when he looked upon her, very pretty was the mystic cloth which the woman had for a skirt. Now, another beaver the man had fetched. Whereupon the woman skinned it, a shinbone (skinner) she used when she flayed the beaver. And then she cooked a meal; not very tidy was she when she cooked, even though very good was the fire. And after she had finished cooking, they ate. Thereupon thought Clothed-in-Fur: "Not very good is she at knowing how to cook," he thought. So then again, after they had gone to sleep, he was also asked by her: "Is it, then, to-morrow that we move camp?" he (thus) was asked.

"Yes, it is really to-morrow that we move camp."

"When you hear me speaking to you after you have gone, promise me that you will do what I shall ask of you!"

So then truly on the morrow upon his way started the man. And when some distance away he was come, he heard her calling to him with a loud voice. "Hey! I am trying in vain to put the pack upon my back," was what he heard her say. But he did not answer her. And he kept right on his way. And when he had seen another place where they were to camp, then there he laid down his bag. Then off he went on a hunt; and when he came back to the place where he had placed his bag, his wife was not there. Again he went back to look for her. Now, when he reached the place where they had been stopping, he saw that his wife had scattered all their goods about; she was not able to make up her pack, and a very great mess she had made of it.

Thereupon again he seized a club to strike her, upon which a raven flew up from the place. And then he said to her: "Behold, a raven shall you be called by the people. Such will be the mess you will make among the poles and leavings wherever people have moved from camp."

Thereupon again on his way started Clothed-in-Fur, alone again was he roaming about. Another time he put down his pack at a place where he was going to camp; again he went off on a hunt for game. When he came back in the evening, somebody had arrived there, (it was) a woman; a wigwam she had put up; very small netted were her snowshoes, and very much turned in (were her feet) as she stepped. Another beaver the man had fetched. So then the woman flayed the beaver. Whereupon the woman cooked a meal, (and) not very good was the fire.

"I say, do build up the fire!" Whereupon the woman built up the fire.

"Work with the fire, work with the fire till it blazes!" Whereupon he angered (the woman).

"You kindle the fire!" said the woman, angry was the woman. And after she had finished cooking, and they had done eating, they lay down to sleep. Again he was asked by his wife: "Is it to-morrow that we move camp?" he was told.

"Yes," he said to her. And then again he was told: "You will hear me speak to you after you have gone away. You must speak to me when I speak to you; do not fail to answer me."

And then on the morrow away started the man. And again he put down his bag at the place where his wife was to camp. Again off went the man on a hunt. When he came back to the place where he had put down his bag, his wife was not there. Again back he went to seek for her; and when he came to where they had been living, he saw his wife trying to lift her pack, but unable was the woman to lift her pack. She would get it upon her back, and then off the pack would fall; too much of a hump she had on the back. So again a club he seized to strike her. And as he was about to go, (there was) a porcupine (which) he began clubbing on the small of the back, whereupon it went into a rocky place. And then he said to it: "Porcupine shall you be called by the people. In that place among the rocks shall you always live."

So again on his way he started alone. And another time somebody came to the place where he was to camp, whereupon the same thing happened to him as before; when he came back, a woman was at the place where he was going to camp. Very short was the dress of the woman, and very small-legged was she, and likewise very white was she at the face. Another beaver the man had fetched home. Whereupon the woman took up the beaver, and likewise a shinbone (skinner) she used in flaying the beaver. And when she opened the belly of the beaver by hitting it, she then began to eat the beaver-entrails. He became disgusted with what she did, and it was a long while before she had finished cooking. Thereupon they ate. And again, after they had eaten, they lay down to sleep. Again he was asked: "Is it to-morrow that we move camp?"

"Yes," he said to her.

"When you hear me speaking to you, then you must give answer to what I shall tell you."

"Yes," he said to her. And then thought Clothed-in-Fur: "Not would I answer her, no matter what she might have to say." And so on the morrow upon his way started the man. And when afar he was come, he heard her calling with a loud voice: "Hey! I am trying to put on my pack!"

But he did not answer her. On his way he continued, again he went and put down his pack where they were to camp. He went off to hunt for game, another beaver he had killed. When he came back to the place where he had put his bag, his wife was not there. And so again he went to look for her; and now, when he was near, he heard the sound of her singing a song:—

"Oh my husband! do fetch me your bow-string, that I may bandage my leg! I am lame, I am lame, I am lame, I am lame!"

And then he saw that her legs were broken, whereupon he gave her his bow-string. Even after the woman had bandaged her legs, she was yet not able to lift her pack, for broken were her legs. So then at last a club he seized to strike her, whereupon a Canada jay flew up. And then he said to it: "Canada jay shall you be called by the people. In nothing will you be of use."

And then on his way continued Clothed-in-Fur. And another time he went and put down his pack. Again he went off on a hunt for game. And when he returned again, a wigwam he saw at the place where he was to camp; a very great heap of fire-wood was outside by the door. And then he saw a woman seated there inside. And she too was another whom he married. A beaver he had fetched home, and the woman prepared the beaver for cooking. Very good at knowing how to cook was the woman. And after she had finished with the cooking, she put the food into a vessel. Now the man ate, but the woman did not eat. "Eat!" in vain he told her.

"Not am I anxious to eat," said the woman. Thus always was what the woman did.

Now, once the man went away on a hunt for game; a stick he carried about with him, and he fetched it home to a place outside, by the doorway; and then there he stuck it into the ground out of doors, (it was) a small poplar (stick).

So, when out of doors went the woman, she was heard to say: "Ah, me! now, then, will I eat."

Thereupon he heard her make the sound, "*Tcąk, tcąk, tcąk, tcąk, tcąk!*" Thereupon the man rose to his feet, he stealthily peeped out of doors to see her; thereupon he beheld a beaver busily eating away. "And so it was a beaver that I married!" he thought. And when the woman came back indoors, again like a person she appeared. And so this was what the man always did, a little poplar he always fetched home on which to feed his wife. And when she had two children, he was told by his wife: "When we move, to open places in the forest do you go!"

And so whenever they moved camp, on ahead went walking the man. And then always he heard his wife come, saying: "To an open place in the forest do you go, to an open place in the forest do you go!" Thereupon truly that was what the man did. So always, when he heard his wife come speaking, then straightway down would the man lay his pack at the place where his wife would make the camp; again off he would go on a hunt for game. And when she came to the place where they were to camp, still would the woman bring along her home. Truly pleased was the man. And that was always what the woman did. And once he was told by his wife: "Now, when you see a brook, wherever you go, always put a (foot) log over it."

And that was always what the man did. Now, once he saw the bed of a brook, even though he remembered what he had been told by his wife, yet he did not place a log over the place of the dried-up water-course; he continued on his way. And then he put down his pack at the place where his wife would make the camp. He went off again to hunt for game; and when he came back to where he had put down his pack, his wife was not there. Thereupon he went back to look for her. He thought of the small, dried-up water-course; and when near by he was come, he heard the sound of a great river flowing along. When he came out upon the view of the river, he saw signs of the footprints of his wife leading into the water, and likewise of his two children. Thereupon he wept aloud. And then he set out down the course of the river. And sometimes he would also see the footprints of his wife coming out of the water, and there he would see where she had been gnawing (upon the poplars). Now, once he came to a lake, (and) a beaver was living there. He beheld a great dwelling, it was a beaver wigwam far out on the water; and now there he saw his wife seated upon the dwelling. Thereupon he went over opposite to where the dwelling was, and then he spoke to his wife: "Come hither, and fetch over here the children!"

But no answer at all was he given. Many a time he tried in vain to speak to her, but he was not answered. Her hair was the woman combing; finally then in went the woman.

Thereupon he saw one of his children come swimming towards him; and just as he was about to take it, back was it withdrawn, for the child was bound to a cord. And so he did not get (his child). And then back home went the child. Another child came swimming towards (him); and when it arrived at the place where he was, he took a shot at it, whereupon he killed it. It was not tied to a cord. And then he took it up dead, and into the forest he went weeping. Somebody he heard come speaking to him in the forest: "Stop crying! Throw away the child you are holding! I am coming to get you," he was told. Just then the woman was heard speaking, as she sat there on the dwelling: "Ta, ta, ta, ta! Let him alone! That is my husband!" Thereupon with each other the women began quarrelling; all sorts of things they said to each other. "Do keep quiet!" was said to the one seated on the dwelling. "Like a mat (spread on the bottom of a canoe) is the appearance of your tail."

"You keep quiet too, you without a tail!"

All sorts of things they said to each other about how they looked.

And then he was taken away by the woman, who had come to (where he was). Thereupon he heard the sound of his wife weeping, whereat they set out on their way. And then said the woman by whom he was taken away: "There is a town over there from whence I came, and my father is the chief."

And as they were coming to the town, they saw a staff standing in the centre of the town. "It is over there where my father dwells. Behind me do you walk," he was told. "Don't be looking about everywhere. Where I step do you step."

And when they entered in, she was addressed by her father saying: "Tawat, tawat, tawat! Truly, indeed, like a human being you are, to have this happen to you!"

Now, some time after they had entered, in came a Brown Bear. He sat down. He was angry, for he had once asked in vain for the woman to be his wife; but she was not given to him, and that was why he was angry. He was jealous; he was too much of an old man. And then he took up his tobacco-pouch; he crumpled (his tobacco) to smoke; in a little while he was smoking; after he was done smoking, he put his pipe back into his tobacco-pouch. He rose to his feet to go to the pole that was standing there in the centre of the lodge. And then he broke it in pieces, whereupon he sat down by the doorway. Chief Bear gathered up the pieces of the pole; he breathed upon them, and then back again was the pole made whole.

And so in like manner Clothed-in-Fur took up his bow and arrow. "See what I would do if I should wish to eat up an underground person!" Thereupon he shot at the pole. Every part of the pole was shattered into splinters. Whereupon the Brown Bear became ashamed; at once he took up his tobacco-pouch, and then out of doors he went.

So once more the old man gathered up the pieces of the pole; and after he had breathed upon them, the same as before was the pole made whole.

Another came in, a White Bear, and he too was angry. Now, he also had asked for the woman, but she was not given to him. He also filled up his pipe; after he had finished smoking, he rose to his feet. "See what I could do if I wished to dispose of a human being who dwells upon the earth!" Whereupon he went up to a huge rock; and after he had broken it in pieces, he then went and sat down by the doorway.

So again the old man gathered up the pieces of the rock, whereupon again was the rock completely restored.

And in the same manner Clothed-in-Fur took up his bow and arrow, and then said: "See also what I could do if I wished to dispose of a person of the underground!" And so when he shot at the rock, thoroughly was the rock pulverized.

Whereupon down the White Bear bowed his head, for he was ashamed. And so after he had taken up his tobacco-pouch, then out of doors he went.

Thereupon he was told by his father-in-law: "Be on your guard! Almost, indeed, are you prevailing over them. Therefore for the period of ten days don't go to sleep! If in that space of time you do not go to sleep, then will you prevail over them."

And truly never did the man go to sleep; and when the tenth day was nearly at an end, he had become so very tired that he wanted to sleep. So when it was nearly morning, then he fell asleep. And when he woke from his sleep, no one was there in the town, there were four poles standing, and there he was bound with cords. And so he tried to get loose. And after a long while he was able to loosen himself from the cords. And then he saw the paths by which the Bears had gone away, whereupon he followed after them as far as the great sea out upon which the Bears had come. Thereupon he saw an object like the form of a string floating on the water. He was not able to walk over to the place. Thereupon he heard on the farther shore the sound of his wife crying. At that he then seized his bow and arrow, and then shot straight away from him; and so there upon his arrow he clung as it sped along. Accordingly on the other shore he alighted. And so there he came to his wife, who was seated facing him.

Thereupon once more (he and his wife) came entering into the home of the woman's father. Very much pleased was his father-in-law when the man was seen arriving. And then again he was told: "Behold, son-in-law, for another ten days don't go to sleep!"

And truly for that reason not again did he fall asleep; (he kept it up) till the ten days were nearly ended, when again he became so very tired that he wanted to sleep. And now nearly was the dawn to appear which would mark the end of the ten-day period; almost was the dawn about to appear, when again he went to sleep. In the morning, earlier than before, it was true that he woke. By that time again had all the Bears gone away. And in the same way as before was he bound fast to the posts that were standing, there he was tied. But tighter than ever was he bound with the cords. "I wish that I might quickly get loose!" he thought. And quickly he tried to get free. After some difficulty he was able to loosen the cords. So again he saw the paths along which the Bears had gone. And speedily he went in pursuit of them. "I wish that I might overtake them before they go into camp!" he thought. Accordingly, as he followed after them, he then came to a steep cliff; and only in places here and there did the earth offer a foothold, and it was along by such a way that the Bears had passed. Now, he was not able to walk by that way. So once more he took his bow and arrow. "Would that I might first reach the foot of the hill!" he thought. And so after he had shot his arrow, and by the time he had alighted at yonder foot of the cliff, not yet had the Bears walked by. And so there he waited for them; at last he saw them come walking along. His wife came on ahead, and many he-Bears were coming along. Thereupon against his will he shot at his wife, and at all the Bears he began shooting; save only the very small cubs he did not kill. Thereupon he said to them: "Such shall be your size till the end of the world, because too severely might you ill-treat the people if you were too large." Thereupon he took up some blueberries and some insects and some leaves, and then he fed them. "Now, that is what you shall eat for food till the end of the world," he said to them.

Thereupon he came back home, he thought of his wife that was sitting there on the dwelling. And so at that place he lived again with his wife. Now, his father-in-law was there, likewise his mother-in-law, his brothers-in-law, and his sisters-in-law; so there he lived as a son-in-law. Now, Muskrat was seated there at the doorway. So once thought Clothed-in-Fur: "I wish that I might eat her!" such was the thought he had of his sister-in-law.

At once up spoke Muskrat: "See what Clothed-in-Fur has in mind! 'Would that I might eat my sister-in-law!' he thinks."

Now ashamed became the man. Whereupon said the old man: "Well, let him go ahead and eat her!" Thereupon, after they slew that woman, they cooked her. And so he was fed. "Don't break the joints at any place!" After he had eaten, then the bones were gathered up; to the water then were the bones taken and thrown in. And after a while in came the woman again; she was alive. And that was always what was done to the man whenever he had the desire to eat them; sometimes it was his mother-in-law, and sometimes it was his brother-in-law, he ate. And once he pulled apart the foot (of the one he had eaten). So when the one he had eaten came in, it then had two nails. That was what Clothed-in-Fur had done to it.

Now, once said Muskrat: "To-morrow by a being with a full set of teeth shall we be given a visit." And on the morrow, sure enough, a human being came walking hitherward. He climbed upon the dwelling, whereupon they all gazed upon him to see how he looked. Laughed the beavers when the human being started on his homeward way. They addressed (Muskrat), saying: "Muskrat, do go and listen to what the human being may have to say!"

So Muskrat slid on his feet off the log, and then started away. And when Muskrat came back, they asked him: "What did the human being say?"

" 'Very troublesome is the dwelling-place of the Beavers,' he said."

"Yes," they said. And when evening was come (the stem of) a pipe moved into where they lived (as a sign of invitation to smoke). Thereupon to his wife said the old Beaver: "Come, receive the pipe!"

The old woman then received the pipe; she gave it to her husband; and then all drew a puff from that pipe. Back moved the pipe after they had all drawn a puff.

So on the morrow came the people, they had come to get some Beavers.

And all gave themselves up to be killed. And all were taken away except Clothed-in-Fur; he was not slain. And in the evening they all returned alive. On another occasion up spoke Muskrat: "To-morrow by a being with a full set of teeth shall we be given a visit."

So on the morrow, sure enough, a man came walking hitherward. There was very little water where they lived. Once more climbed the man upon the dwelling. Again they laughed at how he looked. After the man had gone back home, again Muskrat was commanded: "Do go and hear what he may say!"

And truly Muskrat went. And when home Muskrat was come, he was asked: "What did the man say?"

" 'There is very little water where the Beavers dwell, and all we have to do is simply to go to the Beavers,' he said."

Then angry became the old Beaver. "Therefore let us hide!" Thereupon away they went for the dam. They drew along a great tree that was there at the dam, and to that place was where they went. Furthermore, they closed it up. After they had concealed themselves, they made a beaver-hole, into which they went.

On the morrow came the people for the purpose of killing some Beavers, but they did not find them. Back home they went.

On the next morning a pipe came moving in, but they did not receive it.

So on the following day back came the people. All day long they worked in vain to kill the Beavers, but they did not find where they were, even though they had fetched their dogs, that were good at hunting, and even though they went to where the Beavers were. And the Beavers spoke to the Dogs: "Away, away, away!" Yet (the Beavers) were not barked at. In the evening all went back home, they did not kill a beaver.

Even though the pipe came moving inside again, yet they did not receive the pipe. So that was what they always did, till at last the people grew negligent on having lost the Beavers. Once more in came the pipe. To his wife then spoke the old Beaver, saying: "Do take the pipe!" After she had received the pipe, then she said: "The people surely ill-use us," she said. And all took hold of the stem of the pipe.

On the morrow back came the people bringing their dogs. Although all the dogs came there where the Beavers were, yet again, "Away, away, away!" they were told. And so elsewhere went the dogs.

But there was one dog that was of no use at all for the hunt; now, this dog too came there where the Beavers were. Him the Beavers asked: "On what do they by whom we are killed usually feed you?"

Thereupon he said: "Your livers."

"All right! then bark at us."

Thereupon truly bayed the old worthless dog: " 'A^u, 'a^u, 'a^u!'"

Thereupon said the people: "Well, listen to that (dog)! Perhaps some Beavers are there." And so by and by hither they came, whereupon they found that some Beavers were there. All of them they killed, save only Clothed-in-Fur they did not kill.

And so the gizzard of the ruffed grouse now hangs aloft.

3. The Woman Who Married a Beaver

Once on a time a certain young woman went into a long fast, blackening (her face). Far off somewhere she wandered about. In course of time she beheld a man that was standing, (and) by him was she addressed, saying: "Will you not come along with me to where I live?"

Whereupon she went along with him who was in the form of a human being. And when they got to where he dwelt, very pretty was the home of the man; every kind of thing he had in clothing and food. Very well provided for was the man. And this she was told: "Will you not become my wife? In this place will we spend our life," she was told.

And the woman said: "Perhaps sad might be my father and my mother."

"They will not be sad," she was told.

Thereupon, in truth, she freely consented to marry him, whereat the woman lost the memory of her parents. Very beautiful was the clothing given her by him to whom she was married. It was where there was a certain lake that they passed their life. A long while did she have the man for her husband. When they beheld their (first) young, four was the number of them. Never of anything was the woman in want. Of every kind of fish that was, did the man kill; besides, some small animal-kind he slew; of great abundance was their food. Outside of where they dwelt (was) also some fire-wood. And the woman herself was continually at work making flag-reed mats and bags; in very neat order was it inside of where they dwelt. Sometimes by a human being were they visited; but only roundabout out of doors would the man pass, not within would the man come. Now, the woman knew that she had married a beaver.

From time to time with the person, that had come to where they were, would the children go back home; frequently, too, would the man return home with the person. And back home would they always return again. All sorts of things would they fetch,—kettles and bowls, knives, tobacco, and all the things that are used when a beaver is eaten; such was what they brought. Continually were they adding to their great wealth. Very numerous were the young they had; and as often as the spring came round, then was when off went their brood two by two, one male and one female. And this they said to them: "Somewhere do you go and put up a shelter. Do you rear a numerous offspring, to the end that greater may be the number of beavers." Save only the smaller of their young would they watch over for still another year; not till the following spring would their young go away.

Now and then by a person were they visited; then they would go to where the person lived, whereupon the people would then slay the beavers, yet they really did not kill them; but back home would they come again. Now, the woman never went to where the people lived; she was forbidden by her husband. That was the time when very numerous were the beavers, and the beavers were very fond of the people; in the same way as people are when visiting one another, so were (the beavers) in their mental attitude toward the people. Even though they were slain by (the people), yet they really were not dead. They were very fond of the tobacco that was given them by the people; at times they were also given clothing by the people.

And when they were growing old, the woman was addressed by her husband saying: "Well, it is now time, therefore, for you to go back home. I too am going away to some other land. But do you remain here in my house. Eventually, as time goes on, there will arrive some people, (and) you should speak to them."

And the woman all the while continued at her work, making twine. In very beautiful order was her home. Now, once, sure enough, (she saw) a man arriving there; on top of the beaver dwelling the man sat down. Thereupon he heard the sound of some creature sawing in the beaver-lodge beneath, the sound of some one pounding. When the woman picked up a piece of wood, she made a tapping-noise, so that her presence might be found out by the man. And he that was seated out on top learned that some creature was down inside of the beaver-lodge. And so up he spoke, saying: "Who (are) you?"

"(It is) I," came the voice of the woman speaking. "Come, do you force an opening into this beaver-dwelling! I wish to get out," was the sound of her voice as she spoke.

Now, the man was afraid of her. "It might be a manitou," he thought. Then plainly he heard the sound of her voice saying to him: "Long ago was I taken by the beavers. I too was once a human being. Please do break into this beaver-dwelling!"

Thereupon truly then did he break into that beaver-wigwam. And when he was making the hole into it, "Be careful lest you hit me!" (she said). And when he was breaking an opening, in the man reached his hand; whereupon he found by the feel of her that she was a human being; all over did he try feeling her,—on her head; and her ears, having on numerous ear-rings, he felt. And when he had forced a wide opening, out came the woman; very white was her head. And beautiful was the whole mystic cloth that she had for a skirt; worked all over with beads was her cloak; and her moccasins too were very pretty; and her ear-rings she also had on; she was very handsomely arrayed.

Thereupon she plainly told the story of what had happened to her while she lived with the beavers. She never ate a beaver. A long while afterwards lived the woman. There still lived after her one of her younger sisters; it was she who used to take care of her. And she was wont to say: "Never speak you ill of a beaver! Should you speak ill of (a beaver), you will not (be able to) kill one."

Therefore such was what the people always did; they never spoke ill of the beavers, especially when they intended hunting them. Such was what the people truly know. If any one regards a beaver with too much contempt, speaking ill of it, one simply (will) not (be able to) kill it. Just the same as the feelings of one who is disliked, so is the feeling of the beaver. And he who never speaks ill of a beaver is very much loved by it; in the same way as people often love one another, so is one held in the mind of the beaver; particularly lucky then is one at killing beavers.

4. The Boy That Was Carried Away by a Bear

Once on a time there were dwelling some people; and a certain old man had many children, and one of his sons was he continually flogging; small was the boy. Once again he chastised him thoroughly, and the boy started away on the run into the forest. And presently, while running along through a balsam-grove, very close by he saw a bear. Thereupon then was he seized; and the boy, becoming alarmed, cried out with a loud voice. "Iyā!" he exclaimed. While calling aloud, he thereupon lost the memory of his father and his mother; accordingly, then, instead he became fond of the bear that had come to take pity upon him; he was not slain by it. Thereupon he was carried away into the forest, very much was he loved (by the bear). "My grandson," continually was he called. And so all the while, when roaming about, he was ever in the company (of the bear); various kinds of things they ate, all kinds of things in the way of berries that grew in the ground they ate. Now, once he was told: "Come, let us go over in this direction! Ever are the people putting away some kind of food there. Let us go steal it!" said the Bear.

Now, when they came to the place where the cache was, there was a small island off from the water's edge; shallow was the channel in between. "In this place do you remain," he was told. "I will go fetch the (contents of the) cache." Accordingly into the water waded the Bear as he went over to the islet. A noise did the boy hear (of the Bear) tearing up the birch-bark that covered the cache. Then after a while forth from the island down to the water came the Bear, he came holding in his arms a birch-bark box. Thereupon he started off into the forest with it: "In a little while will the people be coming to the place where the cache used to be." And when a long way off they had gone, "In this place let us eat!" (the boy) was told. Whereat he broke up the birch-bark box. Very nice were the fishes dried by roasting that were in (the box); some tallow, too, was inside. Thereupon they ate. After they had eaten, "Let us go to sleep!" (the boy) was told. Exceedingly warm was it.

And so, when they had eaten up all of the fish that had been dried by the fire, they started upon their way; all sorts of things they ate as they wandered about. Now, when it was getting well on into the winter, "Come, let us seek for a place where we are to stay!" So the Bear rolled over upon his face and belly, in order to find out in his mind how many people would be passing by during the winter. So off in a certain place did the Bear seek for a spot. "Now, by this place will no person pass throughout the entire winter." Accordingly he made his lair there, in a grove of little cedars. So, when winter came, it was into that place they went.

Sometimes a person would in fact be coming straight (to where they were); one piece of fish that had been dried by the fire would (the Bear) take, and when he flung it out, then into the form of a ruffed grouse would the dried smoked fish become. Thereupon would the man turn off his course to follow after the ruffed grouse; and so into another direction would the person go. All winter long slept the Bear, with him slept the boy. Sometimes would (the boy) be addressed: "My grandson, are you hungry?"

"Yes," he would say to him.

"Just you look there at my back." So slightly over would the Bear turn. And when the boy looked, very nice was the food he saw. Everything which they had eaten during the summer before was all there. "Do you eat, my grandson!" he was told. Truly did the boy eat.

So that was what (the Bear) did throughout the winter when feeding (the boy). Sometimes the Bear would say: "Even though I take pity upon people, yet I do not (always) give them of my body. Too much harm would I do you if I should be killed." And when it was getting well on towards the summer, while there was yet a little snow on the ground, then out they came. Always did (the Bear) know where the people would be passing, so there would they not remain. And after the summer had fully come, "Now, my grandson, over this way let us go! Some fishes are in a river over there. It is there I always stay during the spring."

People were always going to the place to kill bears. Already had they set the dead-falls. And when they got to the place, very many were the fishes there. Now, when they saw the traps, then did the Bear know what the bait was; so he would not take it. Although they went often to get fish, yet the boy was not able to eat the fish raw; into the forest would he be taken by his grandfather, and for something would the Bear seek, from decayed wood would he obtain something white. Accordingly, when it was put into his mouth by his grandfather, then would it be like something that was nicely cooked; such was the way (the boy) imagined the fish (to be cooked). When there was no longer any more fish there in the river, then off to some other place they went. Continually with him slept his grandfather, never was he cold.

Now, once he was addressed by his grandfather saying: "Well, my grandchild, now therefore will I take you back home. Too sorrowful are your parents. Come, thither let us go where they are!" Accordingly was he then carried away. By and by he was addressed (by the Bear) saying: "Now, nigh to this place is a lake, and there dwell your father and your mother." Along by the edge of the water travelled the Bear. He continued straight up to a certain tree that stood by the edge of the water. Now, this (the boy) was told (by the Bear) from behind the tree, this he was told: "If at any time you are in need of food, then do you call upon me. I will feed you."

And when the boy went forth from behind the tree, then lost he all thought of his grandfather. And when the boy had gone down to the shore of the lake and looked off aside where the beach stretched away, he saw where there were some canoes; going thither, he saw some women who were there at work. And the maidens saw the boy walking thitherward, and barely did they recognize him. So one of the maidens ran up from the shore to her home, she went to announce the news: "Oh, somebody, we see a boy walking hitherward!" And the old folk came rushing out of the lodges (and) came on down to the shore, whereupon they saw that boy of theirs coming back home; ever since the summer before had they lost him. Still yet was he wearing his little rabbit-fur coat, (he was) also without any stockings, he was in bare legs; and he was not thin, he looked just the same as he did at the time he was lost. But of nothing did they question him, for they were afraid of him. Never again did the old man chastise him.

Once while in play he fashioned a stick, like a war-club was it made. But nothing did the old woman say to her son. And once, while he was roaming about in play, the old woman heard the voice of her son saying: "My grandfather, I wish to eat, do feed me!" And in a little while thither came the boy saying: "Oh look! yonder swims a bear."

And when they ran down to the water, they saw a bear swimming along. And the boy hurried over to get his little war-club, he too got into a canoe. And when they got near to where the bear was swimming, slower went the bear as he swam along; lower he bowed his head. And the boy said: "I myself will strike him," he said. And when they drew up to the bear, the boy picked up his tiny war-club, whereupon he struck the bear but once, and then (the bear) was dead.

Such was what always happened to the boy. Whenever he was heard saying, "My grandfather, I am hungry, feed me!" then there, wherever they were living in the winter-time, would he obtain a bear, near by the wigwam. Such was what happened to the boy that was son to He-that-takes-it-up.

That is the end (of the story of the) bear.

5. A Moose and His Offspring

The Moose was about to go into camp for the winter, and also his wife. Two (in number) were their children, and there was a youth among them; therefore they were five. It was so that they were in fear, of people they were in fear. On very long journeys frequently went the youth, whereupon continually was the old man trying to dissuade him (not to go so far). "Upon your trail might come the people." But (the youth) paid no heed. Once (he saw) the tracks of another Moose; he knew it was a cow. Accordingly he followed after her, whereat, on seeing her, he took her to wife. During this time that he had her for wife, by another Moose were they visited; and by her, as by the other, was he desired for a husband; to be sure, he married her. Therefore two were the wives he had.

In truth, very frequently did they fight. And once he went away, to his father he went. After he was come, he spoke to his father, saying: "Verily, my father, two (are) the women I have." He was addressed by him saying: "My son, do not bring it about that there be two women for you to have. Perhaps they might do harm to each other."

"Ay," he said to his father. And then on the morrow he went back home; in a while he arrived at where they dwelt. Whereupon, sure enough, (he found) that one of his wives had been killed.

And once there arrived two other Moose. Presently they spoke to him, saying: "Why did you have two wives? You should not have done so."

Now, in secret the youth had plucked out his testes, afterwards he flung them straight toward the west.

And then said the women: "Therefore we will follow after your testes."

Thereupon he became exceedingly ill, hardly was he able to go back to his father. In time he arrived within (the wigwam), whereupon then he began to undergo treatment from his father. "Such was the reason why I tried to dissuade you from your purpose. Because of this disobedience you became sick. Therefore now you should remain quietly by."

By this time the winter was halfway gone. In certain places roundabout where they lived wandered the calves. When it snowed, (then) sang the young Moose. Truly happy they were when it snowed:—

> *"May more snow fall, may some more snow fall!*
> *May more snow fall, may some more snow fall!*
> *May more snow fall, may some more snow fall!*
> *May more snow fall, may some more snow fall!"*

Thus sang the young Moose. They were heard by their mother, by whom they were then addressed: "Do not sing such a song, lest perhaps you be laid low with a club on the hardened crust, if much snow falls."

Thereupon they ceased.

And in course of time to very much better health was the youth restored. Therefore then he started off, trying to see how he could travel; and very comfortably did he walk along. And once he saw where the cloud had cast a shadow; in truth, he believed that he could outstrip it. Accordingly, when he ran it a race, a very great distance behind he left it. Truly pleased was he to have outrun the cloud. Then on his homeward way he went. When he entered into where they lived, he spoke to his father, saying: "My father, of a truth, you deceived me when you said that speedy is a human being. On this day now past I raced with the cloud, far behind I outran it. Not so swift as that would a human being be." Thereupon he was addressed by his father saying: "My dear son, of a truth, you are greatly to be pitied for regarding with contempt a human being. Of the nature of a manitou is a human being. To-day you shall learn, if very far you intend to go, how it is that a human being is of the nature of a manitou. He makes use of bird-hawks and swans, and on that account speedy is a human being."

It was then growing dark when (the youth) departed, for away went the Moose. And once, while travelling along, he saw the tracks of some one; it seemed as if some one had been dragging two poles, such was the mark of some one's trail. "It must be a human being that has made the trail," he thought. Then he followed in the path behind him. Of a truth, he made great fun (of the human being), he held him in contempt because of the tracks he made. "It is impossible for him ever to overtake any one, too ungainly are his tracks." And then back home he went; when he arrived, a heap of fun he made of his father: "My father, now perhaps" —while at the same time he was laughing at his father— "upon the tracks of a person did I come. No doubt, you must have been beside yourself, my father, when you said that a human being was speedy. When I was on his trail, two poles was he dragging behind. Verily, never anything could that good-for-nothing human being overtake." Thereupon then again he was addressed by his father saying: "In a little while we shall be visited by a human being."

It was now growing dark. And suddenly in came a pipe. First to the girl's mouth came the stem, whereupon then the girl smoked; next to the old woman, and she also smoked; next to the boy, likewise to the old man, who smoked; then next to the youth. The moment that the stem was entering into his mouth, he dealt it a hard blow. Thereupon then he said: "Never can I be slain by a human being." Thereupon then he was addressed by his father saying: "Oh, my dear son! therefore now have you played the mischief with yourself."

And then in a while they lay down to sleep. After they had lain down to sleep, they heard the sound of a kettle-drum beating; and it was on their account that it was beating; they were being overcome with manitou power. The old man then rose from his bed. "It is in the morning that we shall be sought for. My dear son, come, harken to what I tell you! Don't think of trying to flee away, for I am really telling you the truth in what I am saying to you. Of bird-hawks and swans (the people) make use, such are the things the people use."

Early in the morning, while it was yet dark, there came a sudden crunching of the crust of the snow. Not even did he see any one. Very close he heard the sound of some one. "Halloo!" exclaimed the other. It so happened that the dogs were scattered about everywhere barking. The calves rose to their feet; they saw some one walking hitherward. Not at all did they fail to make out every part of him, and exposed to view were his entrails. (They saw) him point the gun at them, whereupon they were then shot at. Now, there were two human beings. When they all had been shot at, then in that place were they all killed. Then for tracks did the man seek. In truth, one (he found) trailing off the other way. Before (following it up), he turned about, he went to where his father was. "Therefore you had better look after the dressing of these moose." Then away he started, following after the lone moose. On his way went the man, keeping over on the trail of the moose. Now, two (in number) were his dogs, and so upon them he depended. Now, with an easy gait at first did the moose move along; and later, while on his way he went travelling, (he) suddenly (heard the dogs) as they came barking. And then with great speed went the moose. And as he was on the point of slowing up, already again was he being overtaken. In lively manner was he barked at, whereupon truly as fast as he could go he went. For a little while he got out of sound (of the dogs' barking). Now, by this time he was very much out of wind, but yet of a truth he tried running. It was impossible for him to outstrip the dogs, for by this time he was very much out of strength. And by and by, "Kän'kän, kän'kän, kän'kän!" he heard. Then it was that he became mindful of what he had been told by his father, who had tried in vain to dissuade him from going. Thereupon truly he tried with all his might to go, but he was not at all able to outrun the dogs. At the same time he cried as he went walking along. And once, when unable to go, he saw back on his trail a human being walking hitherward, he came saying: "Well, Moose, does it seem that you have walked far enough?"

"Not at all have I yet walked enough."

Then at yonder place (the man) leaned his gun; an axe he drew (from his belt), a stick he cut. After cutting the stick, he came over to where (the Moose) was; a hard blow on the back was dealt the Moose. He was addressed by (the man) saying: "Go on! not yet have you walked enough."

Poor fellow! In spite of his efforts, he tried to go, but he was not even able to take a step.

Next (the man) drew a knife from his scabbard. Then he went up to (the Moose); taking him by the nose, he cut it off. After hanging the nose to his belt, he turned the head (of the Moose) about, and said to him: "Yonder is where you shall be eaten by your fellow-dogs." Forthwith then away went the man.

Accordingly then, in truth, he was much disturbed in mind, fearing lest he might bleed to death. Then he became mindful of what in vain he had been told by his father; and of his mother he also thought.

And now, after those were disposed of that had been killed at yonder place, then back again to life they came. Forthwith they fixed up the place where they lived. It was now growing dark. And after a while there came some one to invite them, whereupon all that were there were asked to come. They departed on their way to where the people dwelt. After they had gone inside, then they smoked. They also were fed, and they were given raiment. Truly happy were they. The old woman was given ear-rings and leggings. And all the various things that people have they were given. And the boy was given a cedar-bark pouch to keep powder in. Ever so pleased was the boy after putting over his shoulder the powder-pouch.

And in a while back home they went; after they were come at home, gone was their youth. In a while it began to grow dark, but they would not go to sleep. And by and by in the night the old woman heard the sound of somebody out of doors coming softly up (and) stopping by the door. "That may be my dear son," she thought. "Some evil fate, perhaps, may have befallen my dear son." Rising to her feet, she then went outside.

Poor thing! there he was with his hand over his nose.

"Ah, me! my dear son, what has been done to you?"

"Nothing (is left of) my nose."

When the old woman saw him, very bitterly she wept. After she had finished weeping, she took up some earth that was very black; when she rubbed (it over) his nose, then back as it used to look became his nose. When within entered the old woman, she spoke to her son, saying: "Come inside!" Of a truth, the man accordingly entered.

Then spoke the old woman, saying: "Verily, with my old moccasin will I strike at a human being if he purposes to shoot at me."

Thereupon spoke the old man, saying: "Hush! speak not thus of the people, for they are truly endowed with manitou power."

And so the buttocks of the ruffed grouse now hang aloft.

6. Little-Image

About the manitou that looks from the east I intend to tell, of Little-Image, for such was he called. Now, Little-Image never ate. And concerning the things he did when he came here upon earth is what I am now going to relate. Now, hither he started out of desire to see this earth. When he arrived at this earth, he then saw a lake; he beheld some children that were fasting, a vast number of children. He waited for them to go up from the lake. Not till after a long while did they make an end of their fasting; all sorts of things were they doing; they were running foot-races one with another. When it was noon, then went they up from the lake bound for home. When they had all departed, then went he over to the place where they had been playing; he saw that the ice was very smooth. And when he dug a hole at the place where they had been playing, he then covered himself up.

When it was evening, (he heard them) as they came laughing (and) as they began playing. Presently they almost tramped him under foot. When once they stepped upon him, he heard one say: "Upon somebody have I stepped." Then he was uncovered, and it was in the snow that he was found. When he rose to his feet, there, in truth, (he beheld) a full-grown man among them, and by him he was much liked. Accordingly then (the man) ceased playing, while the others continued racing. "My friend," he said to him, "why have these children blackened (themselves)?"

"Why, my friend, we are in training together to know how to run, this number of us whom you see running foot-races with one another. You now behold these children, and that is all that is left of us. We are in a contest; if we are beaten, then we are slain,—that is, the one beaten in the race (is slain). Now with the bears are we racing. And long ago our fathers of old were eaten up, so too our mothers. Therefore this number of children whom you see is all that is left of them. And to-morrow they will be entered into another race. That is why you see the children painted black; in a fast are the children, that by so doing they may dream of what shall give them life. This is all that I have to tell you."

So it was now getting on towards evening. "Come, my friend, to where we live let us go!"

Verily, up from the lake they went. Presently they entered into where (the man and the) others dwelt. In a while all the children arrived. Oh, truly sorry (for them) felt the man, he that came as visitor. Soon then did his friend begin to cook. After the man had finished cooking, "Come, my friend! do you also eat," he was told.

"Oh, no, my friend! I do not eat. But nevertheless you had better go ahead and eat."

Truly then did the man eat. In a while (the man) lay down to sleep. But of course he never slept or ate. Accordingly, while sitting there, of a sudden he willed: "Behold, 'I left him far behind (in the race),' let my friend dream!"

When in the morning his friend rose from bed, he spoke to him, saying: "My friend, did you not dream of anything?"

"Why, my friend, 'a great distance behind did I leave him with whom I ran,' was the dream I had."

"Yea, truly, my friend, you shall leave behind him with whom you intend to run."

As soon as they had finished eating, they heard the sound of some one coming along; it was a Bear that came entering in. As it came, it spoke to his friend, saying: "It is now time for us to run the race with each other. Thirty of the children do you bring." And then on out of doors it went.

"Well, it is now time for us to be going, my friend. Come (and) watch us!" he said to the man. In truth, then on their way they went. As they arrived, already must the others have come, for there they were seated in a row. Presently he was approached (and greeted) with a shake of the hand.

"It is now time that we were racing one with another." And this was what the man was told: "By what power do you think that you will leave me behind? Tell me by what means you will outrun me."

The skin of a bull-bat the Bear had hanging from his neck. Up spoke the Bear, saying: "While fasting for eight days, I dreamed of this necklace." Again then was the man addressed: "And what is your (power)?"

"Just simply, 'I left him behind,' was what I dreamed last night."

"Come, let us be off as fast as possible!"

A post at yonder place was standing, they passed it both together. Presently willed the man, the one that came as visitor: "Behold, he will outrun (the Bear)." Sure enough, here came his friend leading in the race. Truly happy was the man when they came (to where he was). Now, a war-club did he who was racing have; whereupon he clubbed (the bear) that he had raced with, and also the other thirty bears.

In truth, happy were the children. Accordingly then they dragged home the bears, they carried them into where they lived. Thereupon they set to work cooking. To be sure, they had good food to eat. In the evening they made some grease; oh, truly a good deal (it was)! Verily, they were pleased. Presently, it grew dark, whereupon (the man) tried to prevail upon his friend, for he wanted to feed him; but the other would not eat. So thereupon (the man) was told: "Never do I eat, and I do not sleep. Therefore this, my friend, do you keep in mind: never shall you be beaten (in a race)."

And now it was night, whereupon to sleep went his companion. When it came midnight, he thought: "'A great way behind do I leave him with whom I race,' let him dream!"

In the morning (the man) awoke. After he had eaten, he heard the sound of somebody coming; in came (a bear). By it he was addressed, saying: "It is now time that we were racing with each other. Now, half the number of your children do you bring along," he was told.

Truly they started away, (the man) following after in the track of the bear, on their way to where the children were. Presently they arrived. Then he was addressed by the Bear saying: "It is now time for us to race with each other. On what do you rely to beat me? You declare through what power you will outrun me; for in a fast of twelve days was I blest by this necklace of mine," for the skin of a bird-eagle did he have about his neck. "Now, do you in turn declare by what power you will outrun me."

"Just simply, 'I left him behind,' was what I dreamed last night."

Well, off they started. When they came to where the post was standing, this the man did; as before, he leaped for the place from whence they started; a little while was he leaping to it, as swift as a missile was how fast he went. And then, as he slowed up, here (came) the Bear on the leap. He spoke to it, saying: "Come faster! We are racing with each other!" Very far behind he left it. After (the bear) was come, (the man) took his club; then he smote it till it was dead. Thereupon he laid the other bears low with the club, as many as half their number he clubbed to death.

And then, in truth, were the children taken back home; truly happy they were. In fact, nearly all the night long were they busy preparing the bear-meat. In a while came the dawn; in course of time the sun rose; then it came noon; whereupon no one by that time had come. Little-Image spoke, saying: "Come, my friend, go look for them!"

Then departed the man; when he arrived at yonder place where dwelt the bears, none were there, for whither they had fled (no one knew). Then back home ran the man. When he arrived, he spoke to Little-Image, saying: "Therefore now have they fled."

"Now, then, my friend, get your club! Let us follow after them!"

Then off they started, all the while they kept on the run. By and by (they beheld them) going along in single file. "Now, then, my friend, let us smite them with the club!" Then as fast as they overtook them they clubbed them to death. In truth many they smote along the way. And when they had slain them all, then back they came. After they had arrived at their home, Little-Image spoke, saying: "My friend, this is the measure of help that I have come to give you. This is the way it shall be: people shall even eat bears for food, and they shall also be feared by bears. My friend, therefore, do I now return home; toward the east is the way I return home. On my arrival, greatly pleased shall I be for having helped you."

And then up spoke the man, saying: "(I) thank (you), my friend. Forever shall I remember you, so (will) also the people who shall live in times to come; however long they may be on earth, of your name will the people speak."

And so the buttocks of the ruffed grouse now hang aloft.

7. The Person That Made Medicine

Once on a time a man was engaged in song,—in manitou song of the mystic rite of the serpent. All kinds of medicine he made. Songs in great number he composed. It was over there, at the so-called Place-of-the-Pipe-Stone, where lived that man. By many people was he given ear when he was teaching songs and medicine.

Now at the time there was another man who was doing the same thing, and he who had first been making the medicine was not pleased. Now, all sorts of things were they giving one another when they were asking for medicine. That was the cause of the anger of him who had first made the medicine.

So once they (all) went together to yonder steep cliff, many canoes they used; they went in company with many people. All sorts of things they cast into the water for an offering,—tobacco, and ribbon, and effects; thereupon they sang, and at the same time they smoked. And presently out opened the cliff at the bottom of the water, and thereupon out flowed from thence every kind of medicine there was. Now, the man who had first been making the medicine did not take any of it. So when it was observed by the manitou that he was not taking the medicine, then back into its place went floating the medicine; up closed the cliff. Thereupon they saw many wild pygmies, whereupon that man began to be stoned (by the pygmies); even though he tried to flee far out upon the water, yet not at all got he out of the range (of their stones). The people that were in their canoes heard the whirl of the passing stones. And when he was come a long way off, at a place where there was another cliff, then from that place over there was he pelted again; straight for the mouth of the river was where he tried to flee. Another mountain, one that is called Moose Mountain, was a place from which he was again struck. Straight out for the open water he tried in vain to pursue his flight. Now, there is another island, known by the name of the Place-to-hunt-Moose, an exceedingly high cliff, (which) was another place from where he was pelted by the little wild pygmies. At last he was struck square on the head; (the missile) went into his head, with a piece of metal was he hit; whereupon he was killed.

So back home went all the people. Again they held a great smoker, (and) they made offerings. Again they propitiated their manitous. And that is why people are never allowed to speak nonsense upon a cliff or upon the water; and very seriously do people forbid one another to talk nonsense (in such places); therefore that is why the people are careful.

Such is what I have heard of what happened long ago. But to-day nobody is very careful, even in the composition of songs. Differently nowadays do the people do (things).

8. The Birth of Nänabushu

In a wigwam lived some people, an old woman with her daughter dwelt. Once she spoke to her daughter, saying: "I beg of you, my daughter, be on your guard. I would have you listen to what I am going to tell you. Verily, am I greatly afraid, I am in fear for you. Never bring to pass when you go out that you sit facing toward this westward way. Something will happen to you if toward that way you sit facing. That is what causes me to entertain fears for you. Be careful to give heed to that which I now tell you to do; (or else) you will bring (an evil) fate upon yourself. Now that was what I had to tell you."

Now such was the way it was, for it was true that at the time heedful was this woman who was a maiden. Never with men had she intimate association. But once on a time unmindful became the maiden; so when out of doors she went (and) afterwards sat down facing the west, then heard she the sound of wind coming hitherward. When she felt it, she was chilled there at the place of the passage out. Accordingly she quickly leaped to her feet. "O my mother, behold the state that I am in! It may be that what you told me of is the matter with me."

Then spoke the old woman to her daughter saying: "Exceeding harm have you done to yourself." So therefore then did the old woman weep. "Now therefore, my daughter, have you done yourself a hurt. You shall learn what will happen to you. Certain beings have entered into your body: therefore, my daughter, you are in a pitiable state. They are not human beings that have gone inside of you there. The time is not far distant before they will be born. Therefore it was they whom I feared."

Now, lo, in the course of time did the old women hear the sound of beings that were quarrelling one with another. She knew by the sound of their voices that they were inside. And so without ceasing did the old woman weep. It was true that then was she sure that her daughter would not live. Now, she heard them quarrelling one with another, there in her (daughter's) belly the sound of their voices could be heard. This was what one was heard to say: "I wish to be the first brought forth."

"No," one was heard saying, even did one say, "you cannot be the first-born. I am the one to be the eldest."

It was natural that all the while the old woman should weep as she listened to them quarrelling one with another. Knowledge of them had the old woman as to how many would her grandchildren be.

Hark! this was what they said as they pushed one another back from the place where they tried in vain to go out. But others of them tried, but to no purpose, to say: "Don't, please! We shall surely do injury to our mother. In proper order please let us go out," (thus) in vain they said.

But not content with the idea were they who wished to be the eldest. Therefore then they said that now from different places they wished to go out. One saw where there was light. "Now, straight by this very way do I wish to go." And so while they were debating among themselves as to who should be the first to go out, then was when they burst open their mother.

After a while at a certain place where round about the old woman was looking she found a clot of blood. Thereupon some birch-bark she began peeling (from a tree). And now, after she had put the blood upon the bark, she then folded the bark over it, and laid it away. Naturally, by and by she looked at it. Now, once when she opened the bark she beheld a babe, whereupon she was addressed, and this is what she was told: "O my grandmother!" she was told at the time that she was addressed. So now this was what she was told: "Do you know who I am? Why, I am Nänabushu."

9. Nänabushu Swallowed by the Sturgeon

And so it is said that Nänabushu and his grandmother continued living there. Once on a time they say that while Nänabushu was meditating, he thought: "I am curious to know if I was the only one," thought Nänabushu. Thereupon he thought: "I will ask my grandmother." So, according to the story, he then truly said to his grandmother: "My grandmother," he said to her, "is it possible that you and I are the only ones living?" he said to her. "Have I never had a mother?" he said to his grandmother. "Is it possible that simply without cause I came into being?" he said to his grandmother.

So after a long while he was given reply, he was told: "My grandson," he was told, "it was almost like that, (as you will see from what) I shall say. Be seated, listen, I shall inform you. Listen to me with care," he was told. "Verily, there were some people living; but then as time went on gradually passed away one by one, till at last also went they whom you would call your parents. And there was also one that was your elder brother," he was told. "And he too disappeared. Now about you, listen, (and) I will explain to you from what source you came, and why now you are here. After that elder brother of yours was born, then that which is the last to come when one is born was thrown away; for it is called a place-for-the-babe-to-rest-its-head, such is the name. So it was from that source that you came, my grandson. At the time when your elder brother was born, it was then taken somewhere out of doors and hung up. And so after a while there was heard the cry of a babe at yonder place where hung the little-rest-for-the-head. Thereupon I went to the place, and there I found you. Therefore it was I who reared you," she said to him. "And your mother herself brought up your elder brother. And the name of your elder brother was Näna-`pātạm. And so the name Nänabushu was what you were called," he was told by his grandmother.

Thereupon Nänabushu seriously began pondering, sad too he became at the thought that forsooth he had an elder brother. And then Nänabushu straightaway made up his mind what he would do, and so he said to his grandmother: "My grandmother, it is strange that never did you say anything to me concerning what had actually happened to us."

"It was for a purpose that I told you of nothing," he was told by his grandmother, "that for no cause you should be sad, and that you should not be disturbed in your peace of mind," he was told by his grandmother. "And that in peace you should live; that you should behold with a feeling of contentment the light of day when it comes; and that whenever the sun comes forth, when a sense of gladness pervades all things, you should be joyful too. Now, that was why I never imparted anything to you," he was told by his grandmother.

Thereupon Nänabushu presently said to his grandmother: "My grandmother," he said to her, "I am going to war. I am going to seek those who slew my parents and my elder brother."

And then he was told by his grandmother: "Don't, my grandson. Somewhere will you bring ruin upon yourself," he was told.

"No," he said to his grandmother, "I am determined to look for them." So then off went Nänabushu, he went to seek (for a small straight tree, easy) to split, to the end that he might make some arrows and some spears. And now it is said that on his early return to his home he was then told by his grandmother: "What now, my grandson?" he was told.

"Nothing," said Nänabushu. "My axe does not cut. Please let me have the whetstone, my grandmother. I want to sharpen the axe."

It was true that over leaned the old woman, and from the meeting-place of the wall and the ground she drew forth a whetstone and gave it to him.

Whereupon over reached Nänabushu, taking it, and then he began the work of sharpening (the axe). And so later on, while Nänabushu was at work with the whetstone, he then heard that which he was told: "Your father, your mother," was the sound of the whetstone. "Why does it say that?" he thought. "Perhaps my grandmother for some reason is deceiving me about what I had asked her," he thought. Once more as he began using the whetstone, so again he heard it: "Your father, your father, your father, your mother, your mother, your mother." Exceedingly angry was Nänabushu. "Hark, listen to what the axe is saying to me!" he said to his grandmother.

"Simply are you hearing the sound of what you are always revolving in your mind," she said to him.

"No," to her said Nänabushu, "simply am I chided to anger." Thereupon Nänabushu truly was angry. And so he once more took up the whetstone. While whetting the axe, then again was he told: "Your father, your father, your elder brother, your elder brother," he was told. Thereupon he leaped to his feet; thereupon he grabbed and fastened down the axe; he thoroughly pounded it with a stone right on the sharp edge.

Thereupon truly was he fully prepared to go; many arrows and spears had he made. So far as the story goes, it is not told what he used when he made the great number of his arrows and spears, for he had dulled his axe; it is only told of him how that he had made himself prepared. And so it is said that Nänabushu started away. By the way, this too was what was told of him! He made a canoe; he hewed it out of a log; the measure of himself was the size he made it, so it is told of him.

Thereupon he went to assail the Great Sturgeon. And so they say that Nänabushu set out, bidding farewell to his grandmother. And then they say he was told: "Be careful, my grandson," he was told; "somewhere will you bring harm upon yourself," he was told by his grandmother.

"No, my grandmother, I shall return again to this place," he said to her. And as Nänabushu now shoved his canoe into the water, he proceeded straight out to sea; and when almost at the middle part of the sea he was come, then he cried with a loud voice, singing:

"Oh ye Great Sturgeons, O ye Great Sturgeons,
Come one of you and swallow me, come one of you and swallow me!"

And in a little while was the sea set in motion; like rapids when the current is strong, so was the flow of the waves.

Thereupon truly Nänabushu sang aloud:

"Oh ye Great Sturgeons, come swallow me!
Ye that have slain my parents, come swallow me too!"

As soon as he had finished speaking, then immediately he saw a great sturgeon coming to swallow him. At first round in a whirlpool spun the canoe, and then down into the water he was drawn, swallowed by the Great Sturgeon, canoe and all. All the while they say there was a hissing-sound in the ears; and when he recovered his wits, inside of a fish he was. Thereupon quietly he remained there; and they say that now he knew that the fish was carrying him away.

And so the chief of fishes returned to the home under water on the floor of the sea. And now they say that (Nänabushu) heard them holding a great smoker among themselves, and he also heard them holding forth with much talk; they were giving thanks for that he was swallowed.

Now, once they say that while he was listening, something Nänabushu saw that caught his attention. Well, on with the story. Wonder how he could see! (Nevertheless) they say that Nänabushu saw something in motion, and it happened to be the heart of the Great Sturgeon that was beating. Thereupon they say that softly he moved (and) pulled out a pointed arrow; and then he began pricking it. Whereupon they say that in a little while he heard the voice of him saying: "Oh, truly indeed but I am feeling sick at heart." And then he heard him asking his wife to give him a drink of something to make him vomit. And so presently did he begin trying to vomit, but he was not able to do it. And then he heard him saying: "Impossible, for Nänabushu is making me sick at my stomach," he said.

True was it, indeed, that hard worked Nänabushu to keep from being cast out; so then crosswise he placed his arrows, and so by them he held on.

Thereupon again the Great Sturgeon spoke: "No hope. I am in distress inside on account of Nänabushu," he said. And so in a little while he was dead, him had Nänabushu slain. Even though all that were living there, had come together by invitation for the purpose of bringing their chief back to life, [but] (it was) not (to be); for how could any one live with his heart cut to pieces? And that was why he had died.

And as for Nänabushu, there he remained.

Thereupon truly they were doing wonderful things as they conjured for a miracle. It was no use, for already dead was the great fish. And so it is said that they were going to bury him, for really a long while had they kept him; perhaps he might come back to life, they thought. And so accordingly they say that when they were burying him, farther out upon the sea, where it was deep, they went to bury him. Ever so mightily they conjured for a miracle.

Now, Nänabushu knew everything that was happening, but yet by no one was it known that he was there and alive. They knew that he had been swallowed, but yet they did not know that he was alive. And so after they had finished burying (the chief of fishes), then back they came together to their home again. Exceedingly numerous they were, from every part of the sea had they come to be at the burial of their chief.

In the mean while they say that Nänabushu had been thinking out a plan how he might succeed in getting out from the inside of the fish which now was also lying buried. And so, now that Nänabushu knew what he would do, he thereupon said: "Oh, I would that there rise a mighty storm the like of which there has never been before!" Whereupon Nänabushu made a smoke offering toward the four directions where sit the manitous.

And so his prayer was answered. Thereupon truly there rose a mighty wind, everything that was on the floor of the sea came to the surface by force of the waves. And as for Nänabushu, the sand (of the mound) where he had been was washed away; and then afterwards the fish came to the surface of the water. For ten days the wind raged, and afterwards there was another great calm, whereupon to the surface (came) the Great Sturgeon.

Now once, when Nänabushu was inside of the fish, he heard something that sounded very pleasantly; and as he listened, he then hear: "(cry of gulls)." Very pleasant was the sound of the creature; it turned out to be some gulls. "Well," thus thought Nänabushu, "I will speak to them," he thought. It was true that soon again he heard the sound of them coming hitherward, whereupon again they came with the cry: "(cry of gulls)." And then he said to them: "Hark, O my younger brothers! Please peck an opening for me into the belly of this fish!"

Thereupon the gulls flew up; and as they went, they could be heard uttering a frightful cry, for such was the sound they made. Whereupon

Nänabushu seized his ears (and) closed them with the hands (to keep from hearing the din). And in a little while again he listened, whereupon again he spoke to them, saying: "O my younger brothers! peck an opening for me into the belly of this fish!" he said to them.

Thereupon truly they became silent.

And so again he spoke to them, saying: "Peck an opening for me into the belly of this fish!" he said to them. "In return I will adorn you."

Thereupon the gulls spoke one with another, saying: "Nänabushu is there."

Indeed, by every creature was Nänabushu known. And so again he spoke to them, saying: "Come, my younger brothers, peck an opening for me into the belly (of this fish). In return I shall adorn you; as beautiful as the creature of the air that surpasses (all others in beauty) is how beautiful I shall make you," he said to them.

"We surely could not (make an opening into) him," he was told.

"Yea, (you can)!" He said to them. "You can do it!"

Thereupon truly they began pecking an opening into (the fish); and after a long while they succeeded. And then afterwards Nänabushu crawled out, and he drew out his canoe which he had hewn from a log. And then was the time that he took a careful look to see how big was the great sturgeon which had swallowed him; like an island afloat upon the water was how it looked as it lay upon the deep. Thereupon he took up one of the gulls in his hands; and then he adorned it. And then he whitened it, (white) like snow he made it. Thereupon he said to it: "You shall be called a gull from now till the end of time."

It was true that exceedingly happy was the gull when it looked upon itself and saw how beautiful it was.

"Now, then," he said to them, "now fly away!"

Now, according to the story, there was mentioned but a single gull that he took up in his hands. Yet nevertheless just as beautiful were all the rest when they all started to fly away. And then afterwards Nänabushu began cutting up the fish with a knife. And so when he had finished cutting it up, then he said, at the same time that he was flinging the pieces in every direction: "Fishes shall you be called till the end of time. And you shall be eaten by the people till the end of the world.—And you," he said to the Great Sturgeon, "never again so large shall you be as long as the world lasts, else nobody would ever live," he said to him. Therefore it truly came to pass that he created little fishes in great numbers from that Great Sturgeon.

Thereupon Nänabushu paddled home in his canoe to find his grandmother. And when he got there, he discovered his grandmother grievously sad in her thoughts. And as he peeped into the lodge, he said to her: "O my grandmother! I have now come home," he said to her.

"Oh, I should like to know why they continually say this to me, these little animal-folk!"

"Nay, my grandmother. It is really myself, Nänabushu, your grandson, who has now come home." And then into the lodge he went. Thereupon he saw that his grandmother was barely able to see, (showing) that perhaps all the while she had been weeping. And then afterwards he had made her younger.

10. Nänabushu Slays Hewer-of-His-Shin

Thereupon the old woman was very happy to see her grandson once more. And not at all did she realize that she had been made younger. So then she said to her grandson: "All the time some creatures came to me here; they told me that you were slain. Again by some would I be told, 'O my grandmother! I have come home.' With some design they came speaking thus to me," she said to her grandson.

Thereupon Nänabushu was angry, and he said to his grandmother: "Again shall I leave you. Not yet have I found the probable ones that must have slain all my relatives."

"Alas! my grandson," she said to him, "you are to be pitied. You may not be able to go there where abides the one who made you an orphan," she said to him.

"And where is it?"

"At yonder place in the centre of the great sea is an island. And never has any one gone there. And he goes for good whoever goes there. I don't know whether they have ever arrived at the place, or if they died on the way," he was (thus) told by his grandmother. "And over there is a manitou; he is called Hews-upon-his-Shin, for it is said of him that ever is he hewing upon his shin. It is said of him that if any one should go thither, then at half way to the place would one hear the sound he makes upon his shin," she said to him.

"Really!" was she told by her grandson. Thereupon in truth did Nänabushu make up his mind, he thought that he would go. And so he said to his grandmother: "Determined am I to go look for him," he said to her. Thereupon Nänabushu again made ready by making spear-pointed arrows, enough to last him three days was the number he made. And so after he had finished them, then again Nänabushu put his canoe in order. And then away went Nänabushu straight towards where it had been pointed out to him by his grandmother. Now, by and by, they say, as Nänabushu went paddling alone (in his canoe), presently something he truly heard straight (on the way) whither he was going. He let his canoe go floating quietly along upon the water while he listened to the sound; presently he clearly heard a sound. "Tän, tän," (such) was the sound he heard. Thereupon he thought: "Hark! that is what my grandmother told me," he thought. And so truly he hurried on. Nänabushu later on again listened for the sound, presently again he heard it. "Twän, twän, twän," was what he heard. Nearer it now sounded. Again he hastened on.

Another time, as he was looking about, he saw something in the way ahead of him; it was an object like a line drawn across his course; and then, as he looked, "Perhaps that which is now coming into view is the island for which I am bound," he thought. Thereupon he truly hastened on with his canoe. Farther on he listened again for the sound, and he heard it the same as before. "Twin, twin," was the sound he heard. Straight from yonder place where the land was coming into view he heard the sound. It turned out truly to be (the island) that he had seen. And now, as he continued on, he presently saw the land in plain sight; thereupon again he listened, and then again he heard the sound. "Twin, twin," was what he heard. And then the water trembled, so loud was the Manitou hewing upon his shin.

Thereupon it is said that Nänabushu now drove his canoe straight for the place in the shore from whence he heard the sound come; truly as he went ashore he saw a path leading away somewhere. And as he followed it up from the shore, he saw a small wigwam standing; and so secretly went he up to it; as he peeped in, he saw an old man seated in a squatting pose, facing him, and he had hold of something in his hand. And as he watched him striking upon his shin, it was like hewing upon a log, such was his manner of doing it. And frightful was the sound that he made when he struck. And as for Nänabushu, there he stood observing him.

After a while the other then turned about, and said: "Aha, aha, aha, Nänabushu! Have you come to make war upon me?" he was told.

"Yes," to him said Nänabushu.

"Very well, then!" At the same time he made a pretence at laughing, so deep was his contempt of Nänabushu; he had no doubt but that he would prevail over him.

And as for Nänabushu, too, "Come, make haste."

And so, in truth, up he slowly rose from his couch, up he rose to his feet; and then he came out of doors.

"Well, let us pick out a place where we are to fight each other," (Nänabushu) was told.

"All right," he said to him.

Thereupon they truly sought for a place. "Here is a place," they said. Round about looked Hewer-of-his-Shin. And up into the air looked Nänabushu; he stood in his place, his shield he carried, so too his bow and arrows. And as for Hewer-of-his-Shin, he held in his hand a war-club of stone. Thereupon they now addressed each other, saying: "Ready!" And truly Nänabushu then shot at him, and then in turn Hewer-of-his-Shin struck him with his war-club. Thereupon exceedingly hard at work they truly kept each other. Nänabushu nearly all the while was occupied in dodging the blows, truly was he kept stirring by the other. And as for Nänabushu, he too was active with his shooting. While they now were in the thick of their fight with each other, then the supply of Nänabushu's pointed arrows began to run low. And in the midst (of the fighting) Nänabushu heard the sound of some one calling out to him from above, saying: "Hey, Nänabushu! at the scalp-lock shoot him!" was the sound Nänabushu heard. Though busily engaged, out he also cried: "What!" said Nänabushu.

"At his scalp-lock shoot him!"

Whereupon he was told by Hewer-of-his-Shin: "What (is the matter), Nänabushu? With whom are you speaking?" he was asked.

Nänabushu then said: "Ah, few do you think are my little brothers of the sky who protect me?" he said to him. Thereupon truly Nänabushu shot the Hewer-of-his-Shin there where he was told to shoot him, there where his hair was tied in a bunch at the back; whereupon he hit him (with the arrow). And then he was told: "Alas, O Nänabushu! is it true that now you really intend to kill me?" he was told.

"Ah!" he said to him. "You surely do not think that I am simply trifling with you!" to him said Nänabushu. Once more he shot him in the crown of the head. Whereupon again the same thing he was told: "Alas, O Nänabushu! is it true that surely now you mean to slay me?" he said to him.

"Of course!" said Nänabushu. "You who slew my parents," he said to him, "you too shall I slay!" he said to him. At the same time that Nänabushu was talking, he was all the while shooting. And then presently he brought him down with his shooting. Thereupon he was told again: "Now, O Nänabushu, do leave me alone! In return something will I give you."

"Hurry and give it to me!" he said to him. "Tell me, too, what you did to my father and mother and to all those who used to live in times past!" he said to him. Whereupon truly he was told: "Do you see this island where now we have fought each other? Those trees that you see standing are the same as they who used to live in times gone by. Such is the form I have made them, that they be as trees," he was told. "Now, if you leave me alone, I will give you something to use to make them come back to life again," he was told.

"Make haste and tell me what I shall do to bring them back to life!"

"Go yonder inside to the place from whence I rose to my feet, and you will see there a small wooden pail; and bring it here to me."

Thereupon Nänabushu truly went to fetch it; but he did not lay aside his bow and arrows. And then he was told: "You see what is here contained in this small pail, in this small wooden pail; there is contained here the means by which you are to bring back to life your father and your mother," he said to him, "and all the others. Now, this you shall do: you shall scratch the bark from the tree until you see the part in wood and then a stick shall you dip into this that is contained here in the little wooden pail; and then shall you rub it upon the place where you have scraped the bark from the tree," he said to him.

"Oh! Is that all?" he said to him.

"That is all."

Thereupon again he shot him in the crown of the head, whereupon he slew him. "There, now!' he said to him. "Dog that you are, who was ever bent upon destroying the earth! So now I will derive from you the source by which the earth will be replenished," he said to him.

Thereupon he became slicing him into small pieces with a knife. And as he scattered the pieces about, in all the various directions he flung them; then he named them what they were to be, they that run about upon the earth as the little animal-folk, and they that fly about in the air, and also the large animal-folk. And then next after Nänabushu had taken up the little pail, he did what he had been commanded. As soon as he had done it to one tree, straightway there stood in the place a man. And so to another he did it. Again to many he did (it). And then by and by he found his father and his mother, and his elder brother Nänä`pädạm.

And then Nänabushu was told by his elder brother, for immediately was he here teased by him while the people laughed: "Did you hear me when I spoke to you?"

Whereupon Nänabushu said to him: "Where?" he said to him.

"When the old man was about to prevail over you."

And so it was by him that Nänabushu was called upon while he and Hewer-of-his-Shin were fighting. And now Nänabushu was yet very busy bringing the trees back to life; truly it was they that used to live in a former time. To its full capacity was the island crowded.

11. Nänabushu Leaves His Brother, and Also His Grandmother

Thereupon Nänabushu, according to the story that is told of him, must have set to work to enlarge the size of the island, so great was the throng of them living there on the island. Now, it is also told of him that there was he very content. And after Nänabushu had finished everything, he then spoke to them, and told them upon what they should subsist. And that was also the time he named what (the people) should call the big animal-folk and the little animal-folk and them that crawl upon the ground. And the story is also told of him how that at the time he named the fishes which he had created from the Great Sturgeon which he had cut up, and them that should not be used for food, such is what they tell of Nänabushu.

And then they say that he spoke to his father and mother, saying: "My father," he said to them, "the time is at hand for me to go away. —And you, my elder brother, Nänä`pädạm, do you stay here to watch over them who are here," he said to him; "to be ruler over them," he said to him. "And myself, I shall go away; I wish to seek for my grandmother," he said to him. "I had made her a promise," he said to him. "Anyhow, we both have not had the same kind of birth, so that we should ever be together," he said to him. "You are yourself, my elder brother, like a real human being; and (as for) myself, from what was thrown away (at birth) was the source from which I sprang," he said to his elder brother.

And though Nänä`pädạm was not pleased with the thought that so soon he was to part from his younger brother, yet it was useless for him to beg (Nänabushu) to let him go along. But Nänabushu knew his feelings, and so said to him: "O my elder brother! during this day will I go with you, for I wish to walk round this island, so that larger it may become," he said to him, "and at the same time that you may know how big is the region over which you are to keep watch."

And so they truly started off, they went walking along the shore by the edge of the water. Now, as they thus walked along, of a sudden mindful was the man; as he looked behind, land only did he see. Now, as they went they talked, but nothing to say had he who was the elder brother. "Let us quicken our pace!" he was told by his younger brother, Nänabushu. "Soon will the evening come on, and we shall not have returned to where we live," he said to his elder brother. And then, as they went along, he explained to his elder brother how he should rule over them who were there.

And so at last he was asked by his elder brother: "O my younger brother!" he was asked, "what is the reason that you are not chief over them, you who brought back to life them that now are alive?" he said to him.

Accordingly Nänabushu gave answer to his elder brother: "O my elder brother!" he said to him, "It is you whom I wish to watch over them," he said to him.

"Oh!" he was told.

And now they were arriving at the place from whence they had started; as they were now drawing nigh to the place, then he who was the elder brother beheld a mighty river flowing by. Thereupon he said to his younger brother: "From whence flows this river? Nothing (of a river) did I see before," he said to his younger brother.

Whereupon Nänabushu said to him: "Ay," he said to him. "Do you see the other shore? It is from over there that we started," he said to him.

Astonished then was Nänä`pädam. And then he thought: "Wonder where shall we be able to get across?" thus he thought.

But Nänabushu, on his part, only gave a laugh; as he went he observed, and as he went he was at the same time seeking for some kind of a log to lay across the stream so that they might be able to cross. It was true that he found one on the way. "Come on!" he said to his elder brother. "You first cross over on the log."

"How shall we be able to get over?" he said to him.

"Why, we shall not fail in the undertaking!" he said to him.

Thereupon truly crossed he over upon the log; the moment he put down one foot and then lifted the other, that very instant he stepped on the other shore. And so before he turned about (to see if the other was coming), then was Nänabushu also across. And as he looked, he then beheld how wide was the river which only at a single step he had passed across.

It was there that Nänabushu now meant to part with his elder brother. "The time has come, my elder brother," he said to him, "for me to part from you. Straight yonder way do you go. Over there will you see them whom we have left," he said to him. "And over in this (other) direction I myself will go," he said to him.

Thereupon they parted from each other. According to the story, not is it told if Nänabushu first went to see his parents when he left the island. All that is told of him is that he parted from his elder brother and that he went to see his grandmother. And now they say that when Nänabushu arrived at the home where his grandmother was, he said to her the same thing that he had said to her in times gone by: "I have come home, O my grandmother!"

"Oh, dear me! Oh, dear me! Why should you always desire to afflict me grievously with such words!" said the old woman.

"Nay, my grandmother! It is truly I!" he said to her.

Thereupon, as she looked toward the doorway, then verily she beheld her grandson come entering in. "Ah, me! It is my dear grandson who has actually come back home!" she said to him. "He is dead, such was my thought of him," she said to him.

And so as Nänabushu looked upon his grandmother, exceedingly white was her hair. And this he thought: "In so short a while has her hair whitened," he thought. Whereupon he was told by his grandmother: "My grandson, do you think that you have been absent but a little while? A long time have you been gone," she said to her grandson. "And perhaps the time has come for me to leave you," she said to her grandson.

"Yes, my grandmother. To yonder place from whence I now have come shall you go," he said to her. "At that place have I placed my elder brother, that he might be ruler over you (and the rest)."

And then truly the old woman departed, she followed back the footsteps of her grandson.

And Nänabushu himself went his way, off in some other direction he went; still to this day must he be travelling along, wherever the place he now may be; and perhaps even to this day he may be walking.

12. Nänabushu, the Sweet-Brier Berries, and the Sturgeons

Well, accordingly then went he slowly along his way. And once after he had seen where some people were intending to spend the autumn, he then said to them: "I beg of you, my younger brothers," he said to the people. He saw them engaged in catching fish, so naturally desired to remain there too, and this he said to them: "I beg that you let me spend the autumn with you."

"You may," he was told.

Thereupon he abode with them. Now they killed fish there where they were spending the autumn. In the course of time (the lake) was frozen over, so thereupon there they spent the winter. Now they had some children. As time went on, they ate up (all) their fish. Thereupon this was what (Nänabushu) said to them with whom he lived: "Now, therefore, we will eat your fishes first; and then afterwards, when they are gone, then our fish will we eat."

And so truly that was what they did. Now, it was true that they ate the fish of the others. In course of time they ate up (all) the fish. And so after they had eaten up the fish of his companions, they that were on the opposite side of the (lodge) fire, then gone were all the fish of the other; thereupon he became angry at them, and so moved away. Not far away he made his camp, and so of course thither he took his own fish. So thereby hungry became the others whose fish he had eaten up. Now, as for the man (whose fish had been eaten up), he kept his children alive by means of sweet-brier berries. So once when home came the man, "Now, I fear that we shall starve," he said to his wife.

"I fear so," he was told.

And so on the following day he started on his way again to seek for sweet-brier berries. And once as he was travelling over the ice of the lake, as he went walking along the shore-line, he suddenly heard the sound of something out on the ice. He saw that an object was there, and so went up to it, and lo, it was an arrow! Accordingly he gazed upon it with a desire to pick it up. He was startled at the sound of somebody's voice saying to him: "You fool," he was told; "is that your arrow?" he was told.

And this he said to him: "Nay," he said to him. "I desire only to look at it."

"Come, kindle a fire. It seems as if you are cold," he was told.

And this he said to him: "Yes, truly, I am cold." Accordingly, indeed, he kindled a fire, and so there he warmed himself.

And then the other took off his moccasins, whereupon, "Pray, eat these moccasins of mine," he was told. Accordingly, indeed, he took the other's moccasins, and what was he to behold when he took the other's moccasins but really the dried tails of beavers! Now, one he fully intended to leave, but, "All of it shall you eat," he was told. "Now, very great wrong am I doing them," he thought, "in that I have not saved some for my children." He saw how large the moccasins were, that one bearskin was of a bear surpassingly large, and from that the other had a moccasin; and (the skin of) a young bear was what he used for a patch on his moccasins. And when the other had put on his moccasins, he went to where his bag was, his cedar-bark bag. And so when he poured out his sweet-brier berries, he filled the bag up with beaver berries.

Thereupon by the other was he helped in lifting the pack upon his back. And then, after he had helped in lifting on the pack, this he was told: "When you have come nigh to the place where you (and the others) live, then select a large hollow space of ground, and there is where you should put down that pack of yours. And then you should continue on your way, and look not back behind you. Not till in the morning should you go and look. Exert yourself; make haste as you go on this path; for the sound of somebody will you hear yelling at you, and this you will be told: 'Hey, push him!' will you be told. So look not back; be careful. Do precisely as I have taught you."

And so truly off he started running. And this he was told by them who pursued him: "Hey, push him!" he was told. And now, indeed, he heard them a short distance away; it seemed that now they would overtake him. So out upon the ice of a lake he came fleeing. And notwithstanding that, already was he coming close to the other side in his flight over the ice, yet exceedingly hard was he now being pressed by them who were pursuing him. And then presently was he arriving at the other side of the frozen lake; and when he was come at the other side of the ice, gone were they by whom he was pursued.

And so in peace he then went walking on. Now, this was what he had been told: "For at yonder forest will you no longer be pursued," he was told. It was true that no longer did he feel the pursuit of anybody after he had gone up from the shore. And so truly he continued his way, looking for the place where there was a great depression in the ground. And when he truly saw the place that had a deep depression, it was there that he dropped his pack. It was true that he did not look back. And so on his way back home he went. Now, this he was asked by his wife: "Where are the sweet-brier berries that you went to get?" he was asked by his wife.

And this he said to her: "Why, in no wise should you feel so sad about it, for no doubt you will yet have food to eat," he said to his wife. And then hardly could the man sleep. "This is indeed the feeling I have had, that perhaps, old woman, we shall yet be blessed," he (thus) said to his wife. And so after the day was come, he then addressed her, saying: "All right, come, let us go!"

Thereupon, in truth, they now started on their way, they went to look at the place where he had dropped his pack when coming home; now, what were they to behold when they caught sight of it but a place full of sturgeons! Thereupon were they happy. "Without fail shall we now have food to eat." And so from that moment they began packing from there. And now when they set to work, while it was day and all day long, they packed (and) hauled the sturgeon. And so by the time they had finished hauling it all, not yet had they eaten.

"I say, do you go wait for him at the place where we draw our water." Accordingly they truly waited for him. Naturally without fail would Nänabushu come in; so, after they were ready, then one of the sturgeons they laid across their doorway. Then accordingly waited they for Nänabushu to come in.

Thereupon, truly, Nänabushu at yonder place had this told him: "We lost to the boys in a wager," (thus) by his children was Nänabushu told, this was he told by his children.

So this he said: "Probably he has found something and for that reason they are living comfortably. Surely, indeed, it is sturgeon-roe, for that was what they ate.

It was on that account that they won from us. I think I will go and see my old friend," he said to his children. Thereupon, truly, he soon was off to visit the Pilferer. And so after he had gone in, indeed while he was entering, he saw a sturgeon lying across his way! And this he said to them: "I want to visit my old friend," he said to them. What should he see where the others lived but a wonderful supply of sturgeon! And this he said to them: "Where did you kill them?" he said to him.

So this he was told: "Over here at our water-hole. This my old woman did; she was at work all day long making a line. And after she had tied the line to my foot, I thereupon went down into the water by way of our water-hole. And when I saw (the sturgeon) down there under the water, I then speared it. And when I jerked the line, then on the line pulled the old woman. So thus she drew me out of the water. And so once again I went down into the water. There, that was how I did down there where I got them. Now, that was how I provided myself with food. Therefore have I related to you what I had done."

"Yes, indeed," said Nänabushu. "Possibly that may be a source by which I shall obtain some food."

Naturally he was fed at the place where he was visiting. Now, this he was told; "Take with you the ones that lie across yonder doorway of ours."

It was so that, as he went out, he took up the sturgeons, and then he went his homeward way. Now, this he said to his wife: "I say, to-morrow do you make a line. For it was by way of yonder water-hole of theirs that they killed the sturgeons."

Accordingly that truly was what the old woman did: she worked all day long making a line, while Nänabushu himself worked at making spears. And so after they were ready, then on the morning of the morrow this he was told by the Pilferer: "By way of yonder water-hole of ours do you go into the water." Now, this had the Pilferer done, he had laid a sturgeon in under the water.

And so when into the water Nänabushu went, and when he was looking about, he saw, sure enough, a sturgeon moving in the water. So thereupon he speared it. When he jerked the line, he was then pulled out of the water by his wife. She was amazed to see him actually drawing a sturgeon out of the water. And this he said to his wife: "This is just the place where we shall obtain sustenance."

Well, again he went into the water, but without success; in vain he tried looking about, but not a single thing did he see; (this continued) till he was getting short of breath, and there was no need of his getting out of breath. Then he jerked the line (to be drawn up). So once more he went into the water, but it came to nothing; and so without success he jerked on the line (to be drawn up). After he was pulled out of the water by his wife, why, he would have gone back in again, but it was no use at all. "What can be the matter with us that I do not see any sturgeon?" he said to his wife. For nought was he chilled by the water, so he gave up in failure. It truly was not a place to get (sturgeons); for wittingly had (the sturgeon) been put into the water for him. Thereupon back home they went without success. And so later on, while they were abiding there, they then began to be in want of food.

It was now getting well on towards the springtime, whereupon he took it upon himself to go looking for sweet-brier berries. So when they were exceedingly hungry, he started on his way; some sweet-brier berries he found, for it was only by such means that he was able to keep his children alive. And then he thought: "Wonder if I can take the sweet-brier berries home!" he thought.

Now, once as he was walking along, he saw a lake; then along upon the ice he went, on the ice along by the edge of the lake he travelled. He saw where (the lake) narrowed into a channel. Then farther on the lake, far out upon the ice, he heard some sort of a sound. As he looked, then was he sure that he heard something making a sound. "What (is it)?" he thought. As he went up to it, there was an arrow, a great arrow, with the ear of a bear for the feather! As he reached for it, he heard the voice of some one addressing him: "Fool, is it your arrow, Nänabushu, that you should have the desire to take it?"

"Yea, my younger brother, it is my own arrow."

"Nay, it is mine, Nänabushu, it is my arrow," he was told.

"Nay," to him said Nänabushu.

"Nay," he was told, "it is my own arrow." And he was told: "The Pilferer himself did not say that when I was merciful to him."

"Oh," to him said Nänabushu, "then it is the truth, my younger brother, that the arrow is yours!" he said to him.

Presently again was Nänabushu addressed: "It seems as if you were cold. Pray, kindle a fire," he was told. And this said Nänabushu: "He is surely the man who is cold. I am not cold," said Nänabushu.

"Nänabushu, the Pilferer did not say that when I was blessing him."

"Yea, my younger brother, certainly I am cold."

"Then build you up a fire."

Truly, after that he built up a fire. Accordingly the other then took off his moccasins there. "I say, Nänabushu, eat these stockings of mine."

And this he said to him: "I am not a dog, that I should eat those stockings."

"Nänabushu, the Pilferer did not say that when I was taking pity upon him."

"Yea, my younger brother, truly, will I eat those stockings of yours." And so, after the other had shaken them thoroughly, then this said Nänabushu: "Bring them hither, my younger brother, I will eat those stockings of yours." What was Nänabushu to behold but a wondrous store of dried beaver-tails! Thereupon truly he ate. One he wished to save. "O Nänabushu! go eat it up." Whereupon truly he ate it up.

When the other went and took up (Nänabushu's) bag of sweet-brier berries, he emptied out his sweet-brier berries. Then off he went, going far out upon the ice, where he began chopping the ice (into chunks). And then, after he had filled the sack full (of ice), "Hither, Nänabushu," (Nänabushu) was told. "Carry this ice upon your back. Regard me not in an evil way. 'Oh, the evil that I am done!' do not think. (It is for) your (good) that you should heed what I am telling you. Be careful; I beg of you, try to do what I tell you. Do not disobey me; else you will surely do yourself harm if you fail to obey me in that; for truly will you do yourself harm. I beg of you, be careful, do that which I have told you. When from this place you start upon your way, you will hear the voice of somebody talking. 'Halloo!' you will be told by somebody. Do not heed them. 'Halloo, Nänabushu is passing across on the ice!' they will say of you. Now, then, 'Push him!' they will say of you. Don't look back. That is what you will keep hearing all the while you are crossing this lake on the ice. Run as fast as you can. This is what they will say to you: 'Hey, hey, hey, hey, push him, push him, push him!' they will say of you."

And so then was when he came starting away. As soon as he was come at the place, then truly some one he heard. And as he began running, then truly he heard them, "Hey, hey, hey, hey, push Nänabushu!" was said of him.

Ah, thereupon truly, nothing loath, he ran with all his speed. Soon a long way out upon the ice did he come running. Some distance away he could hear those who were pursuing him. And then all the faster he went, the nearer they came. At times, "Now they sound as if they will overtake me," he thought. From the belt round his waist he pulled forth an axe. As round he whirled, "All right, push him!" he said. In vain he looked round about, but nobody did he see.

Thereupon, as he started running again, it seemed as if he could hear the sound; with all his speed he ran. "Now, I will try running away from them who are making the noise," he thought. Thereupon with all his might he tried to run, and closer still he could hear them again. "I fear that they who are making the noise will now overtake me," he thought. Thereupon ever so close was he now being pressed when again round he whirled, and who was there for him to see? Even though he tried looking round about, yet who was there for him to see?

Then again he started running; and when a certain distance on the way he was come, then again he heard them, whereupon he began running with full speed. And though he could see that near was the other shore which he hoped to reach by running on the ice, though he could see it close by, yet again was he being hard pressed. And when up from the shore he ran, no one then did he hear any more.

Thereupon he walked peacefully on his way. When he perceived that he was approaching home, he then sought for a great depression in the ground. It was true that soon he saw where there was a great hollow. It was there he put down his pack. Now, when he started to go, he was told: "Look not back," thus he was told. But what he did was to look back. What was he to behold when he looked back? A host of sturgeons he saw where he had put down his pack. Truly, was he pleased to have put down his pack there. Thereupon he started on his homeward way. After he was come there where they lived, he was then asked by his wife: "Why did you not bring home the sweet-brier berries?"

"Old woman, I have been blessed." Thereupon he did not sleep during the night, for he was so thoroughly happy. And this he was told by his wife: "I wager that you failed to obey what was fruitlessly said to you."

Now, he longed for the morning before it was time to appear. Soon then came the morning. "Now, then, old woman, get your tump-line. By no means a mere morsel have I seen," he said to his wife.

Thereupon truly on their way they started. When he came out upon the hill, gone was that which he had seen; for previously he had seen great abundance of sturgeons there where he had laid down his pack. So then he addressed the old woman, saying: "The place here was once full of sturgeons." And this he was told by his wife: "I dare say but that you have doubtless disobeyed," he was told by his wife.

"Yea," he said to her; "truly, 'Look not back,' I was told to no purpose."

And then was when he angered his wife. "Really in good sooth you are thoroughly incapable of giving heed to anything one tries to tell you."

And this to her said Nänabushu: "Quite true, I did not do what I was uselessly told." And so then was he repentant.

Now, from there they went searching round about, when truly they found some sturgeon-roe at the place where he had put down his pack. Whereupon they then went back home, so accordingly what they fetched home was what they cooked in the kettle.

And so once more was he already on his way, once more was he looking for (sweet-brier berries). Now, this was the only source he had to sustain his children. So it was every morning that he went to look for the sweet-brier berries. Now once, when they were very much in want of food, he went again to seek for the sweet-brier berries. Accordingly, as he was going across on the ice of the lake, and as he travelled along by the shore of the lake, again he heard the sound of something fall with a thud upon the ice. When he went up to it, he was surprised to see a great arrow that was there, with a bear-ear was it feathered. "Fool," he was told by some one, "is it your arrow, Nänabushu?"

"No," he said to him. "Yea," to him said Nänabushu; "it is your arrow, my younger brother."

"I say, Nänabushu, kindle a fire. It seems that you are cold."

"Yes," he said to him; "my younger brother, truly I am cold," he said to him.

Thereupon the other removed his moccasins. "I say, eat these," (Nänabushu) was told.

Whereupon he then truly ate the stockings.

Now, the other took (Nänabushu's) bag of sweet-brier berries and poured them out. After he had emptied them out, he then started away. (Nänabushu) saw him chopping a hole far out upon the ice, and he was again filling his sack there.

And when by the other he was helped with lifting on his pack, this was he then told: "I beg of you now take pains, and repeat not the same thing. What I have to tell you, that you do. Not again will I give you advice. This is the last time that I shall speak to you," he was told. "So then, start you hence," he was told.

Thereupon truly off he started, off he went running. Presently another one he heard yelling to him. And then he thought: "Under no circumstances will I look, even though some one should hold back on my pack," he (thus) thought. Thereupon truly, as he was coming across on the ice, he then took a straight away course as he ran. Truly was he hard pressed by those whom he heard. "Ho, ho, ho, push Nänabushu!" was said of him. Now, it was true that he was not anxious to look behind. So then at last, after he had crossed the ice, there was then no one there on the land.

As he went walking along, he soon perceived that he was approaching where he lived. So again he sought for the place with a deep depression in the earth. And so after he had put down his pack there, he accordingly did not look back where he had put down his pack. When he was come at yonder place where he dwelt, he accordingly did not speak to his wife. After he had gone to bed, he was not able to sleep. And after he had spent some time merely lying there, this he then said to his wife: "Truly, again to no purpose have I been blessed."

"I fancy that perhaps again you were not long remembering what had been told you. You do our children a hurt by your failure to obey. What, was there something you were told?"

"Yes, but it is uncertain how it will turn out; for according as I was told so I did."

So presently they saw that the morrow was come. "Now, then, old woman!" he said to his wife. Accordingly, after they had started off (and had come) to the place where he had left his pack, truly what was he to behold there where he had left his pack but a place full to the brim with as many sturgeons as the basin could hold. So therefore were they busy lugging throughout the day. "No doubt but that now we shall live through the winter," he said to his wife.

"Yes," he was told; "therefore saved are our children."

And so in comfort with plenty to eat they continued there.

13. Notes on the Mystic Rite

I will give an account of what I have learned concerning the way of the mystic rite. The one that in the beginning founded the mystic rite was a man. By a certain one was I visited, by him was imparted to me the knowledge of what the mystic rite meant. By him was I taught everything appertaining to the mystic rite, to the end that I might become a member of the mystic society.

Behold, this earth in all its length and breadth, such is what is meant as the mystic manitou. So likewise this sea throughout its whole extent, it is the mystic manitou, so I was told. Furthermore, this sky, that too does the mystic manitou overspread, such was what he told me; and this is the extent (of the mystic rite), (as wide as the limits of) this sky. At every place from whence blow the winds is where the manitous are, —at the east, and at the south, and at the west, and at the north; these are the four sources of the wind that are more manifest. Next is the region between the north and east, then between the east and south, then between the south and west, then between the west and north. These are the eight regions from whence blow the winds, each different from the other; while, on the other hand, this earth is as one.

Now, everywhere on the earth, and up above, and in the sea, have been placed the manitous that shall listen to the people. And about everything that is on the earth do the people speak when they perform the mystic rite, especially of yonder place at the east, for it was from thence that came the one who taught (the mystic rite); at that place stands a mystic manitou, it is from thence standing in line that the (row of) sweat-lodges extend which the people use whenever they perform the mystic rite.

And there is a post that stands upright, a mystic post; and now at that place is where the mystic lodge is, from every direction leads a path to that lodge. Now at the centre of the lodge (52) are laid all mystic skins, wampum beads, magic pouches, tobacco, and every kind of thing that is precious; they place them there as offerings.

And they that take the lead discourse at length; they talk about everything that is contained in all the length and breadth of this earth and sky and the whole sea and the entire vault of heaven. And some speak of the big game-folk and fishes. And also about another manitou man, about Nänabushu, do they talk; for it was he who created everything, so they have said; and so they place offerings for him. Furthermore, much food do they cook when they feast together, every kind of food that is nice.

And yet, withal, they know about the great manitou, for he it is who passes judgment upon everything; therefore they speak of what they desire to get by prayer. Now, this is what they wish to obtain by prayer, that long life they may have, or that they may have good health and not be sick, or that more abundant may become the big animal-folk and fishes, or that the weather may be fair, that in plenty may grow all kinds of berries, or that they may live upright lives. Thus accordingly do they plant seed (in the ground); and (thus it is) that they are careful to bring up their children so that they too may be wise. As of a day do they refer to a winter. Therefore this is what they try to obtain: "Would that I might live a long life!" (thus) do they wish. And this is what actually happens to the people, often does one live a long life. And some few of the people too are wise. And not very frequently is any one sick. Such is what they ask for (in their prayers).

Now, when they finish eating, then first to their feet rise they who are performing the mystic rite, they circle about in the lodge, they pick up the mystic skins and the wampum. And one after another they go through the motion of hitting at one another (with the magic pouches), and down falls the one that is struck at. They blow upon the wampum, whereupon away starts the wampum in its flight. Not often do they fling wampum at one another. And later on, when they finish, they again lay away all their magic pouches and wampum. Not till another winter has passed do they then perform again. Yet nevertheless they frequently sing, simply because they like to sing, and not on account of any desire they have for the good of their souls.

This is what they have said: "When any one dies, then to the world of ghosts one will go," so they have said; "for it is there that the ghosts have a town." Many a time, when one has died, from the dead has one risen. Whereupon then of this does one tell: "I have been to the place where the ghosts dwell." One relates how it is in the land of ghosts.

Such is what I have heard from members of the mystic rite. [Added by Dr. Michelson.]

Now, this is what the people have said, like a single day is the measure of one who has lived a long life. They mark the signs of paths which indicate life; some are marked as far as the end; some scarcely so far; some go half way; some paths, however, extend hardly half way; some are only marked but a little way, some exceedingly short. Such is the extent of life that people have lived, so they have said.

They also were able to look like a bear when they wished to do injury to their fellow-men.

That is all that I am able to tell about.

That man of the mystic rite who is at the east, and he who is at the west, are they who pass judgment upon what they use and what it is worth. Accordingly then do they set the price upon what they shall pay the man who is to conjure.

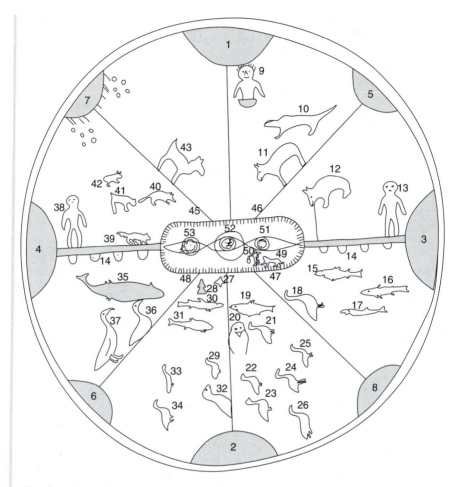

Explanation of Diagram (see Plate I)

Outer circle is the world (*a`ki*)

1. Kīwädin = north.
2. Cāwaṇo = south.
3. Wâbaṇung = east.
4. Nigābī·a·nung = west.
5. Nisawaya·ī·wâbaṇung kīwädenung = northeast.
6. Nisawaya·ī·câwaṇunk negābianuk = southwest.
7. Nisawaya·ī ·nīgābīanung kīwädenung = northwest, the wind the most feared, called also mäcka wāg nōdin = strong wind. The lines and circles before the mound represent much wind.
8. Nisawaya·ī ·wâbaṇunk cāwanunk = southeast.

All the above places are a symbol that manitous dwell everywhere.

9. Wīndigō, called also päbōno`kyä, ruler of the winter region ("he who makes winter").

10. Nīgik = otter.
11. Mōns = moose.
12. Ma`kwa = bear.
13. Midēwineni, one of the ruling manidos of the midewiwin.
14. Madōdusanan are four sweat-lodges, which must first be entered before entering the midēlodge.
15. Adi`kamäg = caribou-fish = whitefish.
16. Kinōnjä = (pike) pickerel ("longnose").
17. Namä = sturgeon.
18. Ni`ka = goose.
19. Namägus = trout.
20. Kū`kūkuhu = owl.
21. Nincip = mallard (?aninicip L.L.— probably Leech Lake).
22. Pi`kwakōcip = whistle-duck, arrow-head duck.
23. Kinugwä·u·wäcip = long-neck duck ("red-head duck").
24. Adcidcāk = crane.
25. Wäwībigwāngä = teel-duck (wäwībigwängä = red head, rather long legs, is not swimmer, but stays near water).
26. Mānk = coon; mānkwak = pl.
27. Mīgis = cowry shell.
28. Mīgis = wampum.
29. Tagwāgicip = fall duck.
30. Māskinō^{n}gä = muskalonge, a kind of pickerel, large, overgrown.
31. Māngamägus = speckled trout.
32. Migizi = bald eagle.
33. Ānzik = fish-duck (anzikwag).
34. Wâbanzik = whitefish-duck.
35. Mbānābä nibānābä = a kind of bear-bird (?) (mbānāba = larger than sturgeon, spouts water up, found in Lake Superior).
36. Cädä^e = pelican (looks like seagull; catches fish and holds it in a rack under the neck; Lake Superior).
37. Kayāck = sea-gull.
38. Nīgābī·a·nisi = westerner (fowl L.L.— Leech Lake).
39. Cigāg = skunk.
40. Ami`k = beaver.
41. Pījy^u = lynx.
42. Wâbōs = rabbit.
43. Adi`k = caribou.
45–48. Pagidciganan = goods, presents.
49. Anicinābä medäwi = a person performs the mystic rite (T.M.).
50. Same act as 49.
51 and 53. Aki`kōk, tcībā`kwan = ·
52. Midēwagān nugisag asämā gayä = mystic lodge, wampum beads, and tobacco (T.M.).

The rectangle represents the lodge of the midewiwin. The winding paths about the circles are the courses taken in the dance.

chapter three

Interpretive Essay

*An Ojibwa Worldview
and Environmental Ethic*

I. Key Cognitive Elements of an Ojibwa Worldview

In the "Introductory Essay" we explained the "cultural worldview" concept and concluded that distinct and different cultures provide their members with distinct and different ways of constructing reality. As one grows up in a culture one appropriates its worldview with, so to speak, one's mother's milk—certainly with one's mother tongue. Peter Berger and Thomas Luckmann (1967) suggest that the "trick" that primary socialization plays on each of us is to convince us that the way we have been insidiously habituated to cognitively organize our experience of the world is the way the world is in sheer actuality. More formally, Hallowell observes that "cultural variables are inevitably constituents of human perception," because culture provides the linguistic structure and conceptual framework through which experience is organized and represented. As an illustration of this process, Hallowell (1951, pp. 171–172) offers the following anecdote:

> Many years ago when I was trying to demonstrate the relation between language and perceiving to a class I used the stellar constellation we call "the big dipper" as an example. I pointed out that this constellation was given a different name in other cultures as, e.g., "the plough" or "the bear," and that, although the constellation itself remained constant in form, the actual perception of it was a function of language and associated concepts, as well as of our organs of vision. The members of the class seemed to have grasped the point, so I was about to pass on to something

else, when one young lady raised her hand and said, "But it does look like a dipper!" And of course it does—to us.

Hallowell suggests that it is best to begin by attempting to appreciate the integrity of each culture's worldview, rather than by assuming that our own culturally conditioned perception and understanding of reality defines the standard from which all others are only more or less intelligible deviations. In the introductory essay we called this "cultural-linguistic relativism." There we also pointed out that cultural worldviews are nevertheless not beyond criticism. Each is subject to criteria of "tenability." A tenable worldview should be comprehensive, self-consistent, pragmatically sustainable, good, and beautiful.

A. The Enculturation Function of Narratives Among the Ojibwa

Every society has a complex suite of means for transmitting its worldview from one generation to the next. As we indicated in the introductory essay, in traditional Ojibwa culture the telling of myths and stories was an integral part of this process. Of course, narratives do not bear the entire burden of transmitting the cultural worldview among the Ojibwa. Much Ojibwa cultural education, particularly in the more practical arts of living, proceeds by way of demonstration and imitation, supplemented by oral instruction. Dreams are also important in reinforcing the Ojibwa worldview, so much so that one could speak of children going "to school in dreams" (Dorson 1952).

Obviously such narratives as we find here are not simply an oral culture's equivalent of a textbook. These stories evidently have considerable entertainment value, and entertainment through a long winter's night was one of the purposes for which they were told. But neither are such narratives an oral culture's equivalent of television. The stories do teach, as well as entertain. Sometimes the "moral" is explicitly stated, as in the case of the ungulate youngster in "A Moose and His Offspring" who, overproud of his own fleetness of foot and unmindful of the advice of his father, is told "Don't try to flee away, for I am really telling you the truth in what I am saying to you. Of birdhawks and swans (the people) make use, such are the things people use." That is, people augment their apparently modest fleetness of foot by magically appropriating the powers of fast-flying birds, not to mention also using hunting dogs and snow shoes. Mainly, however, the narratives educate more indirectly by means of a consistent and coherent set of underlying assumptions about the nature of reality, which in one way or another is repeated in them again and again. And thus the question arises: What is the shape of the world as it is promulgated in these narratives?

When one who has been nurtured in the technologically oriented Western cultural tradition reads a collection of Indian stories like the ones presented here, he or she will inevitably encounter ideas and occurrences that, from his or her perspective, seem quite strange. Some of these will be on the level of everyday life and will represent little more than differences in taste (for example that children would relish eating raw the spinal cord of sturgeons, as in "The Orphans and Mashōs"), but others will have more far-reaching significance. In this section we identify a number of these "strange" ideas, which are essential to a systematic understanding of the Ojibwa worldview as the cognitive context in which an Ojibwa environmental ethic is located.

B. Personification

Among the most striking but also entirely casual features of these stories is the personification of nonhuman beings in all of them. For Hallowell (1960), this was so fundamental an aspect of the Ojibwa worldview that he designated it with a formal term, "other-than-human person." The distinction between an animate and inanimate entity is formally recognized in the Algonkian languages (including Ojibwa) by a semantic indicator (Greenberg 1954). This is roughly similar to the distinction between genders recognized formally in English by the pronouns "he" and "she" and more widely and often seemingly arbitrarily in the Romance languages by gendered definite and indefinite articles and gendered word endings (such as "*el*" and "*la*," "*uno*" and "*una*," and "*—o*" and "*—a*," respectively, in Spanish). By way of comparison, the Ojibwa language does not distinguish persons by gender. In other words, human beings and all animals are linguistically marked as animate in Ojibwa, but not as male or female. And accordingly animals in these stories are always personified and assumed to be endowed with such capacities as volition, reason, speech, and social interaction (with members of their own species, with other species, and with human beings), which are characteristic of persons. In the Romance languages, things (such as the hat and the door—*le chapeau* and *la porte* in French) that have no apparent gender are linguistically classified as male or female (hats are male, doors are female in French). Similarly, in Ojibwa things that are—at least from a Western point of view—not obviously animate are linguistically classified as animate. For example, some, but not all, plants are linguistically animate, and so some plants are sometimes personified in the stories (as is the cedar that saved the son-in-law of Mashōs from careening over a cliff while tied to a toboggan).

Manitous are, of course, also always animate and personal. Manitous are not human, animal, plant, nor mineral beings; they are spirit beings. And such beings come in a wide variety of types. They may sometimes be only heard or even only felt invisible presences (as are the manitous that both bless and harass Nänabushu in the story about the sweet-brier berries and the sturgeons). Manitous may be visible but insubstantial (as Little-Image appears to be—a face looking back at his finders from the smooth surface of the ice). They may manifest themselves in visible, substantial human form (as Little-

Image also eventually appears to do). Manitous may have formerly been human beings (as is the dead mother of the orphans in the story of Mashōs). Manitou-like powers may be obtained by human beings if they possess certain medicines (as do the human moose hunters in "A Moose and His Offspring"). In "Notes on the Mystic Rite," it is implied that the whole of nature is a manitou, which is, perhaps, comparable to pantheism in the West. As did most American Indians, the Ojibwa worldview included the Great Manitou (who is mentioned in "Notes on the Mystic Rite" as well and is also popularly known as the Great Spirit).

For the Ojibwa the most important manitou of them all is Nänabushu— a creator, a culture hero, and a trickster, all in one brash persona. In "Nänabushu Slays Hewer-of-His-Shin," he creates and names small-animal folk of various kinds and, in "Notes on the Mystic Rite," Nänabushu is characterized as "he who created everything." In "Nänabushu Swallowed by the Sturgeon," he benefits the people by reducing the size of fish to make them less dangerous and more numerous, an example of his role as culture hero. In the story of the sweet-brier berries and the sturgeons, he appears as trickster, misbehaving, squandering his blessing—but, getting a second chance to follow instructions and thus save himself and his family from starvation.

One important kind of other-than-human person and manitou is the "Great" whatever (for example, the Great sturgeon(s) and the Great gull in the story of the orphans and Mashōs—who also appear in "Nänabushu Swallowed by the Sturgeon"). Nänabushu himself is the Great hare. These other-than-human persons are the manitous presiding over the species in relation to which each stands as type to token. To risk a cross-cultural comparison, the Great gull bears to all ordinary gulls something of the same relationship as Plato's form of the Gull would bear to all mortal, material gulls. Of course, one must be careful not to take this comparison too far. A Platonic form is not a person or even an active agent of any kind, but an immaterial, impersonal, impassive, abstract, and eternal entity. The Great one(s) of a given species are physical and personal beings distinguished by their size (and sometimes white color) from the mere ciphers of their kind. And among their extraordinary powers is the power to dispense or withhold ordinary specimens of their species (thus, the Great sturgeon and the Great gull in the story of the orphans and Mashōs bestow many sturgeons and many gull eggs, respectively, on Mashōs's son-in-law). These Great other-than-human persons are sometimes referred to as Keepers, Masters, or Bosses of various species—especially game species (Martin 1978).

According to Hallowell (1960), thunder is both linguistically animate and universally personified by the Ojibwa, as are the sun and the moon, and some especially active or dynamic objects of Ojibwa material culture, such as cooking kettles and smoking pipes (in "Nänabushu Swallowed by the Sturgeon," first Nänbushu's whetstone, and then his axe speak to him). Strangely—from a Western point of view—wild stones (in addition to tame ones like whetstones) are linguistically animate (which may help explain why it was plausible for his son-in-law to make it home through the snow with the help of a Great stone after Mashōs had burned the young man's moccasins). Puzzled by the animate linguistic categorization of something seemingly (to him) so inert as a stone, Hallowell went so far as to ask an informant if *all* stones were alive. After some reflection, the reply was "No! But some are" (Hallowell 1960, p. 24). As William Jones (1919) notes, even the stories themselves—as well as the other-than-human characters in them—are animate persons! To tell the story is to invite it into the lodge. As we suggested in the introductory essay, "stories have a life of their own." For the Ojibwa, this is no mere metaphor; these stories are themselves persons and thus do indeed have a life of their own. Hence the telling of them is a matter of some gravity and is circumscribed by an etiquette. For example, they should only be told in the winter season (Jones 1917). And therefore, perhaps we should note, the non-Ojibwa among us who read them should treat them with all the respect due to powerful persons of the other-than-human kind.

C. The Community Concept

Central to the concept of a person is the ability and willingness to enter into social relationships. The difference, of course, is that in the mainstream of Western culture, personhood is limited to humans beings. The Ojibwa narratives, on the other hand, mirror a series of complex often intensely social relationships among a variety of kinds of persons: among manitous and people (as in "Little-Image" and "The Person That Made Medicine"); manitous and animals (as in "Nänabushu Swallowed by the Sturgeon"); manitous and manitous (as in "The Birth of Nänabushu"); people and people (as in "The Orphans and Mashōs"); people and animals (as in "Clothed-in-Fur," "The Woman Who Married a Beaver," "The Boy That Was Carried Away by a Bear"); and people and inert—from a Western point of view—objects (as in "The Orphans and Mashōs"). The impression of a broader-than-human social world is strengthened by the frequency with which the characters of the myths undergo metamorphosis (which will be discussed shortly). A single person, maintaining his or her inner identity, may appear outwardly either as a human or as an animal being.

The stories reveal, indeed, a fundamentally social organization of the integrated natural and preternatural worlds. Most of the animals that appear in the stories are members of societies or communities that are very similar to human communities. Animals live in extended families, just as the Ojibwa do (in "Clothed-in-Fur" and "The Woman Who Married a Beaver" we meet two beaver families, which the hero and heroine of the stories, respectively, join as members, and we meet a moose family in "A Moose and His Offspring"). Some manitous live in families (in some of these stories Nänabushu has a mother, an elder brother, and a grandmother, and in another a wife and children). Other manitou seem to be loners (Little-Image, for example). In any case, the characters in the stories—whether human or other-than-human—frequently address other characters in kinship terms (grandmother, grandfather, my little brother, and so on) even when they are obviously not related by blood. Such discourse intensifies the inherently social reltionships they bear to one another.

The animal families portrayed in these stories are sometimes uncannily similar to human families. The opening lines of "A Moose and His Offspring" suggest the universal unpredictability of having a teenaged family member: "The Moose was about to go into camp for the winter, and also his wife. Two (in number) were their children, and there was a youth among them; therefore, they were in fear." On the other hand, the human families portrayed in "The Orphans and Mashōs" are quite weird and dysfunctional. The mother of the boys who become orphans is having sex all day with snakes and neglecting her domestic duties. Mashōs, for unspecified reasons, perhaps jealousy, plots to kill his son-in-law. Inexplicable family dynamics unfold in "Clothed-in-Fur," who becomes separated from his beaver wife and shoots one of his children with an arrow; for which he is very sorry and mournful, but after which he goes off and apparently courts a prospective bear wife.

The animal families in these stories are sometimes united into larger communities (in "Clothed-in-Fur," the bears live in a tribal village with a chief; and the beaver family includes a muskrat.) What is perhaps most strange—again from a Western point of view—is the not infrequent episode in which a human being marries into a non-human family (as do both Clothed-in-Fur and the woman who married a beaver, as her name announces). (The reason for the prominence of these interspecies marriages will be discussed shortly.) Further, human and other-than-human societies interact in a larger, more formal social context (in "Clothed-in-Fur," "The Woman Who Married a Beaver," and "A Moose and His Offspring," people pay social visits to the several animal families in these stories). There is, as it were, a society of societies or a great community of communities including human communities, animal communities, and manitou communities, all interacting with one another. The whole Ojibwa world, it would not be an exaggeration to suggest, is organized socially. Every being is a member of a family, clan, and tribe; and these families, clans, and tribes—human and other-than-human—are all socially integrated and interactive with one another.

D. Power

Perhaps one of the most striking features of these stories is that so many of their characters, creatures, and objects are pictured as performing actions, which—from a Western point of view—would be considered quite extraordinary. From Mashōs's canoe, which moves under its own power when struck by its master's paddle, to the way Clothed-in-Fur escapes the Foolish Maidens pursuing him by flying away on a tree leaf, we are confronted with a variety of occurrences without analog in the everyday experience of the Western world. These aptitudes and capacities of the various actors may conveniently be designated as manifestations of "power," and they occur in practically every one of the stories here assembled.

Manitous (especially), animals, plants, and even material objects can wield preternatural power. And so can some human beings. Preternatural power is manifested in a variety of ways. Often in these tales its exercise involves metamorphosis or shape shifting (most notably in "Clothed-in-Fur"). Sometimes preternatural power is manifested as knowledge about future events (as when the boys' grandmothers in "The Orphans and Mashōs" tell them what to expect from their mother's pursuit and how to avoid being overtaken, and when the boy's adoptive grandfather in "The Boy That Was Carried Away by a Bear" divines how many people will pass by his winter den). Sometimes power is manifested as the ability to bestow a blessing (as do the Great sturgeon and the Great gull in "The Orphans and Mashōs," and as does Little-Image). Some people have a special capacity for hunting a particular species, such as bear (which appears to be the main point of "The Boy That Was Carried Away by a Bear"). For their part, animals have the power to withhold or voluntarily to give themselves to the people who hunt them (a major theme of "Clothed-in-Fur" and "The Woman Who Married a Beaver").

The source of preternatural powers is often not specified. Such powers are a defining characteristic of manitous and, we may suppose, is in their case intrinsic or inherent to the kind of being they are. Among the manitous, however, power is unevenly distributed. Nänabushu, one of the most powerful of all manitous and the source of many blessings, is often pictured as himself being blessed (as in the story about the sweet-brier berries and the sturgeons)—thus putting him in a power-under rather than power-over position in relationship to the being who is the source of the blessing. Relative power relationships are often indicated in the stories by age-sensitive kinship terms. If one character refers to another as "younger brother" (as does Nänabushu, inappropriately under the circumstances, to the being who was trying to bless him with a gift of sturgeons) that indicates that he or she regards him- or herself as more powerful. Whereas if one character refers to another as "grandfather" (as does the elder orphan in the "Orphans and Mashōs" to Horn-Grebe) that indicates not only respect, but also deference to one who has superior power. As for people, the stories indicate that any special powers they may acquire tend to come as a blessing from another being, such as a manitou, and to be earned as a result of fasting, dreaming, or otherwise soliciting the "pity" of more powerful beings (which will be discussed shortly).

That every one of these tales makes mention of the exercise of some unusual (in Western experience) power suggests that such powers are conceived of by the Ojibwa as a regular part of the world of everyday experience. Indeed, in some respects it might be said that the quality of life depends on the personal acquisition of special powers or—just as well—on being the beneficiary of the special powers wielded by others. Not only do some beings have more power than others, these tales document what Black (1977) refers to as a "hierarchy of power." Sometimes this hierarchy is simply assumed (the Great sturgeon is obviously more powerful than Mashōs's son-in-law whom it blesses and rescues). Fear of more powerful beings motivates humans to make offerings (as in "The Person That Made Medicine"). In "Little-Image," both the man and the bear dream and have power, but in their contest the power of the former—thanks to the beneficent manitou—proves greater than that of the latter. The wife and mother in "The Orphans and Mashōs" who had sex with snakes seems to have had unsavory preternatural powers all along. After she was thoroughly killed by her vengeful husband, she became an even more powerful manitou. She was ultimately unsuccessful in the exercise of her manitou powers, however, because she did not respect a being more powerful than she—Horn-Grebe, whom we may assume belonged to the Great class of manitous—that is, more generally, because she did not respect the hierarchy of power. Sometimes the particular order of this hierarchy is raised to the level of conscious reflection (as when Nänabushu appears to reflect on the relative power-over/power-under relationship between himself and his elder brother in "Nänabushu Swallowed by the Sturgeon"). Perhaps another aspect of this hierarchy of power is that one cannot use powers that one knows to exist—because one has seen others employ them—but that one does not possess or have access to (Mashōs, for example, is unable to use heated stones, as did his son-in-law, to make a path home through the snow after he mistakenly burned up his own moccasins).

Much about this conception of power has a familiar ring. Indeed, the word *power* serves so well to characterize this feature of the narratives because its commonest connotation in English is the capacity to act efficaciously—and that's what these powerful beings do. In English, the plural, *powers*, even refers frequently to a special and sometimes slightly mysterious capacity for such action, as in the phrase "powers of persuasion" or "powers of concentration." In contemporary Western culture, however, the term often has a decidedly naturalistic bias—as in "electric power plant" or jet engines that "power" airplanes. Also in Western culture, power often has a political connotation. Americans sometimes boast that the President of the United States is the most powerful person on Earth—and they do not mean that the President has preternatural manitou power. Reflecting on the powers of the President brings to the fore another central connotation of power in contemporary Western culture—military power—for among the President's political powers is to be Commander in Chief of the armed forces of the United States. Combining the political and military senses of power, historians speak of the "great powers" of, say, nineteenth-century Europe. In the twentieth century there were two so-called "superpowers," the United States and the Soviet Union. At the beginning of the twenty-first century, only one remained.

The analysis of political and more generally social power and of power relationships and power hierarchies of this kind is a major preoccupation of postmodern and feminist philosophizing (Foucault 1979). One confrontation of power in the primarily preternatural Indian sense and power in the primarily naturalistic Western sense is infamous—the massacre at Wounded

Knee. There, on December 29, 1890, a desperate band of freezing, starving Sioux—believing that a shirt painted with runes seen in a dream would protect its wearer from bullets—confronted a Ghost-dance spooked contingent of the U.S. army with tragic consequences (Overholt 1978). In Western culture, the sense of "power" most akin to the preternatural sense of power in the Ojibwa narratives are the powers of such super-heroes as Superman (flight, extraordinary strength, and x-ray vision) or those of the Invisible Man (whose name, in good Ojibwa style, indicates exactly the nature of his preternatural power).

E. Metamorphosis

In these tales, changes in bodily form and appearance are a characteristic way in which power is exercised. Prominent among the powers of a human sorcerer is metamorphosis. The narrator of "Notes on the Mystic Rite" says that some men "were able to look like a bear when they wished to do injury to their fellow men." The Ojibwa sometimes simply referred to such malefactors as "bear walkers"; and there may be some question whether a particular bear that one encounters, especially at night, is a real bear or a bear walker.

The metamorphoses occurring in these stories are striking not only in number, but also in their variety and in the apparent fluidity and even ambiguity that exists between what seem to be distinct kinds of entities. Most frequently, human beings change into animals and animals into human beings. These transformations sometimes seem to be considered permanent and may be either gradual (as the younger brother gradually becomes a wolf, permanently, in "The Orphans and Mashōs") or instantaneous (as Clothed-in-Fur's rejected wives immediately become a wolf, a raven, a porcupine, and a jay, permanently, although it is more likely that each was originally the animal it became and only temporarily appeared to be human). An example of reversible transformation is the woman who married a beaver; she began her life as a human woman, presumably metamorphosed into a beaver, and then finished her life as a human woman. Sometimes the metamorphosis is neither gradual nor instantaneous, but involves a process of middling temporal scale (as when Clothed-in-Fur goes into a ball as a human being and comes out as an animal). Unliving things (from a Western point of view) can become either living or other unliving things (in "The Boy That Was Carried Away by a Bear," dried fish become live grouse; in "Nänabushu, the Sweet-Brier Berries, and the Sturgeons," a moccasin becomes a dried beaver tail and chips of ice become freshly killed sturgeons; in the "Orphans and Mashōs," an awl, a comb, and a flint become spiky mountain ranges, and a punk becomes a great mountain of fire). And large animals can be made small (as the bears in "Little-Image" and "Clothed-in-Fur" and the sturgeons in "Nänabushu Swallowed by the Sturgeon").

The circumstances under which such transformations take place are just as varied. The younger orphan is apparently adopted by wolves and gradually becomes a wolf himself in the story of Mashōs, ultimately because the wicked old man deprived him of his older brother's care. The dried fish become live grouse, in the story of the boy that was carried away by a bear, for purposes of deception. The transformations of the moccasin and the chips of ice in the Nänabushu trickster tale are for purposes of relieving hunger and averting starvation. Beyond these adventitialities, however, three circumstances recur in these tales: (1) metamorphoses occur in order to establish and maintain a marriage relationship between an animal and a human (as in "Clothed-in-Fur" and "The Woman Who Married a Beaver"); (2) they occur as part of a character's escape from a dangerous situation (as in "The Orphans and Mashōs" and "The Boy That Was Carried Away by a Bear"); (3) metamorphoses from large to small animals (as in "Little-Image," "Clothed-in-Fur" and in "Nanabushu Swallowed by the Sturgeon") occur for the safety and convenience of future human generations.

It should be noted that in most of these tales the temporal context in which metamorphoses occur is the mythic time—the world at the time of its origins, in which the order of things is not yet firmly fixed. It is the time at which the wolf, raven, porcupine, and jay (of "Clothed-in-Fur") come into being with their signal characteristics; a time at which a manitou (such as Little-Image or Nänabushu) can undertake to fundamentally reverse a previous situation, so that now people will eat bears and sturgeons instead of the other way around. Because the changes they bring about result in the world assuming the form in which later humans experience it, the characters of the myths sometimes appear in the role of creators and culture heroes. Mythic time is more complex, however, than the linear progression from a start-time as found in the Western biblical account of origins. Remember that the characters and the very stories themselves are other-than-human persons. Telling the stories reprises the world at the time of its origins—so that mythic time is at once both past and, at least during the telling of the tale, also a time parallel to the present.

The traditional Ojibwa thus finds him- or herself in a world in which the inner subjective dimension of experience is more fixed and permanent than the outward physical dimension. One notices in reading these narratives that the bodily form of the actors is sometimes ambiguous. The woman who eventually married a beaver, for example, beheld a "man" standing before her and inviting her to accompany him. The text says that cluelessly "she went along with him who was in the form of a human being" and became his wife. After some intervening description of her new life we are told that only then "the woman knew that she had married a beaver." So the man was a beaver all along, despite his initial appearance. The inner, subjective dimension is more defining of his being—his species identity—than his outward, physical appearance. It is doubtless for this reason that both "Clothed-in-Fur" and "The Woman Who Married a Beaver" explicitly state that the human emissary to the watery world of the beavers is not killed and eaten by the people when they come to hunt the beavers ("Now, the woman never went to where the people lived"; "And all were taken away except Clothed-in-Fur; he was not killed"). Being essentially human but appearing in the form of a beaver, if these people were killed and eaten, those who did so would be guilty of cannibalism; they would have become unwitting "Windigos," or cannibal monsters.

F. The Situation of Blessing

In the stories, power is often pictured as flowing from one "person" to another, the more powerful of the two assuming the posture of a bestower of blessings. We therefore need to turn our attention to the characteristics of what we might call the "situation of blessing." First of all, upon receipt of a blessing an individual's circumstances are altered (or at least potentially so) for the better. For example, Mashōs's beleaguered son-in-law was aided, when Mashōs attempted to kill him, by beings who had "blessed" or "pitied" him in the past (a Great sturgeon, a Great gull, a Great stone, and a cedar tree). The recipient of a blessing may be given food (as Nänabushu is in the story about the sweet-brier berries and the sturgeons) or the ability to successfully acquire that precious commodity (as is the boy who was carried away by a bear) or may obtain the promise of a long life for an individual or community (as are the people—*anishinabe*—in "Little-Image").

A second characteristic of the situation of blessing is the aforementioned fact that the movement of the blessing is from the more to the less powerful person. Such action can, of course, involve relative amounts of power just among human beings (as in the case of the "grandmothers," who "pitied" the fleeing orphans, and one of Mashōs's daughters, who subsequently became the protector and wife of the elder of them). Usually, however, blessing flows from other-than-human persons, be they manitous or mortal animals and plants (that is, from beings like Nänabushu, the Great sturgeon, the Great gull, cliff-dwelling manitous, beavers, bears, and the cedar) to humans. Because people are relatively powerless, in comparison with the ambient powers in the surrounding world, people are inherently "pitiable," and the act of blessing can be seen as motivated by "pity" (in "The Boy Who Was Carried Away by a Bear," for example, the little hero of the story was continually flogged by his father and was adopted, provided for, and blessed by a bear who had "come to take pity upon him").

Though the bestowal of blessing is often a more or less spontaneous occurrence, a third characteristic of the situation of blessing is that it can be—and frequently is—solicited (or at least facilitated) by the human recipients. Our tales certainly indicate one major way in which this is accomplished—by fasting. It was after a "long fast" that the woman who married a beaver gained both a special husband and the knowledge of the proper relationship between beavers and the people who hunt them, which she was ultimately able to carry back to her human relatives. And the man and children in "Little-Image" fasted to gain long life and the specific powers needed to be successful in their mortal contest with the bears. Fasting for a blessing of (dreamed) power is ritually symbolized and announced by the faster blackening his or her face with charcoal. So strong is the association of face-blackening with fasting that undertaking the latter is often indicated in the stories by reference to the former (in "Little-Image," for example, the manitou asks the man, "why have these children blackened?"). Gift giving appears to be another way of effecting the proper situation for receiving a blessing (as the cliff-spirits' response to the gifts of tobacco, ribbons, and other goods indicates in "The Person That Made Medicine"). In the tales that deal with the hunting of animals by humans, gifts seem to be a *quid pro quo* for the blessing of flesh and fur provided by game animals (those who allow themselves to be slain in "The Moose and His Offspring" get presents, as do the slain beavers in "The Woman Who Married a Beaver").

Gift giving, with the expectation of something of equal or greater value to be received in return, must be undertaken with care in Ojibwa culture—as, for that matter in Western culture. A gift should not appear to be given in a *quid pro quo* spirit, but in a spirit of genuine generosity or even personal sacrifice. A beautiful woman—whether Western or American Indian—is likely to be offended if she receives a gift of expensive jewelry from a man who appears to expect her to express her gratitude by giving him sex in return. Such a gift given in such a spirit is likely to be rejected. Further, the exchange of gifts—say an animal's flesh and fur in exchange for a gift of tobacco—seems most appropriate between parties who are more or less equal in the hierarchy of power. Among unequals, the less powerful (human) being is better advised to seek to be pitied by the more powerful (manitou) being and for the blessing to flow from that motive—pity—rather than from a desire for gain. The reasoning may be like that of Socrates in Plato's *Euthyphro* who asks what possible benefit the gods—who are in need of nothing—could get from the form of "traffic" constituted by people praying to the gods to get what they they want and offering sacrifices to the gods in return. For example, in "The Orphans and Mashōs," the evil old man effectively tries to barter with the Great sturgeon and the Great gull by offering his son-in-law as a "gift." To use a very apt old saw, he tries to kill two birds with one stone—get rid of his son-in-law and curry favor with preternaturally more powerful manitous. But these Great beings rebuff his thinly disguised attempt to barter with them because they have previously blessed the son-in-law, presumably in response to his fasting or to some other acknowledgement of his own helplessness and need. (More will be said on the subject of gift exchange further on in this section and in the next section.)

Our tales make it clear that the mode by which awareness of a blessing frequently comes to consciousness is a dream (as most emphatically in "Little-Image"). At least one—if not the most—important function of fasting is to induce dreaming (which is suggested by the narrator's statement that the children in "Little-Image" were fasting precisely in order to dream "of what shall give them life"). Objects dreamed of may be obtained in waking life and worn on one's person to realize the power gained by fasting and dreaming (presumably what is implied in "A Moose and His Offspring" when the father moose tells his wayward son that the human hunters coming for them make use of "bird-hawks and swans"). Thus the situation of blessing highlights again the fact that for the Ojibwa preternatural power is to be considered more efficacious than natural strength and skill. The children in "Little-Image," for example, train for their races with the bears not by a physical regimen of diet and exercise—as would a Western person in similar circumstances—but by the fasting-dreaming regimen summed up with the word "blackening."

Finally, one should note that in the story of Nänabushu, the sweet-brier berries, and the sturgeons over-confidence in the blessing one has received—taking it for granted, so to speak—is explicitly frowned upon. The contrast between Pilferer, who follows all the manitou's instructions perfectly but does not aggressively assert his claim to the blessing ("perhaps . . . we shall yet be blessed"), and Nänabushu, who is disobedient but still confidently claims the blessing ("I have been blessed. . . . By no means a mere morsel have I seen") is sharply drawn. Only after coming up empty-handed does Nänabushu display the requisite obedience and deferential reticence ("Yes, but it is uncertain how it will turn out; for according as I was told so I did."). One wonders whether such an attitude is bad in itself (Mashōs's tormented son-in-law seems, once he has grown to manhood, to be the picture of confidence), or whether it is so only in conjunction with the kind of foolish disobedience to the terms of the blessing for which Nänabushu is notorious (as would also be indicated by the fate of the manitou-mother of the orphans in that story). To this matter of obedience we now turn.

G. Disobedience and Its Consequences

The manitou-mother in pursuit of her children in "The Orphans and Mashōs" disobeys Horn-Grebe's instructions not to step over him as he is ferrying her across a river. She disobeys and the river's waters become a great lake into the middle of which she falls—and drowns, apparently. Similar episodes occur in other tales. The headstrong teen-aged moose in "The Moose and His Offspring" is warned by his father not to run away from the hunters, but he does so anyway and is mutilated and humiliated as a result. In "Nänabushu, the Sweet-Brier Berries, and the Sturgeons"—and many many other stories in the large collection of Nänabushu tales in the Ojibwa cycle of stories—this lovable trickster is constantly getting in trouble because he ignores the instructions of his benefactors. As our representative story here indicates, obedience, if only partial, is not good enough. Also in "Clothed-in-Fur" and "The Person Who Made Medicine," obedience is an important issue.

Receiving instructions is the predominant context for lessons about obedience. In "Nänabushu, the Sweet-Brier Berries, and the Sturgeons," the instructions seem nonsensical or pointless, as do those of Horn-Grebe to the manitou-mother pursuing her children in "The Orphans and Mashōs." The reason for that seems to be this: one demonstrates respect and faith by obeying instructions whether they seem to make sense to you or not. Often the instructions are disobeyed and the offender suffers negative consequences (as in the case of Nänabushu, as already noted, but also in the case of Clothed-in-Fur, who lost his beaver wife and children because he failed to obey her instructions). But, on the other hand, when instructions are obeyed, however ridiculous they may seem, positive rewards are forthcoming (Pilferer and the chastened Nänabushu—who was given a second chance—receive a blessing of sturgeons to tide them over the starvation months of late winter). Indeed, the main theme of "Nänabushu, the Sweet-Brier Berries, and the Sturgeons" seems to be one of rewarded obedience contrasted sharply with punished disobedience to entirely clear but seemingly pointless instructions. Less central, but present nevertheless in "A Moose and His Offspring," the calves, who are singing exuberantly to conjure more snowfall, heed their father's instructions not to do so. That sets them in stark contrast to the arrogant teen-aged moose, whose disobedience and failure to follow advice leads to his humiliation and deprivation. In this story, the moose-father's instructions do have a rationale behind them. A crust forms on snow in the late winter and, if the snow is deep, the sharp hooves of the moose break through and the animal is mired and trapped—while dogs and human hunters wearing snowshoes can walk over the hard crust. The importance of obeying instructions—whether apparently rational or otherwise—is sometimes stated explicitly in the stories (as when in the one about the sweet-brier berries and the sturgeons, Nänabushu's wife says presciently, "I wager that you failed to obey what was fruitlessly said to you").

H. Reciprocity, Life, and Death

Closely related to the elements already discussed are the notions of reciprocity and of the fluid line that exists between life and death. We encounter these conceptions chiefly in stories that deal with the venatic relationship between people and animals. Toward the end of the tale about Clothed-in-Fur we learn that the beavers are willing to give themselves to humans for food and fur, but only if the humans live up to a certain set of obligations centering around the giving of gifts and the proper treatment of the bones of the dead beavers. Considering all these stories, four things seem to be required of human beings who would successfully and sustainably hunt animals: reciprocal gifts, right attitude, genuine need, and the proper disposal of bones.

First, people must make gifts to the animals, who are said to be "happy" with what they receive (utensils, clothing, body ornaments, and the like) and wealthy because of their accumulation. Such gifts are a prominent feature of "The Woman Who Married a Beaver" and "A Moose and His Offspring." In the former story, the beaver are said to like tobacco. And several times the pipe, apparently acting under its own power, is pictured as playing the role of mediator between humans and animals (both in "Clothed-in-Fur" and "A Moose and His Offspring"). Gifts are offered to the cliff manitous in "The Person That Made Medicine."

The second requirement is that people have the right attitude toward the animals they intend to hunt. Several things are involved here—for one, the caution against crediting one's own hunting ability too highly. In "Clothed-in-Fur," the people initially recognize the physical difficulties involved in successfully hunting the beaver and send a pipe full of tobacco as a token of respect; as a result, they hunt successfully. But then one of them notices the low water level around the beavers' lodge and reports this to the others. Confident that the taking of beavers will now be easy, that is, within their own unaugmented abilities to accomplish, they fail to offer the pipe and are unsuccessful in their hunt. The prohibition against thinking disparaging thoughts about the one upon whom you depend is another aspect of the required proper attitude. "Never speak you ill of a beaver!" said the woman to her own people after returning from years as the beaver's wife, for "should you speak ill of (a beaver), you will not (be able to) kill one." On the other hand, it seems to be all right for the beavers to make fun of their human pursuers (in "Clothed-in-Fur," "a human being . . . climbed upon the dwelling, whereupon they all gazed upon him to see how he looked. Laughed the beavers when the human being started on his homeward way."). Once again, personification is prominent: the emotions attributed to the beaver in "The Woman Who Married a Beaver" are quite human in character. The beavers love those who love them, but tend to retaliate in kind against those who do not. Similarly, the cliff-manitous in "The Person That Made Medicine" from whom the people received "every kind of medicine there was," demand respect. The jealous first maker-of-medicine proudly would not take the medicine that the manitous offered—and he suffered dire consequences for this breach of etiquette. And the moral rule governing subsequent human behavior is explicitly stated: "people are never allowed to speak nonsense upon a cliff or upon the water." Finally, one may infer from the concluding remarks in "Little-Image" that a continual, appreciative remembrance of the blessings received from a benefactor also constitutes part of the right attitude.

The third requirement is that people should genuinely need to take the lives of animals and not do so frivolously. A passing detail in "A Moose and His Offspring" seems to illustrate the need requirement. As one of the men is coming to kill the moose, "exposed to view were his entrails." This may suggest that the man was hungry—as indicated by the state of his entrails—and in need of the mooses' meat. A hunter should only kill animals when in genuine need and, in that circumstance—provided that the other courtesies and reciprocities have been observed—the animals should be willing to give themselves up to be killed. The story of the bear that adopted the boy who was abused by his father also demonstrates the willingness of animals to give themselves to human hunters in need—in this case more in the spirit of "pity" than expectation of reciprocal rewards. After he returned to his people the boy had only to say, "My grandfather, I am hungry do feed me!" and a bear would appear for the boy to kill.

The fourth requirement is that people must properly dispose of the animals' bones—a requirement so singular as to warrant separate discussion in the next section.

For their part, when the people fulfill their obligations faithfully, the animals will give themselves willingly to the hunters to be killed. In both "Clothed-in-Fur" and "A Moose and His Offspring," the coming of the pipe into the animals' dwelling seems to be the symbol of a deal being struck. The people offer the pipe; if the animals take it and smoke it, they have agreed to the bargain. (Of course both parties must maintain the appearance of graciously exchanging gifts—not bargaining—as already indicated.) In "Clothed-in-Fur," the beavers refuse the pipe for the good reasons already indicated, but in "A Moose and His Offspring," the surly young moose refuses the pipe without good cause. Just as human beings must not be overconfident in their own abilities, so the moose-father admonishes his brash young son about his unfounded confidence in his ability to outrun any human who may pursue him. Indeed, the main point of "A Moose and His Offspring" seems to be the obverse of the point of "Clothed-in-Fur" and "The Woman Who Married a Beaver." In the latter two stories, needy people can only successfully hunt animals if they provide the animals with reciprocal benefits, respect them, and properly treat their bones. In the former, if hunters show the animals respect (by offering them the pipe and inviting them into the lodge to enjoy the feast) and give them gifts, then the animals are symmetrically obliged to give themselves up to be slain.

The subtle difference between the relationship of the moose hunters and the beaver hunters to their quarry in "A Moose and His Offspring" and "Clothed-in-Fur," on the one hand, and the young bear hunter to his in "The Boy That Was Carried Away by a Bear," on the other hand, probably has to do with the preternatural power that the Ojibwa believed bears to possess. The moose seem to be in possession of only natural powers such as fleetness of foot (which is rendered useless by deep, crusted snow). The beavers similarly must eavesdrop on the people to know what they are saying and must ask the people's hunting dogs about what their masters are doing. But the boy's bear grandfather is able to divine the number of people that will pass near his winter den and is able to transform dried fish into ruffed grouse to decoy such intruders. He also knows how to use a white substance obtained from decayed wood to make raw fish taste cooked.

I. Immortal Bones and Spirit

How, in any case, could the animals possibly enter voluntarily into a compact in which they themselves die? Because the death of animals killed under the proper circumstances is not final; rather, they will come back to life to enjoy the offerings they receive (as vividly portrayed in both "The Woman Who Married a Beaver" and "A Moose and His Offspring"). The proper treatment of a slain animal's bones is essential to its ability to return to life (as most clearly detailed in "Clothed-in-Fur"). The essence of proper treatment seems less ceremonial than preeminently practical. If the bones are broken or destroyed by fire or by feeding them to dogs, the dead animal will, in the former circumstance, come back maimed or, in the latter, perhaps not at all. Further, for the animal's literal reincarnation to be facilitated, the unbroken bones should be returned to the element in which the animal lives—water in the case of beavers and muskrats.

The last episode of "Clothed-in-Fur" illustrates some of these points nicely. Clothed-in-Fur learns that it is all right for him to kill and eat his beaver and muskrat relatives, as long as he preserves their bones intact and gathers them up for deposit in a watercourse. If the bones are broken, the revived individual will be deformed. Now other (unmetamorphosed) people appear on the scene (who are, from the beavers' point of view simply beings "with a full set of teeth"). At first, these beings offer the pipe and the beaver allow themselves to be killed, but eventually, as previously noted, they think that they can simply come and take the beavers without having to bother with such courtesies. As a result, the beavers withhold themselves. This state of affairs continues for some time because the beavers are reluctant to accept the pipes that the hunters have once again started to send. One of the beavers seems to express at least part of the reason for this reluctance to reestablish the reciprocal relationship with the people when she says, "The people surely ill-use us." But to what, more specifically, does she refer? The answer is suggested in the passage that follows. The next day the people come again with their pipes and hunting dogs who, as usual, the beavers shoo away. But of one old dog they inquire, "On what do they by whom we are killed feed you?" When the dog replies, "Your livers," the beavers are satisfied and again allow themselves to be killed. The implication is that because they are fed on the beavers' livers, the dogs must not be getting the beavers' bones to eat, and the people are therefore not disrespectfully ill-using the beavers.

The literally vital importance of not breaking or destroying the slain animals' bones invites some speculation on a deeper ethnometaphysical level. In the Western cultural worldview, the immortal part of a person is the soul, which is either conceived to be perfectly immaterial by philosophers such as Plato and Descartes, or more popularly conceived to be of a diaphanous material substance like smoke. That's how ghosts are often portrayed in the Western cultural worldview. And, in the subcultural Western worldview that includes belief in reincarnation, what reincarnates is the immaterial or quasi-material soul. According to Jenness (1935), the Ojibwa also believed not only in a soul, but also in a "shadow" (ghost?) that could roam outside a person's body—although none of the stories found here document such doctrines. Rather, these stories suggest that the role played by the soul in the Western cultural worldview is played by the bony skeleton in the Ojibwa cultural worldview. The immortal part of a person—quite reasonably and plausibly—is the more, not the less, concrete and material part. After all, an animal's bones clearly outlast its softer more ephemeral flesh. Why not suppose that if carefully preserved and returned to its generative element of water or earth, the bones would reclothe themselves with the softer, more perishable materials of the body—flesh and fur? The bones may even be supposed to be the seat of consciousness and identity, that is, the very spirit of the person—either human or other-than-human. In "The Orphans and Mashōs," the wayward wife and mother is shot in the heart with an arrow and then burned by her angry husband until she finally dies. She is thus killed, but pursues her children as both a manitou and a skeleton. Perhaps in the Ojibwa mind, to be a skeleton is to be a manitou, a spirit being. If so, the spirit and essential inner person is more, not less, material than the outer body.

II. Ojibwa Environmental Ethics

From the narratives themselves and certainly from the analysis of them already provided, it should be obvious that the Ojibwa had a strong environmental ethic. Indeed the Ojibwa ethos, embedded in the Ojibwa worldview, seems much more oriented to setting out the proper way that people should treat other-than-human persons—including animal and plant persons, as well as manitous—than the way they should treat each other.

As to ethical censure of improper human-to-human relationships, these narratives have little to say. Some seem to assume that such are personal and idiosyncratic issues to be settled by the parties that are immediately concerned. For example, the wayward wife and mother in "The Orphans and Mashōs" offended her husband, and he took the matter into his own hands and killed her. Afterward, he abandoned their children. Nothing in the story suggests that he was morally wrong to do either of these things. On the other hand, Mashōs is indeed described as "evil." He is a kidnapper and would-be murderer, but it's up to his victim—with, of course, the help of his wife and a host of other-than-human benefactors—to overcome the malefactions that the evil old man directs at him. The Foolish Maidens harass Clothed-in-Fur and he takes it upon himself to avoid their attentions. No particular moral condemnation of the abusive father who was "continually flogging"—apparently for no reason—one of his many children (and a small and vulnerable one at that) is evident in "The Boy

That Was Carried Away by a Bear." His father stopped ill-treating him out of fear of his apparent preternatural powers, which had, his family seemed to believe, sustained him in good health for the year that he secretly spent with his bear grandfather. Little-Image is definitely a good Samaritan, but he is a manitou, leaving us to wonder if a mere mortal would be expected altruistically to help the children in their deadly races with the bears, if he or she could. Professional jealousy seems offhandedly censured in "The Person That Made Medicine," but the main "moral" of the story has to do with proper conduct toward cliffs and water. No moral condemnation of what Nänabushu did to Pilferer is found in the story about the sweet-brier berries and the sturgeons. Nänabushu got Pilferer to agree that both families would eat Pilferer's store of fish first, and then eat Nänabushu's. But when Pilferer's fish were all gone, Nänabushu contrived some pretext for getting angry and moving away. The real reason presumably was so that he would not have to share his own fish. That's not ethical, but the story moves on—without registering any moral outrage for this betrayal—to it's main concern with the relationship between beneficiaries and their other-than-human benefactors.

A. Animal Rights

So, what kind of environmental ethic do we find here? Animal rights? Yes, animals do have rights, but they are not the same rights as we find attributed them by Western nonanthropocentrists. According to Tom Regan (1983), what having rights amounts to is having justifiable claims on the behavior of others. For example, if one has a property right—in a book, a car, a house, a piece of land—one can limit the access of other people to whatever it is that one owns. Regan (1983) argues that wild animals have rights to life and liberty, just as human beings do; that is, they have a justifiable claim on us not to kill or confine them. Thus to hunt or trap them, he argues explicitly, is a violation of their rights. In these stories, animals have no such rights. They may be hunted, trapped, and killed—provided the hunter needs to do so. The hunter must also accede to the animals' justifiable claims—that is, rights—to be compensated and respected, not to have their bones mutilated or destroyed, and to have their bones returned to the element from which the animals were taken. If these rights are honored, then the animals have a correlative obligation to allow themselves to be killed and eaten. Although the specific rights that the Ojibwa accord animals are different from those accorded them by Regan and other nonanthropocentric animal-oriented philosophers, the metaphysical foundation, as it were, of animals' rights in the Ojibwa environmental ethos is quite similar to that in contemporary Western animal-rights theory. According to Regan (1983) animals are "subjects of a life"—that is, they have some sense of self, some memory of the past and anticipation of the future, desires, hopes, and fears—a subjective life in short that can be better or worse from their own point of view. In the Ojibwa stories, animals are all this and more; they are other-than-human persons, capable of reason, reciprocity, revenge, and even speech. Personhood or many of its aspects is thus the ultimate ground of animals' rights in both contemporary Western nonanthropocentric ethics and in the traditional Ojibwa worldview and ethos.

As for "animal liberation" (in contradistinction to animal rights), nothing is found in these stories suggesting anything of the kind. According to animal liberationist Peter Singer (1975), above all, people should not cause animals to suffer unnecessarily. While need or necessity certainly is required for a human being to rightfully kill animals in the Ojibwa environmental ethos, no story in this sample (nor for that matter in any others in the Jones collection) is in the least concerned with animal pain and suffering. On the contrary, in "A Moose and His Offspring" a hard blow on the back with a stick was justly inflicted on the uncooperative young moose by a rightfully aggrieved human hunter, who then cut off the poor young moose's nose. Both those acts of violent retribution must have hurt a lot, but the story gives more attention to the young moose's humiliation (having her nose cut off was sometimes an Ojibwa wife's punishment for adultery) and deprivation (he got no tobacco, food, or presents) than to his pain (Hilger 1939). And, it might be added, after having been beaten and denosed, the young moose is *not* killed—as if to kill him would be to do him a favor that he did not merit!

B. Human-Animal Marriages as a Means of Community Building

In addition to personhood, the Ojibwa environmental ethic has a conceptual foundation in community membership. Communitarianism is the view that one's ethical duties and obligations arise because one is a member of a community. That different community memberships give rise to different duties and obligations is a corollary to this lemma. For example, as a family member one has duties and obligations to one's parents, grandparents, children, grandchildren, siblings, aunts, uncles, and cousins that one does not have to unrelated fellow members of one's country. Similarly, one has duties and obligations to one's fellow citizens and to one's country as such that one does not have to one's fellow human beings on a global scale. In the Ojibwa worldview and ethos, duties and obligations do seem to arise among persons—human and other-than-human—because of mutual community membership.

One of the most striking and strange—from a Western cultural perspective—aspects of these stories is human-animal marriage (a core theme of both "Clothed-in-Fur" and "The Woman Who Married a Beaver"). Indeed, from a Western cultural perspective, these unions may even seem to involve the type of sexual deviation called "bestiality"—cross-species sexual intercourse—that many Westerners regard as not only disgusting, but immoral. Sex, however, is not what these marriages are all about. Yes, these human-animal marriages produce offspring, which would imply sex between the human and animal partners to such marriages, but the "children" of these marriages are mostly incidental characters in the stories. To establish communal or social bonds between people and animals is the main reason for these marriages—which is often exactly the function of "arranged" marriages among human beings. Marriages arranged by parents or other authority figures between young men and young women who are not even acquainted with one another are customary in some cultures, precisely in order to create alliances between families, clans, tribes, or—at the royal level—nations. That's the main purpose of the human-animal marriages in these stories.

"Clothed-in-Fur" is almost altogether about making the right marriage. The hero is destined to be the human groom to an animal wife. But of what species? His search for a wife of the right species is the plot line of the story. First he is pursued by the Foolish Maidens. Perhaps they are "foolish" precisely to think that Clothed-in-Fur is an eligible bachelor for either of them—human women. Then he undergoes a rebirth. He goes into a ball. When the Foolish Maidens give up and go away after unsuccessfully trying to crack it open and get him out, he emerges all bloody (like a newborn) and washes his fur coat in two lakes until it is clean. Now he has metamorphosed into an animal form of indeterminate species. He then immediately meets and "marries" a "woman" who turns out to be a wolf; following that, he meets and marries "women" who turn out to be a raven, a porcupine, and a Canada jay. Each of these wives has some deficiency indicating that they are not of the appropriate species. The wolf woman was unable to carry their packed belongings to a new camp; the raven woman was messy; the porcupine woman was unwilling to build a fire or carry her pack; and the Canada jay woman's legs were broken under the weight of her pack. Then Clothed-in-Fur meets a woman who turns out to be a beaver, and she is a very good wife indeed. She gathers lots of firewood, cooks the beaver he kills for dinner (but refuses to eat it—doubtless because to do so would be an act of cannibalism), and capably carries her pack and relocates camp very well.

Because "Clothed-in-Fur" once failed to make a footbridge over a stream for his wife and beaver children, they entered the water and returned from their hybrid and (dry) human-beaver world to the watery world of beavers, and he lost them—temporarily as it turns out. After killing one of his own children (quite inexplicably), he goes away with a bear woman to her "town" where her father is "chief." There follows what appear to be marriage competitions between himself and a couple of bear suitors—a brown (grizzly?) and a white (polar?) bear—for the woman's hand (or paw). He succeeds in marrying the bear woman, but she and her fellow bears leave him after he fails to stay awake for ten days straight—another test. When he catches up with them at last, he kills all the adult bears, including his wife, but spares the cubs. The point of this ultimately failed bear-marriage episode in "Clothed-in-Fur" seems to be to reduce the size of bears and establish a largely vegetarian diet for them. The implication here, as in "Little-Image," is that in the distant past, the balance of power between people and bears was inverted. Bears were once larger and preyed on people. Now—thanks to Clothed-in-Fur and Little-Image—they are smaller and people prey upon bears instead of the other way around.

C. The Human-Animal Gift Economy

After finishing up his bear business, Clothed-in-Fur, returns to his beaver wife and family. There follows the concluding episode about the importance for successful hunting of reciprocity, respect, and proper treatment of the slain animal's bones. Unstated but implied throughout is that Clothed-in-Fur is the communal link between the people and the beaver. His matrimonial presence among them makes it possible for the people to "visit" the beavers. And when people of different clans visit one another they exchange gifts. Indeed, among traditionally gathering-hunting peoples such as the Ojibwa, economic exchange was effected, not by exchanging goods for money, nor even by bartering goods for goods, but by exchanging goods as gifts (Cheal 1988). The people give the animals what they have plenty of and what the animals lack—horticultural and manufactured articles (tobacco in "Clothed-in-Fur," "The Woman Who Married a Beaver," and "A Moose and His Offspring"; also kettles, bowls, knives, and clothing in "The Woman Who Married a Beaver"; and raiment, earrings, leggings, and a birch-bark pouch in "A Moose and His Offspring"). All that the animals have to give in return is their flesh and fur.

Although longer and in many ways richer, "Clothed-in-Fur" is less explicit about this visitation/gift-economy relationship than "The Woman Who Married a Beaver," where it is plainly stated that "in the same way as people are when visiting one another, so were (the beavers) in their mental attitude toward the people." That everyone involved—especially the other-than-human persons—is very happy with and much enjoys these visits and exchanges of gifts is clearly indicated in "The Woman Who Married a Beaver" and "A Moose and His Offspring" (the former states that the beavers were "continually adding to their great wealth" and "were very fond of the people"; and the latter states that "truly happy were" the compliant mooses after smoking, eating, and being showered with gifts during their post-mortem visit to the lodge of the people).

D. The Land Ethic

This foundation in community and the multiple and distinct rights, duties, and obligations generated by community membership and relationship suggests that the Ojibwa environmental ethic most resembles the land ethic, first articulated by Aldo Leopold. Leopold (1949, p. 202) points out that during the three thousand years of recorded Western history it appears that "ethical criteria have been extended to many fields of conduct" that had formerly not been covered by such criteria. For example, slavery was once tolerated in the Western ethos; later it was not. Leopold (1949, p. 202) suggests that "this extension of ethics . . . is actually a process of ecological evolution. . . . An ethic, ecologically, is a limitation on freedom of the action in the struggle for existence . . . a differentiation of social from anti-social conduct . . . [which] has its origin in the tendency of interdependent individuals or groups to evolve modes of co-operation." The direct reference here to evolution and the allusion, more especially, to the works of Charles Darwin with the phrase "struggle for existence," suggest that Leopold is informed by Darwin's account of the origin and development of ethics.

In the *Descent of Man,* Darwin confronted the apparent evolutionary anomaly of ethics. From an evolutionary point of view, it would seem that the most ruthlessly selfish individuals would better succeed in the competition for resources and mates, and thus their qualities of character and behavioral traits would be represented in ever-greater degree in future generations. How could those who loved their neighbors as themselves, who turned the other cheek, who kept promises, who endangered themselves to help their fellows, have survived and reproduced? Darwin's answer was simple and elegant. Individual survival and reproduction are enhanced for many primate species—and especially for *Homo sapiens*—by membership in a well-knit society or community, which can exist only if their individual members refrain from anti-social conduct; that is, from behavior that we now call immoral or unethical. As Darwin (1871, p. 93) so memorably put it, "No tribe could hold together if murder, robbery, treachery, &c., were common; consequently such crimes 'are branded with everlasting infamy.'"

In addition to the evolution of ethics by natural selection, Darwin envisioned a kind of social evolution or development. The first human societies, which the first generation of post-Darwinian anthropologists called "clans" or "gens," were little more than extended families. As time went on, these merged to form "tribes," which in turn merged to form nationalities, then eventually republics (or nation-states). In the late twentieth century, republics merged into regional confederations, such as the European Union. Also during the late twentieth century most of the peoples of the world, if not politically united, were united economically, and by transportation and communications technologies, into a global village. At each stage of this process of social development, Darwin (1871, pp. 100–101) noted that ethics develops correlatively: "As man advances in civilisation, and small tribes are united into larger communities, the simplest reason would tell each individual that he ought to extend his social instincts and sympathies to all the members of the same nation, though personally unknown to him." As the scope of ethics expands to the boundaries of each emergent society, the content of ethics changes to accommodate and foster the new social order. Thus, corresponding to the emergence of republics, there developed the virtue of patriotism, and corresponding to the recent emergence of the global village, there developed the concept of universal human rights. Incidentally, Darwin himself anticipated the development of a species-wide human ethic. He continues, "This point being once reached, there is only an artificial barrier to prevent his sympathies extending to the men of all nations and races. If indeed such men are separated from him by great differences in appearance or habits, experience unfortunately shews us how long it is before we look at them as our fellow-creatures" (Darwin 1871, pp. 100–101).

Aldo Leopold built his land ethic squarely on these Darwinian foundations. He merely observed that ecology portrays plants and animals, soils and waters, as members, with human beings, of a *biotic* community. As in the past, acknowledgement of the existence of and membership in this newly recognized biotic community, should engender in *us*—though, for Leopold, not necessarily in its other, nonhuman members—an ethical response. In short, according to Leopold (1949, p. 203), "All ethics so far evolved rest upon a single premise: that the individual is a member of a community of interdependent parts." That, in a nutshell, is Darwin's account of the origin of ethics. Leopold (1949, p. 204) then observes that ecology "simply enlarges the boundaries of the community to include soils, waters, plants, and animals, or collectively: the land." From that realization there follows a "land ethic" that "changes the role of *Homo sapiens* from conqueror of the land community to plain member and citizen of it" and that "implies respect for . . . fellow-members and also for the community as such" (Leopold 1949, p. 204).

E. Animal Communities in the Leopold and Ojibwa Land Ethics

Certain similarities and differences between contemporary Western ideas and traditional Ojibwa ideas about animal rights were just noted. The foundation of animal rights in both is personhood or many of its aspects. Animals are "subjects of a life," according to Tom Regan, and other-than-human *persons*—more or less the same thing, in other words—according to the Ojibwa. Some animals do have rights—in the sense of justifiable claims on human behavior—in the traditional Ojibwa environmental ethos, but they are not the same rights as are ascribed to some animals by Regan and other contemporary Western animal-rights theorists. Contrary to contemporary Western ideas about animal rights, in the traditional Ojibwa environmental ethos, animals may be killed and eaten by genuinely needy human beings. But the animals who are killed and eaten may justifiably claim to be compensated for their gift of flesh and fur by receiving horticultural and manufactured gifts in return, by being treated respectfully, and, perhaps most importantly, by having their bones returned intact to the element from which they were taken, in order that the slain animals may be reincarnated whole and intact. Further, in the traditional Ojibwa ethos, animal rights arise in the context of mixed human-animal societies or communities, which are forged by ties of marriage between certain heroic people and certain kinds of animals. In contemporary Western animal-rights theory it is not necessary that human beings and animals belong to a common community for animals to have rights. This theoretical difference makes for an important practical difference. Kinds of animals with whom no communal ties have been forged (by marriage or otherwise) appear to have no rights in the Ojibwa environmental ethos. Consider the harsh way Clothed-in-Fur treats the "women" (a wolf, a porcupine, a raven, and a Canada jay) in his several failed marriages. He not only abandons them, he beats them. One may also note similarities and differences between the two communitarian land ethics we are comparing—the one sketched by Leopold, the other embedded in the Ojibwa narratives.

One similarity between Leopold's communitarianism and that revealed in the Ojibwa narratives is that some animals are portrayed as living in communities that are very like human communities. But the likeness of animal communities to human communities is less complete in Leopold's portrayal than in that of the Ojibwa narratives. We have already amply illustrated how such anthropomorphic animal societies are portrayed in the Ojibwa narratives. How are they portrayed by Leopold? The very first essay in *A Sand County Almanac* portrays a meadow "mouse-engineer," who is "a sober citizen who knows that grass grows in order that mice may store it as underground haystacks, and that snow falls in order that mice may build subways from stack to stack: supply, demand, and transport all neatly organized" (Leopold 1949, p. 4). In another essay, Leopold (1949, p. 20) portrays geese as at once being members of a flock (vaguely compared to a gathering of Shriners or Republicans) and within the tribe-like flock also members of families: "In thus watching the daily routine of a spring goose convention, one notices the prevalence of singles—lone geese that do much flying about and talking. One is apt to impute a disconsolate tone to their honkings, and to jump to the conclusion that they are broken-hearted widowers, or mothers hunting lost children." But neither the meadow mouse-engineer nor the geese at the goose convention smoke tobacco or have any desire for human artifacts.

F. Personification in the Leopold and Ojibwa Land Ethics

Leopold's personification and anthropomorphizing is also more restrained than that found in these Ojibwa tales, and backed up with empirical observations of animal behavior. He insists, for example, that "the geese that proclaim the seasons to our farm are aware of many things, including the

Wisconsin statutes." Upon reading this, one becomes immediately skeptical—how could geese possibly know about something so culturally sophisticated as written law? But the claim is corroborated by the ensuing description of the different way the same geese behave in the fall and spring seasons: "The southbound November flocks pass over us high and haughty, with scarcely a honk of recognition for their favorite sandbars and sloughs. . . . November geese are aware that every marsh and pond bristles from dawn to dark with hopeful guns." The geese are aware, one soon begins to realize, not of any written law per se, but rather of the effect of the Wisconsin statutes that govern waterfowl hunting—which allow it in the fall and prohibit it in the spring. "March geese are a different story . . . they know that the spring truce is now in effect. They wind the oxbows of the river, cutting low over the now gunless points and islands, and gabbling to each sandbar as to a long-lost friend" (Leopold 1949, p. 19).

In the Ojibwa narratives, the personification and anthropomorphizing of animals is more liberal, but the difference is one of degree, not kind. And often too, the personification of animals is based on empirical observation: beavers are very industrious and they do build lodges that are actually very similar in appearance to the kind of sappling-and-bark lodges that the traditional Ojibwa built for themselves; ravens make messes; Canada jays have relatively weak legs; bears, as omnivores, eat a wide variety of animal, plant, and fungal foods; moose and deer yard ("go into camp") in winter—to mention but a few examples afforded in these stories. Leopold, it may be worth noting, was himself behind one of those guns hoping to kill his bag limit of geese in November. Like the Ojibwa, his personification of animals was not a reason to refrain from killing them.

Leopold suggests that he might have good scientific grounds for personifying and even—in a restrained sort of way—anthropomorphizing animals (and so by implication might the traditional Ojibwa). After imputing grief to the lone honkers, he notes, "The seasoned ornithologist [a kind of scientist] knows, however, that such subjective interpretation of bird behavior is [not preposterous, absurd, or even flatly false, but] risky" (Leopold 1949, p. 20). Leopold then constructs a quantitative argument to confirm his subjective (that is, his personifying) conjecture:

> After my students and I had counted for half a dozen years the number of geese comprising a flock, some unexpected light was cast on the meaning of lone geese. It was found by mathematical analysis that flocks of six or multiples of six were far more frequent than chance alone would dictate. In other words, goose flocks are families, or aggregations of families, and lone geese in spring are probably just what our fond imaginings had first suggested. They are bereaved survivors of the winter's shooting, searching in vain for their kin. Now I am free to grieve with and for the lone honkers (Leopold 1949, p. 16).

More generally, the theory of evolution provides a scientific justification of personification. *Homo* is, from an evolutionary point of view, a primate, one of five genera of great ape (along with chimpanzees, gorillas, orangutans, and gibbons). If we human beings have a conscious, inner, subjective life of desire, emotion, imagination, and thought, why should we not suppose that other apes, primates, mammals, and vertebrates have such a life as well. One might reply that we cannot directly observe animal consciousness and, from a scientific point of view—or rather from the narrow point of view of Logical Positivism, a largely discredited but powerfully influential philosophy of science—we cannot legitimately posit the existence of that which we cannot directly observe. Neither, however, can we directly observe the consciousness of other human beings, yet only the most extreme solipcist supposes that other human beings lack conscious experiences similar to one's own. On the basis of what, then, does one normally so confidently infer the state of another human being's consciousness? On the basis of their behavior. Other human beings look more or less like oneself and they act more or less like oneself. One knows how one feels or thinks when one acts a certain way; when one see others acting in similar ways one imputes (to use Leopold's word) similar states of consciousness to them.

If we accept the evolutionary supposition that human beings too are animals, we may be no less confident of imputing similar conscious states to animals than we are to other human beings—to the extent that they look and act as we do. Because our fellow apes most resemble us in anatomy and behavior, we may be more confident in our "subjective interpretations" of their behavior than in, say, our subjective interpretations of beaver, bear, or bird behavior. When it comes to snake or fish behavior, we think that we may be confident that such animals have some sort of inner subjective lives—that is, some states of consciousness—but because they are so far removed from us phylogenetically, speculation on just what they are thinking or feeling is very risky indeed.

In any case, the purportedly "scientific" refusal to acknowledge the existence of animal consciousness—that is, to personify animals—turns out to be a pre-scientific prejudice lingering from the biblical belief that human beings are uniquely created in the image of God and endowed with an immortal soul and the allied Cartesian dogma that animals are merely sophisticated automata or machines and human beings are the only such animals inhabited by a "thinking thing." Leopold (1949, p. 110) puts this point quite succinctly: "It is a century now since Darwin gave us the first glimpse of the origin of species. We know now what was unknown to all the previous caravan of generations: that men are only fellow-voyagers with other creatures in the odyssey of evolution. This new knowledge should have given us, by this time, a sense of kinship with other creatures; a wish to live and let live; a sense of wonder over the magnitude and duration of the biotic enterprise." Because the traditional Ojibwa were not prejudiced by the religious and philosophical dualism infecting Western thought, they quite naturally—and from a contemporary scientific point of view, quite correctly—assumed that human and other-than-human animals were similarly (and equally) conscious beings.

G. Biotic Communities in the Leopold and Ojibwa Land Ethics

The land ethic is much less about animal persons, animal communities, and certainly animal rights (which Leopold discusses not at all), than about *biotic* communities. A biotic community is a community composed of many species, some of which exist in their own sub-communities, which biologists call populations. So important is this kind of community—the biotic community—that it is the focus of the land ethic's oft-quoted golden rule or, more technically put, summary moral maxim: "A thing is right when it tends to preserve the integrity, stability, and beauty of the biotic community; it is wrong when it tends otherwise" (Leopold 1949, pp. 224–225). In addition to single-species animal communities, do we find any notion of a multi-species biotic community in these Ojibwa narratives? Certainly the larger biotic community is not as vividly portrayed in the narratives as are the single-species sub-communities (in "Clothed-in-Fur," "The Woman Who Married a Beaver," and "A Moose and His Offspring") that it comprises. But something like the biotic-community concept is there—more implicitly, to be sure, as a kind of background assumption, than as the object of explicit portrayal.

One place it shows up implicitly—but, nevertheless, quite plainly, after a little analysis—is in "The Orphans and Mashōs." First, the elder orphan is kidnapped by the evil Mashōs and is taken away from his little brother for whom he had dutifully cared. His little brother is adopted by wolves and gradually becomes a wolf; thus, after the elder brother has become Mashōs's grown-up son-in-law, his wolf-brother remains his occasional companion and ally. In Mashōs's various attempts to kill him, his son-in-law is variously saved or aided by a Great sturgeon, a Great gull, a Great stone, and a cedar tree. This is because the son-in-law has previously humbled himself to these various powerful other-than-human persons and they have pitied him. But why just these other-than-human persons and not some others? Perhaps it is a coincidence—but probably it is not—that these beings represent land animals (the wolf-brother), animals of the water (a Great sturgeon), animals of the air (a Great gull), a representative of the plant kingdom (the cedar tree) and a representative of the mineral kingdom (the Great stone). According to Leopold, as already noted, "the boundaries of the biotic community . . . include soils, waters, plants, and animals, or collectively: the land." The correspondence is not perfect, but it is pretty close. Unlike Clothed-in-Fur or the woman who married a beaver—both of whom are special human emissaries to specific animal communities—Mashōs's son-in-law is a shining example of a good boy grown up to be a good man. He is indeed a very good plain member and citizen of both his human and his biotic communities. "The Person Who Made Medicine" concerns not animal communities but respect for cliffs and water, which is pretty similar to Leopold's idea that we should respect not only plants and animals, but soils and waters as well.

Perhaps most expansive of all is the communitarian vision set out in "Notes on the Mystic Rite." There the earth, the sky, the sea, and the four winds, along with the winds intermediate to those blowing from the cardinal compass points, are all the body of the mystic manitou. Within this living cosmic community the initiates pray not only for long life and personal health, but for the health as well of the biotic community: "that more abundant may become the big animal-folk and fishes . . . that in plenty may grow all kinds of berries."

H. The Fur, Flesh, and Bones of the Land Ethics

As noted, in some of these narratives (especially "The Orphans and Mashōs" and "Clothed-in-Fur"), the spirit-essence of a being is its bony skeleton, something more enduring and substantial than its soft tissues and hide. And the same spirit-essence can assume different outward forms. Clothed-in-Fur and the woman who married a beaver were human, but metamorphosed into beavers. As "Notes on the Mystic Rite" indicates, a preternaturally powerful human person can metamorphose into a bear—for nefarious purposes. Think of the skeletal spirit-essence outwardly clothed—now this way, now that—with the furry coat and flesh of various species as a philosophical metaphor. Think of the bare bones of the land ethic as a skeletal spirit essence and think of the scientific vocabulary of Western culture and the mythic vocabulary of Ojibwa culture as the outwardly different flesh and fur clothing it. This comparative exercise is a kind of metamorphosis translating its outward appearance in one vocabulary into that of the other. The same skeletal spirit-essence of the land ethic appears in Leopold's *A Sand County Almanac* clothed in the language of evolutionary biology and ecology and in these narratives in the language of edifying fiction. The essential ideas—the bare bones—are the same (or at least nearly the same) irrespective of the idiom in which they are expressed.

One element of the essential spirit-essence of the land ethic is this. There is no great metaphysical and psychological gulf separating human beings from other-than-human beings—as there is in the still-lingering, die-hard prescientific Western cultural worldview. Human beings and other-than-human beings are equally natural beings. In the scientific idiom of Western culture, this idea is conveyed through the phylogentic location of *Homo sapiens* as a twig on a branch of the evolutionary tree of life (Wilson 1992). In the Ojibwa stories, it is conveyed through many devices, the just-mentioned phenomenon of metamorphosis whereby human beings assume the shape of animals and animals the shape of human beings, the dreams and visions of animal and plant spirit beings, talking thunder, and so on and so forth. In Leopold's already quoted words—which are neither the idiom of science nor of myth, really, but something in between—we human beings and other forms of life are all equally "fellow-voyagers in the odyssey of evolution."

A second element of the spirit-essence of the land ethic is this. Human beings and other-than-human beings are mutually dependent, and if we should specify who is more dependent on whom, then we should have to say that human beings are more dependent on other-than-human beings than they are on us. In the contemporary idiom of Western ecology, human beings are dependent on plants and animals to provide us not only with "natural re-sources," but also with "ecological services." Expressed in Leopold's inter-mediate poetic idiom,

> Plants absorb energy from the sun. This energy flows through a circuit called the biota, which may be represented as a pyramid consisting of lay-ers. The bottom layer is the soil. A plant layer rests on the soil, an insect layer on the plants, a bird and rodent layer on the insects, and so up through various animal groups, to the apex layer, which consists of the larger carnivores. . . . The lines of dependency for food and other services are called food chains. . . . Man shares an intermediate layer with the bears, raccoons, and squirrels which eat both meat and vegetables. The pyramid is a tangle of food chains so complex as to seem disorderly, yet the stability of the system proves it to be a highly organized structure. Its functioning depends on the cooperation and competition of its diverse parts (Leopold 1949, p. 215).

The Ojibwa narratives express similar ideas quite emphatically. Human beings and bears are quite on a par, so much so that the balance of power be-tween them has shifted in the past and remains precarious (as both "Clothed-in-Fur" and "Little-Image" suggest). A "pitiful" human being is virtually doomed without the aid of preternaturally powerful other-than-human per-sons. The Ojibwa narratives convey even more graphically than Leopold that the functioning of nature "depends on the cooperation and competition of its diverse parts," and that the human species is but one—and a relatively in-significant one at that—of those parts.

A third key element of the spirit-essence of the land ethic is the hierarchi-cal social structure of nature in which the human economy is embedded in the larger economy of nature. In the idiom of Western ecology, animal and plant populations interact to form "biotic communities." The inherently social struc-ture of the biota is "hierarchical" in scale; that is, local biotic communities are incorporated into regional biotic communities, which are in turn incorporated into biomes, which are ultimately incorporated into the global biosphere (Allen and Hoekstra 1992). And, according to Leopold, *Homo sapiens* is but a "plain member and citizen" of the hierarchically organized congeries of biotic com-munities. More vividly than anything one might find in an ecology textbook—

or in *A Sand County Almanac,* for that matter—the Ojibwa narratives portray human beings and other forms of life as belonging to a hierarchically organized inherently social order of nature. Calvin Martin (1978, p. 187) corroborates the impression one gets from reading these stories: "Nature, as conceived by the traditional Ojibwa, was a congeries of societies: every animal, fish, and plant species functioned in a society that was parallel in all respects to mankind's."

Finally, at the core of the spirit-essence of the land ethic is, in Leopold's words, "respect for . . . fellow-members [of the hierarchically organized biotic community] and also respect for the community as such." And he goes on to say, "It is inconceivable to me that an ethical relation to land can exist without love, respect, and admiration for land" (Leopold 1949, p. 223). In most of the Ojibwa narratives ("The Orphans and Mashōs" and "The Boy That Was Carried Away by a Bear" are good examples), the expression of love and respect for fellow members of the biotic community and also for the community as such is implicit. But in some (most notably, "The Woman Who Married a Beaver" and the "Person That Made Medicine"), it is spelled out. As to love and respect for fellow members, "Just the same as the feelings of one who is disliked, so is the feeling of the beaver. And he who never speaks ill of a beaver is very much loved by it; in the same way as people often love one another, so is one held in the mind of a beaver." And as to the community as such, "That is why people are never allowed to speak nonsense upon a cliff or upon the water; and very seriously do people forbid one another to talk nonsense (in such places)."

I. Pimadaziwin

Returning to the matter of a more human-oriented ethic, we might now say that, in this regard, the Ojibwa ethos is perhaps most illuminatingly compared with Aristotle's teleological ethic. Aristotle posited a single overall *telos* (that is, end, goal, or purpose) at which all human action should aim: *eudaimonia.* This word is usually translated as "happiness," and might be more literally rendered "well-spirited," but is best left merely transcribed from the Greek alphabet into the Roman, because there is no precise equivalent in English. Here we have done something similar with the word *manitou,* an Ojibwa word that we have prefered to leave untranslated rather than to risk distortion of its meaning by translating it as, say, "spirit." Like Aristotle, the Ojibwa seem to have posited a single overall end at which all human action should aim, namely *pimadaziwin* (Hallowell 1960). And "happiness" is just as inadequate a rendering of the Ojibwa notion of *pimadaziwin* as it is of the Greek notion of *eudaimonia.* Fortunately "Notes on the Mystic Rite" provides us with a ready-made translation of *pimadaziwin.* The narrator says, "Now this is what they [initiates in the mystic rite] wish to obtain by prayer, that long life they may have, or that they may have good health, and not be sick."

The mystic rite to which these "notes" relate is otherwise known as the *Midewiwin* or Grand Medicine Lodge. It was a body of lore about the causes of and cures for all the ills that flesh is heir to. Initiates acquired this lore and the associated medicines in four stages from novice to master practitioner (Hickerson 1970). According to Hickerson (1962), the *Midewiwin* originated in the post-Columbian period. Martin (1978) argues that it was a response to the terrible ravages of European pathogens introduced to the Western Hemisphere soon after the voyages of Columbus. Diseases such as smallpox and influenza were originally contracted by ancient Europeans from their domestic animals, such as chickens and pigs (Crosby 1994). American Indians had few domestic animals, mainly only dogs, and so had been free of most of the diseases that had jumped from livestock to human hosts in the Old World. Because their ancestors had long co-existed with such diseases, latter-day Europeans had evolved resistance to them. However the indigenous peoples of the Americas were so much more vulnerable and succumbed in such great numbers that perhaps their population was ultimately reduced by ninety percent after exposure (Thornton 1987). In any case, the *Midewiwin* was certainly focused on achieving *pimadaziwin*—good health and long life.

For the Ojibwa, however, human *pimadaziwin* was intimately connected with what Leopold (1949) called "land health" (and what is now called "ecosystem health"). In "Notes on the Mystic Rite," the narrator immediately goes on to say that the initiates of the mystic rite also pray "that more abundant may become the big animal-folk and fishes, or that the weather may be fair, [or] that in plenty may grow all kinds of berries." Of course, all these environmental things they pray for are tributary to *pimadaziwin*, to human good health and long life—abundant game animals and fishes, edible plants, salubrious weather. But that helps us to see another important point of similarity between the Leopold and Ojibwa land ethics—that ultimately human well-being (*eudaimonia* or *pimadaziwin*, in other words) is inseparable from environmental well-being, and that ultimately an environmental ethic is not opposed to or even distinguishable from a more directly human-oriented ethic. Because human communities are embedded in biotic communities, human health is dependent on environmental health. Ultimately, the Leopold land ethic, no less than the Ojibwa land ethic, is therefore about *pimadaziwin*: human health and longevity—not only for each of us personally, but for all of us collectively and in perpetuity. As Leopold (1949, p. 203) puts this point, "An ethic may be regarded as a mode of guidance for meeting ecological situations so new or intricate, or evolving such deferred reactions that the path to social expediency is not discernible to the average individual." That is, Leopold sees his land ethic as ultimately serving "social expediency"—collective and sustainable human well-being—which cannot, however, be realized apart from environmental well-being.

III. The Controversy About American-Indian Environmental Ethics

A. Proponents and Skeptics

The idea that traditional American-Indian human-land relationships are governed by an environmental ethic goes back at least to Henry David Thoreau, who is among the first Western thinkers to suggest that human-land relationships should be governed by an environmental ethic. According to Roderick Nash (1967, p. 92), Thoreau once imagined "the Indian" to be a "child of nature"—perfectly, if innocently, attuned to the environment. However, after actually meeting some Indians on his excursion into the Maine woods, crowned by his ascent of Mount Katahdin, Thoreau changed his tune. The Indians he met "appeared to be 'sinister and slouching fellows' who made but 'a course and imperfect use of Nature'" (Nash 1967, p. 92). Thoreau's ambivalence about the existence of American Indian environmental ethics foreshadows a long-running debate about this issue.

Thoreau's initial impressions were based, as suggested, on little more than his own creative imagination. In the 1930s, however, anthropologists William C. McCloud and Frank G. Speck based their opinion that American Indians were "conservators" (the phrase "environmental ethics" had not yet come into currency) on some actual evidence. According to McCloud (1936, p. 562), "To primitive man there is a soul in all things animate and (to us) inanimate. . . . [Thus] they appear to have rationalized their rude conservation in spiritual terms." According to Speck (1939, p. 23), who worked among the Ojibwa, "The hunter's virtue lies in respecting the souls of the animals necessarily killed, in treating their remains in a prescribed manner and in particular, in making use of as much of the carcass as is possible. . . . The animals slain under the proper conditions and treated with the consideration due them return to life again and again. They furthermore indicate their whereabouts to the 'good' hunter in dreams, resigning themselves to his weapons in a free spirit of self-sacrifice."

When the widespread perception of an "environmental crisis" emerged in the 1960s, many concerned Westerners turned to traditional American Indian culture searching for a precedent or even a model for an environmental ethic, something up until then completely foreign to the Western worldview. Stewart Udall (1963, p. 16), Secretary of the Interior in the John F. Kennedy administration, claimed that "the most common trait of all primitive peoples is a reverence for the life-giving earth, and the native American shared this elemental ethic: the land was alive to his loving touch, and he, its son, was brother to all creatures." After Udall revived and popularized the Thoreauvian image of an environmental ethic in traditional American Indian culture, he was followed by many others (for example Grieder 1970). But equally as many skeptics emerged to discredit that idea as neo-Romantic hog wash, just Jean-Jacque Rousseau's noble-savage nonsense with a new environmental spin. An article in *BioScience* by Daniel Guthrie (1971) was especially influential in raising doubts about the existence of environmental ethics among traditional American Indians. J. Donald Hughes (1983) provides the most extensive case for environmental ethics in traditional American-Indian culture; Shepard Krech III (1999) provides the most extensive case against the same proposition.

B. A Debate about Apples and Oranges

It is hard to imagine how the two sides to this certainly impassioned, often bitter, and seemingly zero-sum debate can be reconciled. But on closer inspection, one notices that the evidence offered by the two parties to this debate is of different kinds.

Proponents of American Indian environmental ethics offer—as is offered here—cognitive or ideational evidence. We focus on the *attitudes* toward and *values* respecting nature that various American Indian peoples evince. Sources for such cognitive or ideational evidence vary from personal testimonials by contemporary Indians about the attitudes and values of their ancestors (such as that by Hester, McPherson, Booth, and Cheney 2000), to empirical anthropological research (such as that by McCloud 1936 and Speck 1939), to ethnohistory (such as that of Martin 1978), to ethnometaphysics and literary criticism (such as that offered by Hallowell 1960 and by this book).

On the other hand, skeptics offer behavioral evidence. They focus on what American Indian peoples *did (and do)* in and to nonhuman natural entities and nature as a whole. For example, Guthrie (1971) cites midden heaps (which one might as well call garbage dumps) at the foot of Anazazi cliff dwellings; buffalo driven off cliffs and only partially butchered, the rest left to rot; the extinction of a number of large animals shortly after the arrival from Siberia of the ancestors of the peoples who would become American Indians; and the litter alleged to be found on contemporary Indian reservations in the United States. Krech (1999) cites the same "Pleistocene extinctions" by the Siberian big game hunters who were the first to discover America; bad hydraulic farming by the Hohokum in the Southwest; over-exploitation of natural resources—forests for fuel and building materials; animals and plants for food among pre-Columbian woodland peoples from the Eastern Seaboard to the Midwestern prairies; deliberately set fires in both forests and grasslands all over North America; indiscriminate and wasteful slaughter of bison; and the fur trade, in the course of which Indian trappers (the Ojibwa prominent among them) extirpated the populations of beaver and other fur-bearing animals in some locales to the point of threatening these species on a continental scale.

C. Ethics and Behavior; Ideals and Actions

In short, proponents of the traditional American Indian environmental ethics point to ideas, skeptics point to actions. Ethics is indeed about human behavior, but not in the way that history, sociology, and psychology are often about human behavior. Historical, sociological, and psychological treatments of human behavior are largely descriptive, while the treatment of human behavior in ethics is largely normative. For example, a history of the conquests of Alexander the Great might recount all the relevant facts—describe what happened—and refrain altogether from moral judgment: that, for example, the burning of Persepolis was wrong and Alexander ought not to have done it. Or a sociological study of the increasing number of marriages that end in divorce might simply describe the trends and never indicate whether this phenomenon is good or bad, whether in an ideal world marriage should be so casual. Or a psychological study might describe the higher incidence of abusive behavior toward their children of adults who themselves suffered from parental abuse as children, without morally condemning such a cycle of violence and insisting that it ought to be interdicted. Traditional Western ethics, on the other hand, sets out to determine how people ought to behave toward one another. In so doing, it portrays ideals of human-to-human behavior; it does not describe actual human-to-human behavior—except incidentally, by way of instruction or example. Similarly, environmental ethics sets out to determine how people ought to behave toward nature; it portrays ideals of human-to-nature behavior; it does not describe actual human-to-nature behavior—except, again incidentally, by way of instruction or example.

Therefore, simply describing how people actually behave—toward one another or toward nature—does not provide a decisive answer to the question whether people subscribe to a humanitarian or environmental ethic, as the case may be. People may subscribe to an ethic and yet not live up to the ideals it envisions or fulfill the obligations it imposes. To conclude from a catalogue of egregious past American-Indian environmental behavior that therefore American Indians subscribed to no environmental ethic would be like assembling a catalogue of human-to-human atrocities in Western history—Roman gladiator shows, the Crusades, the Spanish Inquisition, the slave trade, the German Third Reich, the U.S. invasion of Iraq—and concluding that there was no human-to-human ethic in the West.

Indeed, rarely do people live up to the ideals their ethics envision or the duties and obligations their ethics impose. But that doesn't mean that ethics have no effect on actual human behavior. Despite Roman gladiator shows, the Crusades, the Spanish Inquisition, the slave trade, the German Third Reich, and the U.S. invasion of Iraq, on the whole people in the West treat one another better because of the Greek Golden Mean, the Christian Golden Rule, the Kantian categorical imperative, and the utilitarian greatest happiness principle than they would if such ethics did not exist in Western culture. In any culture, actual human behavior will never measure up to the moral norms or ideals envisioned by its worldview and ethos, but in striving toward them, however far short actual human behavior may fall, some overall movement in the direction of those norms and ideals will have been achieved. Similarly, despite the Pleistocene extinctions perpetrated by Siberian immigrants to the Americas and the alleged litter on contemporary Indian reservations—as if such "evidence" were relevant to the existence of traditional American Indian environmental ethics—and despite the existence of buffalo jumps, midden heaps, soil salinization, resource depletion, and the fur trade, on the whole American Indians probably treated nature better because of their environmental ethics than otherwise they might have. One of these environmental ethics—the Ojibwa land ethic—has been explored here.

Literature Cited

Allen, T. F. H. and T. W. Hoekstra. 1992. *Toward a Unified Ecology.* New York: Columbia University Press.

Berger, P. and T. Luckmann. 1967. *The Social Construction of Reality.* Garden City: Doubleday.

Bidney, D. 1949. "The Concept of Meta-Anthropology and Its Significance for Contemporary Anthropological Science." *Ideological Differences and World Order.* Edited by F.S.C. Northrop. New Haven: Yale University Press.

Bishop, C. 1970. "The Emergence of Hunting Territories Among the Northern Ojibwa." *Ethnology,* 9:1–15.

Bishop, C. 1976. "The Emergence of the Northern Ojibwa: Social and Economic Consequences." *American Ethnologis,* 3:39–54.

Black, M. 1974. *The Northern Ojibwa and the Fur Trade: An Historical and Ecological Study.* Toronto: Holt, Rinehart and Winston of Canada.

Black, M. 1977. "Ojibwa Power Belief-Systems." *The Anthropology of Power.* Edited by R. D. Fogelson and R. N. Adams. New York: Academic Press. pp. 141–51.

Boas, F. 1911. *Handbook of American Indian Languages.* Bureau of American Ethnology, Bulletin 40. Washington, D.C.: Smithsonian Institution.

Boylan, M. 2000. *Basic Ethics.* Upper Saddle River, N. J.: Prentice Hall.

Callicott, J. B. 1989. *In Defense of the Land Ethic: Essays in Environmental Philosophy.* Albany: State University of New York Press.

Callicott, J. B. and R. T. Ames. 1989. *Nature in Asian Traditions of Thought.* Albany: State University of New York Press.

Cheal, D. 1988. *The Gift Economy.* London: Routledge.

Copway, G. 1850. *The Traditional History and Characteristic Sketches of the Ojibway Nation.* London: Charles Gilpin.

Crosby, A. W. 1994. *Germs, Seeds, and Animals: Studies in Ecological History.* Amrock, NY: M. E. Sharp.

Darwin, C. 1871. *The Descent of Man and Selection in Relation to Sex.* London: J. Murray.

Dobzhansky, T. 1963. "Anthropology and the Natural Sciences." *Current Anthropology,* 4:138, 146–148.

Dorson, R. M. 1952. *Bloodstoppers and Bearwalkers: Folk Traditions of the Upper Penninsula.* Cambridge: Harvard University Press.

Einstein, A. 1916. *Relativity: The Special and General Theory.* New York: Crown Publishers, Inc.

Foucault, M. 1972. *The Archaeology of Knowledge.* New York: Pantheon Books.

Foucault, M. 1979. *The Birth of the Prison.* New York: Vintage Books.

Gare, A. 1995. *Postmodernism and Environmental Crisis.* London: Routledge.

Geertz, C. 1957/1973. "Ethos, World View, and the Analysis of Sacred Symbols." *The Antioch Review,* 17:4. Reprinted in *The Interpretation of Cultures.* New York: Basic Books, Inc. pp.126–141.

Geertz, C. 1973. "Thick Description: Toward an Interpretive Theory of Culture." *The Interpretation of Cultures.* New York: Basic Books, Inc. pp. 3–30.

Ghiselin, M. 1974. "A Radical Solution to the Species Problem." *Systematic Zoology,* 23: 536–544.

Goodenough, W. 1956. "Componential Analysis and the Study of Meaning." *Parabola* 2, No. 2:6–12.

Goodpaster, K. E. 1978. "On Being Morally Considerable." *Journal of Philosophy,* 75: 308–325.

Greenberg, J. 1954. "Concerning Inferences from Linguistic to Nonlinguistic Data." *Language in Culture.* Edited by Harry Hoijer. Chicago: The University of Chicago Press. pp. 3–19.

Greenberg, J. 1977. *A New Invitation to Linguistics.* New York: Doubleday.

Grieder, T. 1970. "Ecology before Columbus." *Americas,* 22:21–28.

Guthrie, D. 1971. "Primitive Man's Relationship with Nature." *BioScience,* 21:721–723.

Hallowell, I. 1951. "Cultural Factors in the Structuralization of Perception." *Social Psychology at the Crossroads.* Edited by J. H. Rohver and M. Sherif. New York: Harper.

Hallowell, I. 1955. *Culture and Experience.* Philadelphia: University of Pennsylvania Press.

Hallowell, I. 1960. "Ojibwa Ontology, Behavior, and World View." *Culture In History.* Edited by S. Diamond. New York: Columbia University Press. pp. 19–52.

Hallowell, I. 1963. "Ojibwa World View and Disease." *Man's Image in Medicine and Anthropology.* Edited by Iago Galdston. New York: International Universities Press. pp. 258–315.

Hallowell, I. 1966/1976. "The Role of Dreams in Ojibwa Culture." *The Dream and Human Societies.* Edited by G. von Grunebaum and R. Callois. Berkeley: University of California Press. Reprinted in 1976. pp. 449–474.

Hallowell. I. 1976. *Contributions to Anthropology.* Chicago: The University of Chicago Press.

Hambly, W. D. 1926. *Origins of Education Among Primitive Peoples.* London: Macmillan.

Havelock, E. 1963. *Preface to Plato.* Cambridge: Harvard University Press.

Heidegger, M. 1938/1977. "The Age of the World Picture." *The Question Concerning Technology and Other Essays.* Translated by William Louitt. New York: Harper and Row.

Hester, D., D. McPherson, A. Booth, and J. Cheney. 2000. "Indigenous Worlds and Callicott's Land Ethic." *Environmental Ethics*, 22: 273–290.

Hickerson, H. 1956. "The Genesis of the Trading Post Band: The Pembina Chippewa." *Ethnohistory*, 3:289–345.

Hickerson, H. 1962. *The Southwestern Chippewa: An Ethnohistorical Study*. American Anthropological Association Memoir No. 92. Menasha, Wisconsin.

Hickerson, H. 1970. *The Chippewa and Their Neighbors*. New York: Holt, Rinehart, and Winston.

Hilger, I. 1939. *A Social Study of One Hundred Fifty Chippewa Families of the White Earth Reservation of Minnesota*. Catholic University of America, Washington, D.C.

Hoijer, H. 1954. "The Sapir-Whorf Hypothesis." *Language and Culture*. Edited by H. Hoijer. Chicago: The University of Chicago Press. pp. 92–105.

Hughes, J. D. 1983/1996. *North American Indian Ecology*. El Paso: Texas Western Press.

Jenness, D. 1935. *The Ojibwa Indians of Parry Island, Their Social and Religious Life*. Ottawa: Canada Department of Mines, Bulletin 78, National Museum of Canada Anthropological Series No. 17.

Johnson, L. 1991. *A Morally Deep World: An Essay on Moral Significance and Environmental Ethics*. Cambridge: Cambridge University Press.

Jones, W. T. 1917, 1919. *Ojibwa Texts*. Publications of the American Ethnological Society, Vol. 7, pts. 1 and 2. Leyden and New York.

Jung, H. Y. 1972. "Ecology, Zen, and Western Religious Thought." *Christian Century*, 88:1153–1163.

Kelly, W. H. 1972. "Culture and the Individual" [typescript for classroom use, University of Arizona].

Kinietz, W. V. 1965. *The Indians of the Western Great Lakes 1615–1760*. Ann Arbor: University of Michigan Press.

Kluckhohn, C. 1949. "The Philosophy of the Navaho Indians." *Ideological Differences and World Order*. Edited by F.S.C. Northrop. New Haven: Yale University Press. pp. 356–384.

Kluckhohn, C. and D. Leighton. 1946/1962. *The Navaho*. Garden City: Doubleday and Co. (Originally published by Harvard University Press.)

Krech III, S. 1999. *The Ecological Indian: Myth and History*. New York: W.W. Norton.

Latour, B. 1999. *Pandora's Hope: Essays on the Reality of Science Studies*. Cambridge: Harvard University Press.

Leopold, A. 1949. *A Sand County Almanac: and Sketches Here and There*. New York: Oxford University Press.

Lumsden C. L. and E. O. Wilson. 1981. *Genes, Mind, and Culture: The Coevolutionary Process*. Cambridge: Harvard University Press.

Lyotard, J-F. 1984. *The Postmodern Condition*. Minneapolis: University of Minnesota Press.

Martin, C. 1978. *Keepers of the Game: Indian-Animal Relationships and the Fur Trade*. Berkeley: University of California Press.

McCloud, W. C. 1936. "Conservation Among Primitive Hunting Peoples." *Scientific Monthly*, 43:562–566.

McIntosh, R. P. 1998. "The Myth of Community as Organism." *Perspectives in Biology and Medicine*, 41:426–438.

McKenney, T. L. 1827. *Sketches of a Tour to the Lakes, of the Character and Customs of the Chippeway Indians, and of Incidents Connected with the Treaty of Fond du Lac*. Baltimore: Fielding Lucas.

McTaggart, F. 1976. *Wolf That I Am: In Search of the Red Earth People.* Boston: Houghton Mifflin.

Naess, A. 1973. "The Shallow and the Deep, Long-range Ecology Movements: A Summary." *Inquiry*, 16: 95–100.

Nash, R. 2001. *Wilderness and the American Mind.* New Haven, C.T.: Yale University Press. (2001, fourth edition)

Overholt, T. W. 1978. "Short Bull, Black Elk, Sword, and the 'Meaning' of the Ghost Dance." *Religion*, 8:171–195.

Passmore, J. 1974. *Man's Responsibility to Nature: Ecological Problems and Western Traditions.* New York: Scribner's.

Quimby, G. I. 1960. *Indian Life in the Upper Great Lakes: 11,000 B.C. to A.D. 1800.* Chicago: The University of Chicago Press.

Rabb, J. D. and D. H. McPherson. 1994. *The Lakehead University Native Philosophy Project.* Thunder Bay Ontario: Department of Philosophy, Lakehead University.

Radin, P. 1927. *Primitive Man as Philosopher.* New York: Dover Publications, Inc.

Redfield, R. 1941. *The Folk Culture of the Yucatan.* Chicago: The University of Chicago Press.

Regan, T. 1983. *The Case for Animal Rights.* Berkeley: University of California Press.

Ritzenthaler, R. 1978. "Southwestern Chippewa." *Handbook of North American Indians.* W. C. Sturtevant (general editor). Vol. 15, *Northeast.* B. G. Trigger (volume editor). Washington, D.C.: Smithsonian Institution. pp. 743–59.

Ritzenthaler, R. and P. Ritzenthaler. 1970. *The Woodland Indians of the Western Great Lakes.* Garden City: Natural History Press.

Rogers, E. S. 1962. *The Round Lake Ojibwa.* Royal Ontario Museum-University of Toronto, Art and Archaeology Division, Occasional Paper No. 5.

Rogers, E. S. 1978. "Southeastern Ojibwa." *Handbook of North American Indians.* W. C. Sturtevant (general editor). Vol. 15, *Northeast.* B. G. Trigger (volume editor). Washington, D.C.: Smithsonian Institution. pp. 760–771.

Rolston III, H. 1975. "Is There an Ecological Ethic?" *Ethics*, 85:93–109.

Rorty, R. 1979. *Philosophy and the Mirror of Nature.* Princeton, N. J.: Princeton University Press.

Routley, R. 1973. "Is There a Need for a New, an Environmental Ethic?" In *Proceedings of the XVth World Congress of Philosophy*, Vol. 1. Edited by Bulgarian Organizing Committee. Varna: Sophia Press. pp. 205–210.

Sapir, E. 1929/1964. "The Status of Linguistics as a Science." *Language*, 5:207–214. Reprinted in *Culture, Language and Personality.* Edited by David G. Mandelbaum. Berkeley: University of California Press.

Sapir, E. 1931. "Conceptual Categories in Primitive Languages." *Science*, 74:578.

Schoolcraft, H. R. 1851–1857. *Historical and Statistical Information Respecting the History, Condition and Prospects of the Indian Tribes of the United States.* Philadelphia: Lippincott, Grambo and Co. (Vols. 1–4); Lippincott (Vols. 5–6).

Shrader-Frechette, K. S. 1981. *Environmental Ethics.* Pacific Grove, Cal.: Boxwood Press.

Singer, P. 1975. *Animal Liberation: A New Ethics for Our Treatment of Animals.* New York: Avon.

Skinner, A. and J. V. Satterlee. 1915. *Folklore of the Menomini Indians.* American Museum of Natural History Anthropological Papers, Vol. 13, No. 3. New York.

Speck, F. 1939. "Savage Savers." *Frontiers*, 4:23–37.

Swanton, J. R. 1909. *"Tlingit Myths and Texts.* Bureau of American Ethnology, Bulletin No. 39. Washington, D.C.: Smithsonian Institution.

Taylor, P. 1986. *Respect for Nature: A Theory of Environmental Ethics.* Princeton, N.J.: Princeton University Press.

Thornton, R. 1987. *American Indian Holocaust and Survival: A Population History Since 1492.* Norman: University of Oklahoma Press.

Udall, S. 1963. *The Quiet Crisis.* New York: Holt, Rinehart & Winston.

Warren, W. 1970. *History of the Ojibwa Nation.* Minneapolis: Ross and Haines.

White Jr., L. 1967. "The Historical Roots of Our Ecologic Crisis." *Science,* 155:1203–1207.

Whorf, B. 1950/1956. "An American Indian Model of the Universe." *International Journal of American Linguistics,* 16: 67–72. Reprinted in *Language, Thought, and Reality.* Edited by John B. Carroll. New York: John Wiley & Sons, Inc. pp. 57–64.

Wilson, E. O. 1978. *On Human Nature.* Cambridge: Harvard University Press.

Wilson, E. O. 1992. *The Diversity of Life.* Cambridge: Belknap Press of Harvard University.

Index

A
aboriginal:
  American peoples, 11
  mode of life, 35
  times, 35
Achilles: 20
adapt(ation)(ed)(ive):
  cultural, 15–17
  genetic, 17
aesthetic(s): 12, 25
  criterion, 30
  Kant's, 25
  quality, 30
Alaska, 18, 34
Alexander the Great: 134
Algonkian:
  culture, 33
  languages, 18, 102
  Ojibwa as, 28
  peoples, 33
  speakers, 18
Allen, T. F. H.: 129
American(s):
  aboriginal peoples, 11, 22, 107
  Anglo-, 29

anthropology, 25
  cultural studies, 20
  European-, 1, 35 *See also* American
    Indians
American Indian(s) 1, 33–34, 36, 103,
    111, 131–135
  as conservators(ionists), 132
  culture, 132–133
  cultural world views, 1
  environmental behavior, 134
  environmental ethics, 132–135
  ethical traditions, 6
  languages, 20
  of Yucatan Penninsula, 11
  philosophy, 9 *See also* Indian(s)
Ames, Roger: 6
Anazazi: 133
animal(s): 3–4, 7, 11, 15, 102, 104–106,
    108–111, 113–133
  ancestors of *Homo sapiens*, 17
  behavior, 124
  communities (societies), 105,
    123–124, 127–128
  consciousness, 126–127
  cruelty to, 11

cultural, 15
domestic, 131
experience of pleasure and pain
    (sentient), 4
families, 105
-folk, 84, 87–88, 97, 103, 128, 131
fur-bearing, 133
game, 29, 111, 131
groups, 129
Homo sapiens (human beings) as,
    15, 126
human-gift economy, 121–123
human- marriages, 119–121
-kind, 68
land, 127
land ethic and, 123–124
liberation, 119
marked as animate in Ojibwa, 102
of the air, 127
of the water, 127
-oriented philosophers, 118
person(s)(ification) (of), 124–127
populations, 3
predatory, 15
rights (theory, theorists), 118–119,
    123–124, 127
species, 13
social communication among, 15,
    104–105
subjects of a life, 118–19, 123, 126 *See
    also* game animals
animate(ism): 28, 102–104, 132
Anishinabe: 32, 99, 110
Anglo:
-American, 29
-phone, 36
anthropocentric(ism)(ist)(s): 3–5
environmental ethics, 3–4
non-, 4–5, 118–119
anthropology(ical)(ist)(s): 1, 9, 12,
    15–16, 29, 31, 132
American, 25
conventions, 13
discussions, 12
empirical research 133
post-Darwinian, 122
relativity in, 26–30
William Jones as, 1, 34

Apache: 18
Apollo: 12
Aristotle(elean): 7–8, 130
ethics (eudaimonia), 130–131
Asia(n): ethical traditions, 6
traditions of thought, 2
axe: 35, 59–60, 74, 81–82, 94, 103

B
bear(s): 65–66, 70–72, 76–78, 90, 93, 97,
    99–100, 105–112, 115, 118,
    120–121, 125–126, 128–129
bear-ear as arrow feather, 93, 95
Brown, 65, 120
Chief, 65
clan, 13
hunting of, 70–72
meat, 78
skin, 90
social structure of, 105, 120
-walk(ers), 108
White, 65, 120
beaver(s): 61–64, 67–69, 99, 104–105,
    110–111, 114–116, 120–121,
    125–126, 128, 130
berries, 90
dried tails of, 90, 93, 108
entrails, 62
-hole, 67
lodge (dwelling, wigwam), 64, 67,
    69, 114
marriage between humans and, 63,
    67, 68–70, 104–105, 108–109, 113,
    120–121
reciprocity (ethics) between humans
    and, 69–70, 109–110, 113–116,
    121, 130
the fur trade and, 133
treatment of the bones of, 113, 116
being(s): 9, 20, 79–80, 102, 105, 106–111,
    116, 127, 128
animal, 104
conscious, 127
Great, 111
human, 5, 9, 15–17, 20, 24–25, 64–65,
    67–69, 73–75, 79, 88, 102–110,
    113–115, 118–120, 123–124, 126,
    128–130

living, 4
mineral, 102
natural, 128
non-human, 102, other-than-human,
    128–129
personal, 103
physical, 103
spirit, 102, 106, 117, 129
thunder, 28, with a full set of teeth,
    67, 116
belief(s)(ieve)(ed)(ing): 1, 3, 5–6, 8,
    11–12, 14, 17, 19, 21–22, 24, 26,
    28, 33, 36, 58, 108, 115, 118, 130
biblical, 126
dis-, 23
in reincarnation, 117
in souls, 117
structures, 31
systems of, 30
Bentham, Jeremy: 7
Berger, Peter: 100
Berkeley, George: 24
berries: 70, 97, 128, 131
blue-, 66
sweet-brier, 90–95, 102–103, 106, 110,
    112–113, 118
**bestiality (from the Western
    perspective):** 119–120, examples
    found in Chapter 2
Bidney, David: 9
biology(ical)(ist)(s): 5, 9, 13–15, 26,
    127–128
and pragmatic value of worldviews,
    26
evolution(ary), 4–17, 128
macrocosm, 17
organization, 5
philosophers of, 5, 14
point of view, 15, 17
species, 14, 17–18
unity of human species, 16
biosocial(ly): 16–17
biosphere: 129
biota: 129
biotic: community(ies), 5, 123,
    127–129, 130–131
enterprise, 126
mutual dependence, 129

birch(-bark): 59–60, 70, 80, 121
bird-hawk(s): 73–74, 101, 112
Bishop, C.: 32
Black, Mary: 30, 106
blessing: 110
situation of, 110–112
Boaz, Franz: 20
bone(s): 22, 43–44, 66, 113, 115–118, 121,
    124, 128
fish-, 22
proper treatment of, 114–117
shin- skinner, 61–62
Booth, Annie: 133
Boylan, Michael: 8, 11–12, 30
buffalo jump: 133, 135
Bungee Ojibwa, 32

C
Callicott, J. Baird: 5–6
Canada: 22, 36
Jay, 63, 108–09, 120, 124–125
cannibalism: 110, 120
canoe(s): 46–52, 58, 64, 71–72, 78–79, 82,
    84–86, 105
caribou: 99
Carnegie Foundation: 34
Cartesian: 126 *See also* Descartes
category(ical)(ies)(ization):
European conceptual, 23
grammatical (lingustic, semantic),
    19–21, 104
Kant's imperative, 134
Kant's of understanding, 24–25
mistake, 5
principles of in ecology, 18
cedar(s)(-bark): 57, 71, 75, 90,
    102, 110
Cheal, D.: 121
Cheney, Jim: 133
Chippewa: 32, 35
Christian(ity)(ization): 10, 34–35
Golden Rule, 134
Judeo- ethical tradition, 3, 7
un-, 36
view of animals, 126
worldview, 10
clan(s): 105, 113, 120–122
nomenclature, 13

cliff-spirit(s): 78–79, 110–11, 114, 118, 128, 130
Clothed-in-Fur: 58–68, 105, 108, 110, 113, 116–117, 120–121, 124, 127–128
cognitive(ly)(tion): 24
  arrangement of (conditions of, systems for interpreting, organizing) (human) experience, 2, 24–25, 28, 100
  complex (context), 1–2, 102
  culture (dimension of) (cultural research) 2, 6, 12–13, 22–23, 27, 30
  dissonance, 11
  diversity, 11
  elements of Ojibwa worldview, 100–115
  evidence of American Indian environmental ethics, 133
  foundations for recognition and perception, 19
  mental apparatus, 25
  orientation(s), 6, 8–9, 18, 20, 25–26, 29, 31
  outlook, 19
  peculiarities of current Western wordview, 26, 31
  pluralism, 11
  semantic- (domains), 30–31
  structures, 15
  synthesis of given, 25
  system(s), 29
Columbus(ian): 131
  post-, 9, 131
  pre-, 35, 133
Coming-Dawn: 56
Communication(s): 15–16, 18, 20
  social, 15
  technologies, 122
communitarian(ism): 119, 124, 128
  land ethic, 124
  vision, 128
community(ies)(al): 5, 20, 104–105, 110, 119, 122–123, 130
  animal, 105, 123–124, 127–128
  biotic, 5, 123, 127–131
  bonds, 120
  building, 119

  community of, 105
  concept, 104–105
  cosmic, 128
  foundation in, 121
  human, 104–105, 124, 131
  land, 122
  link between people and beavers, 121
  manitou, 105
  membership(s), 119, 121
  mixed human-animal, 105, 124
  sub-, 127
  ties, 124 *See also* society(ies)(al)(ly)(io)(ization) (ology)(ical)
comprehend(sive)(ly)(ness): 2
  criterion of tenability, 11, 30, 101
  definition of culture, 13
  explanation, 6
  ideas of order, 12
  worldview, 11, 30, 101
consciousness: evaluating human and non-human, 124–127
consistent(ly)(cy): 4, 11, 32
  criterion of tenability, 2, 11, 30, 101
  in-, 2, 11
  self, 27, 30, 101
  set of assumptions, 37
construct(s)(ed)(ing):
  an argument, 125
  de-, 29–30, 37
  Huron of experience, 23
  nonanthropocentric environmental ethics, 4
  reality, 100
  socially, 29–30, 37
Copernicus(an): 8, 24–5
Copway, George: 34
cowry shell: 99
crane: clan, 13
Crosby, Alfred W.: 131
Crusades: 134
culture(al)(s): 1, 6–33, 35–36, 100–101, 120, 135
  a- vantage point, 32
  absolutism, 21
  adaptation, 16–17
  American (cognitive, worldview(s)) 1, 22, 132–133

and biology, 14–15
attitudes and values, 3, 6
boundaries, 17–18
change, 35
Chippewa type, 35
cognitive 2, 6, 22–23, 30
comparison(ative study of) (cross-
    interpretation of) 6, 31, 103
cross-fertilization, 6, 18
developments, 17
diffusion, 18
disruptions, 35
diversity (differences, variation),
    16–17
eu-, 15–16
education (enculturation), 101
European-American worldview(s), 1
evolution (Lamarkian), 6, 14–17
families (grouping) of, 18
Greek, 19
heredity, 16
hero(s) (Ojibwa's principal), 35,
    103, 109
information, 15, 31
material, 35, 103
native, 33
non-Western, 9
Ojibwa (cognitive, worldview), 2,
    36, 109, 117, 128
oral, 10, 18, 101
proto-, 15–16
relativism, 20–32, 101
skills, 17
"studies," 9, 20, 22–23
sub-, 9, 27, 116–117
transmission of, 10
units, 17
universal characteristic, 16
variables, 100
Western (perspective, tradition,
    worldview), 3, 8, 11–12, 29–30,
    36–37, 101, 104, 107–109, 116, 119,
    128, 134
worldview(s), 1–2, 6–14, 22, 31,
    100–101
Woodland Algonkian, 32
written (literate), 10
custom(s): 33–34

D
Darwin, Charles: 5, 8, 15–16, 122–23, 126
    notion of ethics, 122
death:
    life and, 113–116, of William Jones, 37
Democritus: 24
Descartes, Rene: 8, 22–23, 25, 29, 116
    view of animals, 126 *See also*
        Cartesian
disease(s): 7, 12
    Old World, 35, 131
Dobzhansky, Theodosius: 14, 16–17
dog(s): 67–68, 74–75, 93, 113, 116, 131
    hunting, 101, 115–116
Dorson, R. M.: 101
dream(s): 13, 76–77, 106–108, 111–12
    cultural relevance, 101, 106, 112, 132
drum: kettle, 74
dualism: 126–127
duck(s): 48
    arrow-head, 99
    fall, 99
    fish, 99
    long-neck, 99
    mallard, 99
    red-head, 99
    teel, 99
    whistle-nose, 99
    whitefish, 99
duty(ies): 4, 7, 44, 105, 119, 121, 134

E
eagle: 77, 99
ear-rings: 65, 79, 121
earth: 75, 117
    the 8, 12, 21, 59–60, 65–66, 76, 78, 87,
        95–96, 107, 128, 132
east(ern): 32, 75, 78, 96–98
ecology(ical)(ly)(ists): 3, 5, 16, 18,
    122–123, 128–131
ecosystem(s): 5, 16
    health (of), 5, 131
    services, 3, 129
education(al): function of narratives,
    33–34, 101
    cultural, 101
    oral, 33–34, 101
    un-, 33

Einstein, Albert: 25–28
end(s): 4–5, 53, 69, 81, 96, 130
engine(s)(eer)(s): 3, 107,
    mouse-, 124
English: 21, 30–31, 102, 107, 130
    Jones's translations from Ojibwa,
        34–37
entity(ies): animate, 28
    distinct kinds of, 108
    eternal, 103
    inanimate, 102
    occult, 13
    separate, 21
    socio-political, 32
    species as actual, 14
environmental crisis: 2–3, 5, 132
environmental ethic(s): 1–6, 9, 134
    American Indian, 132–136
    anthropocentric, 3–4
    as actions or values, 133–135
    comparative, 5–6
    holistic nonanthropocentric, 4–5
    individualistic nonanthropocentric, 4,
        nonWestern approach to, 5
    Ojibwa, 1–2, 7, 31, 37, 100, 102, 117–131
    subdiscipline of moral philosophy, 2
        See also land: ethic(s)
    Western theories of (approaches to),
        2, 7
environmentalist(s): 1, 4
epistemological:
    problems, 25
    reasons, 30
Eskimo: 34
ethic(al)(s): 4–5, 7–8, 13, 15, 117–119,
        119, 122–123, 130, 134
    American Indian (environmental), 6,
        132–136, Aristotle('s), 7, 130
    Asian traditions of, 6
    behavior and, 134
    Darwin(ian)('s) and, 5, 122–123
    definition of, 122
    environmental, 1–7, 117–136
    expansion of, 122–123
    Greek, 7
    Hume('s) 5
    Judeo-Christian tradition of, 3
    Kant(ian)('s), 4, 8

land (Leopold) 5, 121–124, 127–131
    Ojibwa environmental (land) 1–2, 7,
        31, 37, 102, 117–131
    Ojibwa human-to-human, 117–118
    philosophical systems of, 7
    Plato('s), 7
    rule-oriented theory of, 8
    traditional (contemporary) Western
        (anthropocentric), 3–5, 7, 119, 134
    utilitarian, 4
    See also environmental ethics, ethos,
        and land: ethic(s)
ethno(-): botany, 9
    -grapher(s), 6, 14,19–20, 31, 37
    -graphic semantics, 30
    -history, 133
    -linguists, 21
    metaphysics(al), 9, 13, 31, 116, 133
    -ologists, 25
    -science(tific) 30–31
    -semantics, 30, 35
ethos: 12–13, 19, 117, 122–124
    Ojibwa (environmental), 117–119,
        123–124, 130
    Western, 122
    worldview and, 12–13, 119, 135
Euclid(ian): 25–26
    non-, 25
evolution(ary):
    and personification, 126
    anomaly of ethics, 122
    biology(ical), 5, 14–15, 128
    cultural (social), 6, 14–17, 122
    Darwinian, 14–17
    Darwin's epic, 8
    ecology(ical), 5, 122, 128
    genetic, 17
    human trajectory, 15
    Lamarckian, 14–17
    odyssey of, 126, 129
    of another reality, 2, 37
    of ethics, 122–123
    of language, 16
    of moral sentiments, 5
    of philosophy, 23
    of species, 5
    of Western thought, 23
    point of view, 15, 122, 126

resistance to disease, 131
situations, 131
strategy, 5
supposition of human beings as
    animals, 126
theory of, 126
tree of life, 128
European(s): 22, 32, 35, 131
-American(s) (cultural worldview),
    1, 35
Catholic worldview, 35
heritage, 25
Indo- languages, 21
languages, 25
pathogens, 131
traditions of thought, 2
travelers, 33
Union, 122
worldview (categories), 8, 23
Euthyphro: 111

F
fact(s)(ual): 134
and value, 12
linguistic, 29
of contemporary life, 11
family(ies): 103, 105, 118, 125
alliances between, 120
animal, 105
extended, 104, 122
groups, 32
human, 105
hunting and trapping territories,
    32–33
member (of), 105–06, 119, 124
non-human, 105
of beaver, 104–105, 121
of cultures(al), 18
of geese, 125
of moose, 104–105
relations among languages, 21
fasting: 76–77, 106, 110–112
for power/face-blackening, 68, 76,
    111–112
Field Museum of Natural History: 34
fire(s): 22, 42, 45, 52–56, 61–62, 70–71,
    90, 93, 95, 108, 116, 120, 133
a-, 45

-blaze, 34
-wood, 38–39, 42, 52, 54–55, 63,
    68, 120
fish(es)(ing)(eries): 3, 22, 32, 35, 50, 68,
    70–71, 82–84, 88, 90, 97, 99,
    108–109, 115, 118, 126, 128,
    130–131
preacher of, 22–23
bones, 22
the great (chief of), 83
Foolish Maidens: 35, 58–60, 105,
    117, 120
Foucault, Michel: 29, 107
Fox: 33
French: 102
-men, 23;
Freud, Sigmund: 8
fur: 58, 72, 111, 113, 117, 119,
    123, 128
-bearing animals, 133
Clothed-in-, 35, 58–66, 104–106,
    108–110, 112–117, 119–121, 124,
    127–129
trade, 32, 35, 133, 135

G
game animals: knowledge of, 29
"big-folk," 96
ethics and, 103, 111
hunting of, 38, 48, 52–55, 58, 61–64
Keepers (Masters/Bosses) of, 103
Overkill Hypothesis and, 133, 135
pimadaziwin and, 131
species, 103
games: playing of, 58–59
double-ball, 58
Gare, Arran: 29
Geertz, Clifford: 12–13, 16
gene(s)(tic)(ally): 15, 17
adaptation, 16–17
changes, 17
Darwinian inheritance, 15
evolution, 17
faulty, 26
information, 15–17
mutation, 15
pool 16
proclivity, 17

German Third Reich: 134
Ghiselin, M.: 5
Ghost:
-dance: 108
'shadow,' 117
gift giving: 106, 113–115, 123
economy of, 121
ethics of, 111, 121
for power, 111
global village: 122–123
goal(s): 4–6, 31, 130
G/god(s): 10, 12, 111
fairy -mothers, 36
image of, 3,126
Goodenough, Ward: 30
good(ness)(s): 1, 4–5, 8, 11, 30, 34, 62,
93, 97, 99, 101, 111, 121, 134
greatest, 4
trade, 18 Omitting the adjectival
form, e.g. "good hunter," "good
boy," etc.
Goodpaster, Kenneth: 4
Goose(eese): 124–125
grammar(tical)(ly): 21
categories, 19
deep of different cultures, 6
forms, 21
Great Lakes: 22, 35
Greco-Roman: ethical tradition, 3
Greek(s)(ce):
alphabet, 130
ancient (of classical antiquity, of the
classical period), 6–8, 10, 12
culture, 19
Golden Mean, 134
Helladic, 19
notion of *eudaimonia*, 130
philosophers, 7
world, 19
worldview (outlook), 7–8, 19
Greenberg, Joseph: 26, 102
Grieder, T.: 132
gull(s): 83–84, 103
Great-, 51–52, 103, 106, 110–111, 127
gull-eggs, 50–52, 103
sea-, 99
Guthrie, Daniel: 133

H
habitus: 1, 6, 12
Hallowell, Irving: 6, 9, 13, 19, 28,
31–32, 35, 100–104, 130, 133
Hambly, W. D.: 34
happy(iness): 4, 34, 50, 54, 73, 75,
77–78, 84–85, 91, 94, 114, 121,
130, 134
Havelock, Eric: 19
health(y): 73, 97, 118, 128, 130–131
ecosystem(s), 5, 131
environmental, 131
human, 131
land, 131
of the biotic community, 128
Heidegger, Martin: 23, 29
Hesiod(ic): 19
Hews-upon-his-Shin: 85–87
Hickerson, H.: 32, 131
Hilger, I.: 119
history(ical)(ly)(ico-)(ians): 25–26, 31,
107, 134
ethno-, 133
events, 26
Field Museum of Natural, 34
individual thinkers related, 7
-intellectual context, 22
Ojibwa, 32–33
quality of change in Western
worldview, 8
roots of the worldview concept, 23
tales, 34
Western (intellectual, philosophical),
9–10, 25–26, 31, 122, 134
Hitler, Adolf: 30
Hoekstra, Thomas W.: 129
Hohokum: 133, 135
Hoijer, Harry: 20
Homer(ic): 19–20
Homo sapiens: 15–16, 122–123, 126,
128–129 *See also*
human(s)(ity)(ly)
Hopi: 18, 27
Horn-Grebe: 44–46, 106
Hughes, J. Donald: 6, 133
human(s)(ity)(ly): action, 130
-animal gift economy 121

-animal marriages, 119–121
artifacts, 124
behavior, 3, 26, 114, 123, 134–135
beings 3–5, 7, 9, 15–17, 20, 24–25,
    64–65, 67–69, 73–75, 79, 88,
    102–111, 113–114, 117–120,
    123–124, 127–130
-centered, 3
communities (society(ies), social
    world), 5, 29, 104–105, 122–124,
    128, 131
consciousness, 22
economy, 129
evolutionary trajectory, 15
experience, 2, 22, 109
families, 105
form, 103
future generation, 109
health (good, and long life,
    longevity), 131
hosts, 131
hunter(s), 112–114, 119
infant(s)
knowledge, 29
-land relationship(s), 132
language, 16
mind, 29
nature, 17, 25
needs and wants, 3
non- natural entities (animals,
    families, nature as a whole,
    world), 1, 3, 105, 123, 132
-oriented ethic, 130–131
other-than-, 35, 102–104, 105, 109–110,
    117–119, 121, 123, 127–129
perception, 100
pimadaziwin, 131
place in the world (natural
    environment), 2, 6, 15
pleasure and pain, 4
population(s), 3, 16–17
power, 110
rights, 7, 123
social evolution (phenomena), 14–15
sorcerer, 108
species, 15, 129
species-wide ethic, 123
subjects, 24

-to-human atrocities (behavior, ethic,
    relationships), 117, 134
well being, 131
Hume, David: 5, 24
humiliation:
    moral relevance of, 119
Hunt(ing):
    and animal rights, 118
    and prediction, 29
    animals, learning to, 15
    culture and, 18, 32
    ethics and, 68–72, 110–119, 121, 132
    family territory, 18, 32, 33
    Siberian big game, 133 *See also* Game
        animals, hunting of
    the Ojibwa and, 35
    waterfowl, 125
Huron(s): 22–23
    Lake, 32
hypothesis: 25, 29
    Sapir-Whorf, 21, 35

I
Indian(s): 22–23, 33–34, 107, 132
    American, 1, 6, 9, 11, 20, 33–36, 103,
        111, 131–135
    environmental ethics, 132–135
    human-land relationships, 132
    pan-, 35
    reservations, 133, 135
    stories, 101
    trappers, 133 *See also* American
        Indians
informant(s): 14, 19, 28, 33, 36, 104
information: 15–17, 31
    cultural, 15, 31
    genetic, 15–17
    practical, 33
    sensory, 20
    symbolic, 18
insects: 66, 129
interests: 4–5
intuition(ive):
    appeal, 28
    Kant's forms of, 24–25
    Kluckhone's, 10
investigator: Western, 31–32
Invisible Man: 108

J
Jenness, Diamond: 117
Johnson, Lawrence: 5–6
Jones, William: 1–2, 34–37, 104, 119
Judeo-Christian:
  ethical tradition, 3, 7

K
Kant('s)(ian): 4, 7, 8, 24–25, 134
  categorical imperative, 134
  Copernican revolution in
    philosophy, 24–25
  ethic(s)(al)(theory), 4, 8
  metaphysics, 24–25
Kelly, William: 14, 18
Kennedy, John F.: 132
Kinietz, W. V.: 22–23
Kluckhohn, Clyde: 10, 13, 21
knowledge: 6, 11, 24, 80, 126
  human, 29
  Jones's of native dialects, 34
  of future events, 106
  of mystic rite, 96
  of proper relationship between
    beavers and people, 110
Koyukon, 18
Krech, Shepard, III: 133

L
Lake Michigan: 33
Lake Superior: 1, 32–34, 36
Lamarck(ian): 14–15, 17
land: 49, 69, 85, 88, 95, 118, 123, 127,
    130, 132
  animals, 127
  community, 123
  ethic(s), 5, 121–131
  grass-, 133
  health, 131
  home- of Ojibwa, 32, 35
  human- relationship with, 132
  of ghosts, 97
  wood- indians, 33, 133
language(s): 6, 12, 16–32, 100, 102
  Algonkian, 18, 28, 102
  American Indian, 20
  Athabaskan, 18
  body, 15

  English, 130
  European, 30
  Greek, 130
  habits, 20
  Hopi, 27
  Indo-European, 21
  kinship expressed in, 104–105
  Navaho, 18
  of edifying fiction, 128
  of evolutionary biology, 128
  Ojibwa, 28–29, 33, 35–36, 102, 130
  principles of, 19
  private, 18
  Roman, 130
  Romance, 102
  symbolic, 17 *See also*
    linguist(s)(ic)(ally)
Latour, Bruno: 29
law(s): 7
  Clothed-in-Fur's father (mother,
    brother, sister)-in-, 65–66
  empirical, 25
  Mashōs as father-in-, 49, 53, 55, 57
  Mashōs's son-in-, 48–58, 102–103,
    105, 107, 110–112, 127
  written, 125
legend(s): 18, 34 *See also* myth(ic)(s),
    narrative(s), story(ies), tale(s)
Leighton, Dorothea: 21
Leopold, Aldo: 3, 5, 122–131 *See also*,
  ethic
linguist(s)(ic)(ally): 19, 26, 35
  animate category in Ojibwa, 102–104
  classification of gender in Romance
    languages, 102
  constituted worlds, 23
  conventions, 30
  environment, 17
  ethno-, 21
  facts, 29
  formalities, 31
  kinship, 18
  Ojibwa arrangement (organization)
    of experience, 28, 31, 102–103
  phenomena, 18
  relativism, 20–21, 26–30, 101
  structure(s), 29, 31, 100
  William Jones as, 1

worldview (Weltanschauug), 27 *See also* language(s)
literacy(ry)(te): 8, 10, 19–20
   criticism, 31, 133
   non-, 10, 19
   pre-, 19 *See also* writing(ten) and oral
litter: and environmental ethics, 133, 135
Little-Image: 75–78, 103–104, 106, 109, 118, 121
lodge(s): 22, 39, 42, 54, 56, 65, 72, 84, 90, 104, 115, 121
   Grand Medicine, 131
   mide, 99
   mystic, 96–97
   Ojibwa, 125
   sappling-and-bark, 125
   sweat, 96, 99 *See also*, Beaver, lodge of Wigwam
logic(al)(ly): 7, 12
   fallacy of "Affirming the Consequent," 29
   Kant's, 25
   Positivism(ists), 20, 126
Luckmann, Thomas: 100
Lumsden, Charles L.: 15
lynx: 99
Lyotard, Jean-Francios: 29

M
Maine Woods: 132
Malabranche(ian): 11
manitou(s): 44–45, 69, 73–75, 78–79, 83, 85, 96–98, 102–107, 109–114, 117–118, 130
   as skeleton, 117
   mystic, 96, 128
   the great, 97, 103
marriage:
   between species, 119–121 Examples in Chapter 2. *See also*, community, human
Martin, Calvin: 103, 130–131, 133
Mashōs: 46, 57–58, 102–105, 107, 109–111, 117, 127
McCloud, William C.: 132–133
McIntosh, Robert: 5
McKenney, T. L.: 33
McPherson, Dennis: ix, 36, 133

McTaggart, F.: 33
medicine(s): 103–104, 131
   classifications of, 33
   Grand Lodge, 131
   the person that made, 78–79, 104, 107, 111–112, 114, 118, 128, 130
member(s)(ship):
   non-human, 123
   of biotic communities, 5, 123, 128–130
   of class, 100
   of cultures, 6–8, 14, 16, 18, 20, 31, 100
   of families, 104–105, 119, 124
   of flock of geese, 124
   of human communities, 5, 128
   of mystic rite (society), 96–97
   of one's country (nation), 119, 122
   of societies (communities), 104, 119, 121–122
   of species, 102
Menomini: 33
Mesquakie: 33
metamorphosis: 104, 106, 108–110, 128
   Examples found in Chapter 2.
metaphysic(s)(al): 27
   alternate, 27
   ethno-, 9, 13, 31, 116, 133
   foundation of animal rights, 118
   gulf separating human beings, 128
   Kant's, 24
method(ology)(ical)(ly): 14
   Descartes' *Discourse on*, 22–23
   of discovering a culture's worldview, 14, 30
   of hunting, 14
   of identifying cultural units, 17
   of philosophers and anthropologists, 9
   of tool making and tool use, 15
   problem(s) (questions), 13–14, 18–20
Michelson, Truman: 34, 97
Michigan: 32
Micmac: 18
midden heap(s): 133, 135
Midewiwin: 99, 131
mission(aries): 35
   Jones's anthropological to the Philippines, 34
moose(es): 72–75, 79, 99, 103–105, 112–115, 119, 121, 125

moccasins: 52–56, 69, 90, 93, 95, 104, 107

moon: 8, 12, 103

moral(ly): aspects of culture, 12
  behavior, 7
  condemnation, 117–118, 134
  criterion, 30
  enfranchized, 3
  im-, 120, 122
  judgment, 134
  maxim, 127
  norms, 135
  of the story, 101, 118
  outrage, 118
  person, 11
  philosophy, 2
  reasons, 25
  rule, 114
  sentiments, 5
  way of life, 11
  worth, 7
  wrong, 4, 117

Mount Katahdin: 132

muskrat(s): 66–67, 105, 116

Mystic Rite: 78, 96–99, 130–131

myth(ic)(s): 18–20, 31, 33–34, 101, 104, 109, 129
  Greek, 19–20
  Ojibwa, 34
  time, 109
  Tlingit, 33
  vocabulary, 128 *See also*, legend(s), narrative(s), story(ies), and tale(s)

N

Naess, Arne: 4

Nänabushu: 35, 80–94, 104, 106–107, 109–110, 112–113, 118
  as Manitou (Great Hare), 103, 106, 109–110
  birth of, 36, 80
  Ojibwa cultural hero (creator, trickster), 35, 102–103, 112
  stories (tales, narratives) about, 79–96

Nana'patam: 81, 88–98

narrative(s): 1–2, 12, 18–19, 31–37, 101, 104, 107–109, 117, 124–125, 127–130

approach, 31
authenticity of Ojibwa, 35–37
content, 29
enculturation function of, 101–102
entertainment value of, 101
legacy, 31
of Jones (William), 1–2, 34–37
Ojibwa, 1–2, 12, 32–37, 38–99, 104, 107–109, 117, 124–125, 127–130
oral (culture), 19, 36, 101
provenance of Ojibwa, 34–35
role in oral education, 33–34, 101
tradition(al), 31, 34 *See also* legend(s), myth(ic)(s), story(ies), tale(s)

Nash, Roderick: 132

nature(al): 24, 29, 80, 130, 132, 135
  as a whole, 1, 133
  attitudes toward and values respecting (toward), 6, 133
  beings, 128
  child of, 132
  concept of, 12
  creative thought about, 8
  divisions and arrangement of experience, 21
  economy (of), 18, 129
  entities, 1
  environment(s), 3, 6, 26
  functioning of, 129
  History (Field Museum of), 34
  Homo sapiens a part of (set apart from), 15
  human, 17
  human behavior toward, 134
  mastery of, 26
  non-human entities, 133
  of a manitou, 73
  of events, 6
  of objective (physical) reality, 21, 23, 101
  of the world of being, 9
  pace of Darwinian evolution, 16
  philosophy (of), 8
  powers, 115
  realm of, 15
  relationship between people and, 1
  resources, 3, 129, 133
  selection, 5, 26, 122

social order of, 130
strength and skill, 112
structure of, 129
variation of cultural forms
whole of as a manitou, 103
world (nonhuman), 3, 104
Navaho: 18, 21
Newton(ian), Isaac: 8, 25
New World: 17–18, 22
Nietzsche, F.: 29
nonanthropocentric(ist)(s): 4–5,
    118–119 *See also*
    anthropocentric(ism)(ist)(s)
norm(s)(ative): 1, 134–135
moral, 135
orietation, 5, 13
north(ern): 26, 32–34, 96, 98
America(n), 9, 133
plains, 32
northeast, 98
northwest, 98 *See also* American
    Indians
Ojibwa: Northern

O
obedience(dis-): 7, 73, 112–113
object(s)(ive): 12, 23–25, 27, 30, 36, 44,
    65, 85, 90, 103–106, 127
dreamed of, 112
European worldview as, 23
information gathering, 31
material (physical), 15, 106
measure of truth, 26
of Ojibwa material culture, 103
orientation, 25
place to stand, 32
reality, 23
subjec- dualism, 23–24
world, 20, 22–23
Ojibwa 1–3, 8–9, 13, 18, 22, 28, 32–36,
    100–108, 111, 117, 123, 125–126,
    130, 132–133: Bungee (Plains) 32
cognitive culture (orientation) (mind)
    2, 29, 117
culture, 36, 101, 111, 128
education (cultural), 101–102
environmental (land) ethic(s) (ethos),
    1, 7, 31, 100, 102, 117–131, 135

ethos, 117, 119, 124, 130
gift economy, 121
Jones materials (*Texts*), 34–36
language (linguistic/semantic/
    syntactic structure of) 28, 29, 31,
    35–36, 102–103, 130–131
material culture, 103
narratives, (myths, stories, tales) 1, 2,
    32–37, 38–99, 101, 104, 106, 112,
    119, 124–130
non-, 104
Northern 32, 137
raconteurs, 2
Southeastern, 32
Southwestern, 32, 34
territory, 36
theory of the cause of (interpretation
    of) thunder, 29
world(view) (cultural worldview)
    (outlook) (way of perceiving the
    world) (reality) 2, 8, 9, 12, 19, 36,
    100–117, 119 *See also* Anishinabe
    and Chippewa.
Old World: 17–18, 131
diseases, 35, 131
ontological(ly):
problems (questions), 13–14, 25
status of culture, 13–14
oral: culture(s), 10, 18–19, 101
education (instruction), 33, 101
heritage, 19
means of cultural transmission, 10
narrative(s) (materials), 19, 31, 36
peoples, 9, 13, 18, 25
poetry, 19
tradition, 10
organism(s): 3–5, 14, 17
super-, 5
orphan(s): 34, 38, 42, 85, 103, 105–106,
    109–110, 112, 127
other-than-human: animals, 127
being(s), 105, 128–129
benefactors, 117
characters, 104
person(s), 35, 102–104, 109–110, 117,
    119, 121, 123, 127, 129
societies, 105
Ottawa: 18

otter: 99
owl: 99

P
pain(s)(ful): 4, 7, 95, 119
Passmore, John: 3
Pasteur, Louis: 8
patriotism: 123
pelican: 99
perceive(d)(ing)(eption)(ual): 6, 8, 13,
    19–20, 28, 94–95
  culturally conditioned, 101
  human, 100
  language and, 100
  of an environmental crisis, 132
  Ojibwa way of, 37
  orientations, 25
  un- 24
Persepolis: 134
person(s)(al)(ity)(hood): 2, 7, 11, 19, 28,
    34, 47, 52, 63, 65, 68–69, 71, 73,
    99, 102–104, 107, 110–111, 119
  acquisition of power, 106
  adjustment, 6
  animal, 127
  assumptions, 1
  attributes of, 28
  beings, 103
  body of a, 117
  character(istic)(s)(of), 8, 102
  concept of, 104
  health, 128
  -hood, 104, 119, 123
  human, 123
  -ification(-ified)(fying), 102–104, 114,
    124–127
  im-, 103
  immortal part, 116–117
  lay- 8
  married, 11
  moral, 11
  of European heritage, 25
  of Nanabushu, 103
  other-than-human, 35, 102–104,
    109–110, 117, 119, 121, 123, 127,
    129
  plant 117
  property of, 7

  sacrifice, 111
  spirit (soul) of a, 117
  stories as, 103
  that made medicine, 78–79, 104, 107,
    111–112, 114, 118, 128, 130
  testimonials, 133
  thunder as, 28, 103
  underground, 65
  Western, 12, 112
  worldview (imperative), 10–12
personification: of non-humans,
    102–104, 124–127
  science and, 125–126 See entire
    Chapter 2
phenomenon(a)(l)(ism): 24–25
  cultural, 8, 15
  excitation, 24
  experience as, 23
  kind of significance, 29
  linguistic, 18
  of divorce, 134
  of metamorphosis, 28
  orientation, 25
  reality, 24
  social, 15
  world, 24–25
Philippine(s) Islands: 34
philosophy(ical)(ies)(ers): 1–5, 7–13,
    18, 21, 23–26, 29–31, 107, 116, 118,
    126, 128
  analytic 12
  and anthropology(ists), 9, 12, 31
  and fine arts, 18
  animal-oriented, 4, 118
  competing systems of, 10
  contemporary postmodern,
    29–31
  Continental, 29
  deconstructive postmodern, 30
  Descartes', 23
  discipline of, 9
  dualism, 126
  Einsteinian revolution in, 25–26
  environmental, 4
  ethical, 7
  ethno-metaphysics as subdiscipline
    of, 9
  feminist, 107

Greek (ancient), 7, 25
Kant's Copernican revolution of,
  24–25
Medieval Western, 10
modern, 23, 25
moral, 2
native, 18, 36
of biology, 5, 14
of nature (natural), 8
of science, 126
Ojibwa, 2
relativism of postmodern, 29
systems of ethical, 7
traditional American Indian, 9–10
Western history of, 9
Western tradition of, 10
worldview and, 7–9
physic(s)(al): 13, 15, 26–27
  appearance, 109
  beings, 103
  difficulties in hunting beaver, 114
  dimension of experience, 109
  objects, 15
  reality (world), 21–22, 24
  regimen, 112
  relativity in, 26–28
  un-, 13
pickerel: 99
Pilferer: 92–93, 112–113, 118
pimadaziwin: 130–131
  land health and human health, 131
pipe(s): 65, 67, 74, 78, 103, 114–116
pity: 33, 42, 49, 51, 57, 70–71, 93, 106,
  110–111, 115
Place-of-the-Pipe-Stone: 78
planet(s): 8, 12
Plato(nic): 7–8, 13, 18–20, 103, 111, 116
  theory of the forms, 103
pleasure: 4, 46
poet(s)(ic)(ry): 19
  idiom, 129
  oral, 19
poplar tree: 60, 63–64
porcupine: 62, 108–109, 120, 124
  quills, 55
Potawatomi: 18
power: 22, 30, 49, 115, 118, 121, 126,
  128–29

hierarchy of, 106–107, 110
importance of, 105–108, 110–112
manitou, 74–75, 103, 111
preternatural, 106–108, 111–112, 115,
  118, 128–129 *See also*, fasting gift-
  giving.
preference(s): 4
Prescott, Philander: 33
preternatural(ly): power(s), 106–108,
  111–112, 115, 118, 128–129
  worlds, 104
primate(s): human relationship to
  other, 126
primitive(s): 25
  man, 132
  peoples, 132
principle(s): 9, 13
  greatest happiness, 134
  of categorization, 18
  of honor, virtue, and bravery, 33
  of language, 19
  of natural selection, 26
  of relativity in physics, 27–28
  uncertainty in worldview analysis,
    30–32
psychology(ical)(ly): 134
  gulf separating, 128
  image, 22
  processes, 6
  things difficult to accept, 25
  treatments of human behavior, 134
punk: 44–45, 108
purpose(s): 53, 67, 73, 75, 80–81, 83,
  94–95, 101, 109, 120, 128, 130
pygmies: 78–79
Pythagoras: 7–8

Q
Quimby, G. I.: 33, 35

R
Rabb, Douglas: ix, 36
rabbit: 99
raccoon: 99, 129
Radin, Paul: 9–10
raven: 62, 108–109, 120, 124–25
real(ity): 1, 6, 20–30, 37, 100–101
  and motion, 27–28

bear, 108
harm, 7
human being, 68
moral worth, 7
of species, 13
objective (world), 23
phenomenal, 24
physical, 20, 22–24
reason, 118
social (socially constructed,
    constructing), 20, 29–30, 37, 100
truth and, 25 Omitting the myriad
    occurrences of such rhetorical
    flourishes as "really" in the
    narratives of chapter 2.
reason(ed)(ing): 4, 6–7, 9, 19, 23–24,
    102, 119
reciprocity: 113–116, 119, 121
recognize(d)(ing)(ition): 4, 6, 11, 13, 19,
    33, 48, 71, 102, 114, 123, 125
Redfield, Robert: 11
Regan, Tom: 4, 118, 123
reincarnation: 116–17
relativity(ism)(ized): cultural 20–32
    Einstein('s)(ian) (theory of), 26–28
    in anthropology, 26–29, 31
    in postmodern philosophy, 29–30
    in physics, 26–28
    linguist and, 26
    linguistic (-cultural) (worldview),
        20–21, 27–30, 101
    of twentieth-century cultural
        studies, 22
    phenomenalism, 25
religion(s): 10, 36
Republicans: 124
resource(s): 122
    conceptual, 6, 10
    cultural, 16
    depletion, 135
    for worldview analysis, 19, 31
    natural, 3, 129, 133
respect: 114, 133
    and hunting, 121, 132
    in the land ethic, 123, 130
    moral relevance of, 104, 106–107,
        113–116, 118, 123, 128, 130

revolution(ary): change in worldview
    of Western science, 27
    Einsteinian in philosophy, 25–26
    industrial, 26
    Kant's Copernican, 24–25
    modifications in linguistic
        phenomena, 18–19
    solarcentric, 8
ribbons: as offering/gifts, 78, 111
right(s): 4, 7, 118–119, 121, 123–124, 127
    animal, 118–119, 123–124, 127
    human, 7, 123
    property, 118
Rogers, E. S.: 32
Rolston III, Holmes: 1, 4
Roman gladiator shows: 134
Romantic(neo-)(ism): 132–33
    view of American Indians, 132–133
Rorty, Richard: 29
Rousseau, Jean-Jacque: 133
Routley, Richard: 4
ruffed Grouse: 58, 68, 71, 75, 78, 115
rule(r)(s): 7, 22, 88–89, 98
    Christian Golden, 134
    golden of land ethic, 127
    moral, 114
    -oriented theory of ethics, 8

S
Sagard, Gabriel: 22–23
Sapir, Edward: 20–21, 25–26, 30, 35
Satterlee, J. V.: 33
Sault Ste. Marie: 32
Saulteaux: 32
savage: superstitions, 23
    noble-, 133
Schoolcraft, H. R.: 33
science(s)(ific)(ist)(s): 3, 9, 21, 24–27,
    29, 125–126, 128–129
    affiliations, 21
    ethno-, 30–31
    paradigm, 27
    philosophy of, 126
    pre-, 126, 128
    point of view, 126–127
    social, 9, 26, 31
    Western, 24–27, 31

self: 4, 12, 118
-aware, 4
experience as -grounded, 24
interest, 4
-sacrifice, 132
semantic(s):
Algonkian, 102
categories, 21
-cognitive domain(s), 30
descriptive, 30
discrimination(s), 18–19, 29, 31
English, 31
ethno(graphic), 30, 35
Greek, 19
morphology, 28
Ojibwa, 31, 102
structures, 29, 31
taxonomy, 20
sense(ation)(itive)(ty)(ory)(ous): 2, 12,
20, 27, 29, 113
age-, 106
common, 11, 21–22, 24
data, 20
experience, 22
information, 20
non- (ical), 7, 79, 113–114, 130, 133
of gladness, 81
of kinship, 126
of power, 107–108
of self, 4, 118
of wonder, 126
Shrader-Frechette, Kristin: 3
Shriners: 124
Siberia: 133
Singer, Peter: 4, 7, 119
Sioux: 32–33, 108
skeleton: 43, 117
as manitou, 117 *See also*, bones,
Ghost.
as soul, 117, 128
Skinner, A.: 33
skunk: 99
slave(trade)(ry): 122, 134
smoking: fish, 50, 71
significance of smoke, 116
tobacco (pipe/ritual/offering), 65, 67,
74–75, 78–79, 83, 115, 124

snake(s): 39, 105, 107, 126
snowshoes: 61–62, 101, 113
**society(ies)(al)(ly)(io-)(ization)(ology)
(ical):** 5, 8, 12, 18, 20, 33, 100–101,
104–105, 122, 134
activity, 20
animal, 124, 130
ant- conduct, 122
bio-, 16–17
bonds, 120
class, 11
communication, 15
conduct, 122
congeries of, 130
constructed, 29–30, 37
context, 105
ethics and, 122–123
evolution (development), 14, 122
expediency, 131
folk, 10
habits, 34
hierarchy in, 129–130
human 5, 29–30, 122
instincts and sympathies, 122
institutions, 18
interaction, 102
life, 33
microcosm, 17
mixed human-animal, 124
mystic, 96
of societies, 105
order (of nature), 123, 130
organization, 104
other-than-human, 105
phenomena, 15
-political, 132
power, 107
reality, 20
relationships, 104–105
rolls, 31
science(s)(ist)(s), 9, 26–27, 31, 134
structur(es) (of nature), 14, 129
visits, 105
Western, 8, 11
world, 104 *See also*
community(ies)(al)
Socrates(tic): 7, 10, 111

solipcism(ist): 126
song(s): 63, 73, 78–79
    manitou (mystic rite), 78
Son-in-law of Mashos: 48–58, 102–103,
    105, 107, 110–112, 127
soul(s): 3, 97, 116–117, 126, 132
south(ern): 32–33, 96, 98
    southwest, 98, 133
    southeast, 98
    See also American Indians
    Ojibwa, Southern
space: 5, 14, 24–25, 27, 50
    Euclidian, 25
    of ground, 95
    of time, 65
    probes, 8
    -time continuum, 25
Spanish Inquisition: 134
spear(s): 81–82, 85, 92
species: 4–5, 13–18, 102–103, 106, 109,
    120, 127–128, 133
    animal, 13
    boundaries of, 18
    composing biotic communities, 127
    concept of, 13–14
    cross- sexual intercourse, 119
    endangered endemic, 4
    game, 103
    Homo sapiens (human), 15–17, 129
    inter- marriages, 105, 119–120
    level of biological organization, 5
    origin of, 126
    plant, 130
    primate, 122
    vertebrate, 4
    -wide human ethic, 123
specimen(s): 5, 14, 103
Speck, Frank: 132–133
spirit(s)(ed)(ual): 34, 116–117, 130, 133
    being(s), 102, 117, 129
    cliff- 111
    departed, 133
    -essence, 128–130
    Great, 103
    of generosity, 111
    of pity, 115
    of *quid pro quo*, 111

    of self-sacrifice, 132
    of the person, 117
    terms, 132
    voice of, 34
    well-, 130
spruce tree: 59
    spruce-leaf, 59, 60
stars: 12
stones (pebbles): 46–47
    animation of, 53, 79, 103–104, 107
story(ies): 1–2, 33–36, 42, 46, 48, 50, 53,
    55–56, 58, 69, 72, 80, 82, 84,
    88–89, 101–120, 125, 128, 130
    as other-than-human persons, 104
    Eskimo, 34
    Indian, 101
    of Jones (William), 34–37, Ojibwa,
        1–2, 34–37, 101–120, 125, 128, 130
    tellers, 37 *See also* legend(s),
        myth(ic)(s), narrative(s), tale(s)
sturgeon(s): 48–50, 91–92, 94–96, 99,
    102–103, 106, 108–110, 112–113,
    118
    Great-Sturgeon(s), 49, 82–84, 88, 103,
        106–107, 110–111, 127
    smoking, 50
    sturgeon-roe, 91, spinal cord of, 102
subject(s)(ive): 12, 23–25, 36, 118,
    125–126
    experience, 24, 109, 126
    human, 24
    image(s) of physical reality, 22–23
    interpretation of (bird, beaver, bear)
        behavior, 125–126
    lives of animals, 126
    -object dualism, 23–24
    of a life, 118, 123
    orientation, 25
    -predicate syntactical structure, 19
sun: 12, 78, 81, 103, 129
Superman: 108
superstition(s): 23, 29
swan(s): 73–74, 101, 112
Swanton, J. R.: 33
sympathy(etic): 7, 122–123
syntax(ic)(al): English, 31
    Greek, 19

morphology, 28
relationships (-al scheme), 18, 20
structure(s), 19, 31
structures of Ojibwa language, 29, 35

T
tale(s): 1, 18, 33–34, 36–37, 106, 108–109,
    111–113, 124
  fairy, 36
  of Jones (William), 34
  Ojibwa, 2, 34, 37, 106, 108–109,
    111–113, 124 *See also* legend(s),
    myth(ic)(s), narrative(s),
    story(ies).
Taylor, Paul W.: 1, 4
technology(ical)(ly): 8, 18, 26, 36, 101,
    122
  challenge, 3
  nuclear, 26
  success, 26
tenable(ility): 2, 101, and truth, 29–30
think(er)(s)(ing)(thought): 1, 7–11,
    14–15, 22, 42, 48, 51–52, 57,
    59–60, 66, 74, 77, 83, 86, 89,
    92–93, 114, 116, 120, 126, 128
  Western, 24 132
Thoreau, Henry David: 132
Thornton, R.: 131
thought(s): 9, 19, 21, 23, 25, 28–29, 34,
    38–39, 45–52, 55–58, 60–61, 63–64,
    66, 69, 71, 73, 75, 77, 80–81, 83–85,
    88–90, 93–95, 114, 126
  Asian traditions of, 2
  conscious, 13
  creative, 7–8
  non Western traditions of, 5
  patterns of, 27
  processes of, 20
  speculative, 10
  Western, 23–24, 126
thunder: 28–29, 103, 129
time(s): 5, 14, 24–25, 27
  aboriginal, 35
  end of, 84,
  -less, 20
  mythic, 109
  Newtonian, 25

space- continuum, 25
when beavers were numerous, 69
    Omitting such rhetorical uses as
    "once upon a time" and
    incidental uses such as "at the
    same time.";
tobacco: 65, 68, 99, 119, 121, 124
  as offering/gift, 69, 78, 96, 111, 114
toboggan(ing): 57–58
tool(s): 15
  methods of making, 15
  use, 15
translate(d)(ing)(tion)(s): 128, 130
  Jones's, 34–37
  un-, 130
tribe(s)(al): 13, 18, 29, 105, 120, 122
  culture, 35
  -like, 124
  Ojibwa, 32
  village, 105
trout: 99
true(r)(th): 2, 10, 21–23, 25–27
  and tenability, 29–30 Omitting the
    myriad occurrences of such
    rhetorical flourishes as "truly,"
    "in truth," and "of a truth" in the
    narratives of chapter 2.

U
Udall, Stewart: 132
utility(arian)(s): 4, 7, 134

V
value(s): 3–4, 6, 12, 19–20,
    26, 31
  attitudes and, 3, 6, 20, 133
  cultural, 31
  entertainment, 101
  fact and, 12
  goals and, 6, 31
  intrinsic, 4
  pragmatic, 26
Vico, Giambattista: 29
village(s): 11
  global, 122–123
  Ojibwa, 32–33
  tribal, 105

virtue: 7, 8, 33
  hunter's, 132, of patriotism, 15

W
wampum: 96–97, 99
war: 35, 81, 86
  -club, 72, 77, 86
  U.S.—in Iraq, 134
Warren, William: 32
West(ern)(erners)(ward): 6, 10, 12, 26,
    32, 36, 39, 73, 79, 97–99, 103, 108,
    120, 132, 134
  animal-rights theory(ists), 118,
    123–124
  biblical account of origins, 109
  Christian worldview of, 10
  civilization, 31
  culture(al) (influences, sub-,
    tradition), 3, 8, 11–12, 29–30,
    36–37, 101, 104, 107–108, 111,
    116–117, 119, 128, 134
  countries, 36
  ecology, 129
  environmental ethics, 7
  ethic(al)(s) (theory, traditions), 3–5, 7,
    134
  ethos, 122
  experience, 106
  hemisphere, 131
  history (recorded), 10, 25, 31, 122, 134
  ideas, 123
  influence, 35
  intellectuals, 23
  investigator, 32
  Medieval philosophy, 10
  memes, 26
  -most group of Ojibwa, 32
  nonanthropocentric (ists) (ethics),
    118–119
  non- (alternatives, approaches to
    environmental ethics, conceptual
    resources, cultures, oral peoples,
    traditions of thought,
    worldviews), 5–6, 9, 25, 30–31
  of Lake Michigan, 32
  of Lake Superior, 1, 34
  origin, 35

person, 112
philosophy(ers)(ical) history
    (inquiries, thought, tradition,
    paradigm), 9–10, 23–24
  point of view, 102–105, 108
  science, 24–25, 27, 31
  society, 8, 11
  theories of environmental ethics, 2
  thinkers (thought), 126, 132
  traditional anthropocentric ethics, 4
  traditions, 19
  view of soul, 116–17
  world(view)(s), 8–12, 21, 25–26,
    30–31, 105, 116–117, 119, 128, 132
whetstone: 35, 81–82, 103
whitefish: 99
White Jr., Lynn: 3
Whorf, Benjamin: 21, 27, 30, 35
wigwam: 42, 58, 60–64, 72–73, 79, 86 *See
    also* Lodge(s)
Wilson, E. O.: 5, 14–16, 128
Windigo(s): 98, 110
Wisconsin: hunting statutes, 124–125
Wittgenstein, Ludwig: 18
wolf: 54, 61, 108–109, 120, 124
  boy transforms into, 48, 53, 108, 127
Woman Who Married a Beaver: 68–70,
    105, 108–110, 114, 127–28
Woodland Indians: 33, 133
world(view)(s): 1–2, 6–14, 18–33, 37,
    100–117, 128, 132, 135
  and ethos, 12–13, 19, 119, 135
  and philosophy, 7–9
  and relativism, 20–32
  and uncertainty principle, 30–32
  Catholic, 35
  Christian, 10
  comparative study of, 2
  competing, 11
  conveyed through narrative, 101
  cultural, 1–2, 6–13, 25, 31, 100–101,
    116–117, 128
  dissonance between, 102
  European, 8, 23
  geocentric, 8, 12
  Greek, 7–8, 19–20
  language and, 20–32

Malabranchian, 11
nonWestern, 30–31
Ojibwa, 2, 8–9, 12, 19, 100–115, 117, 119
personal, 10–12
scientific, 26–27
Western, 8–12, 26–27, 30–31, 105, 116,
    128, 132
Wounded-Knee Massacre: 107–108

writing(ten): 11, 18
    law, 125
    means of communication, 10
    means of cultural transmission, 10
    record of philosophical reflection, 9
    word, 10 *See also* literacy(ry)(te)
        and oral

gift-giving III
112 Dickster

102 other-than-human-person